How We Heal and Grow

The Power of Facing Your Feelings

JEFFERY SMITH MD

LIBENTIA

Published by

Libentia Press
10 Stewart Place
Suite 8-GE
White Plains, NY 10603
USA

First Edition
ISBN: 978-0-9898881-0-3 (Paperback)
Library of Congress Control Number: 2014918208

Interior and Cover Designs by John Walker

To Claude

CONTENTS

INTRODUCTION
Why change is not easy, but less hard than one might think. Pg. 1

1   THE CAVE THE BRIDGE AND THE VILLAGE
How overwhelming feelings early in life lead to patterns of avoidance that later cause many of our problems. Pg. 9

2   AVOIDING FEELINGS
A survey of why and how we shut feelings out and how our protective castles can become confining prisons. Pg. 34

3   CATHARSIS: AMAZING MEDICINE
How facing feelings allows them to heal. Pg. 95

4   INFORMATION AND MISINFORMATION
How we use thoughts and ideas to shut out feelings and how knowledge can save us. Pg. 133

5   YOUR CONSCIENCE CAN BE WRONG
How your conscience, too, can become a means of running from feelings and how you can reshape it. Pg. 170

6   VOLUNTARY BEHAVIOR CHANGE
The role of behavior in avoiding feelings and finding them. Pg. 202

7   DREAMS AND QUESTS
How Dreams, quests, and ambition can cover up feelings, too. Pg. 240

8   ARRESTED DEVELOPMENT
About emotional development, how its arrest can cover feelings, and a look at three critical periods. Pg. 259

9   THE FUTURE STARTS TODAY
Encouraging words and the Scarsdale Psychotherapy Self-Evaluation (SPSE), a universal tool for evaluation of therapy effectiveness. Pg. 300
GLOSSARY AND BIOGRAPHIES Pg. 306

ACKNOWLEDGMENTS

Leon Balter, who taught an introduction to theory in residency, Cindy, who, over many years, encouraged me to write, Donna Drown who asked for an article and ended up making editorial suggestions, and all those who patiently supported my efforts and offered great ideas. The many patients who have taught me over the years, John Walker, who did the book and cover designs, Margot, my sister, who edited for content and Laura Kenny, my copy editor and Claude, who never let me down.

FOREWORD

Michael Blumenfield, MD

You are about to embark upon an exciting and fulfilling journey. Your guide will be Dr. Jeffrey Smith, a very experienced psychiatrist who has dedicated his career to understanding how people heal and grow. He will familiarize you with the work of experts in the field such as Sigmund Freud, Margaret Mahler, Otto Kernberg and many others, as well as his own original work. He will not present you with boring, dry psychobabble. Rather he will offer you everyday language and metaphors to which you can relate. He will present conflicts and emotional issues that you know are true to life. This book offers a fresh and sensible way to look at how people develop dysfunctional patterns and how facing feelings that have been avoided is the pathway to healing and growth. Dr. Smith covers the full range of human problems from quirks to serious personality issues. He approaches the subject from a developmental point of view, sharing how most of us have pockets of immaturity and how to outgrow them. He explains how and why the mind resists change and how to stack the deck in our favor.

You can read this book to satisfy your own intellectual curiosity about a fascinating subject. More likely you will find yourself thinking about your own psychological conflicts and difficulties. Some of the insights that come from reading this book may be helpful to you. I suspect that some readers may decide to enter therapy as they realize that they could better fulfill their potential were it not for stumbling blocks from earlier in life. One of the central themes of Dr. Smith's explanation is the phenomenon of catharsis where our underlying raw, unprocessed feelings emerge and lose their power over us and are transformed when we share them with a therapist or trusted other in a context of connection and safety. I can also see the value of this book as a companion as you are going through therapy. It will facilitate your motivation to explore and understand deep-seated feelings and early events in your life. The book will also give you a background and understanding of the therapeutic process that will be unfolding. After reading this book, I have decided to give a copy to some of my own patients as they begin their work in therapy.

Michael Blumenfield, MD

Past President, American Association for Psychoanalysis and Dynamic Psychiatry

Sidney E. Frank Distinguished Professor Emeritus of Psychiatry and Behavioral Sciences, New York Medical College

INTRODUCTION

Why change is not easy, but less hard
than one might think.

Why do self-help readers often end up with a collection of books and new knowledge but not much change in their lives? The answer is that when we try to make changes in our dysfunctional ways we find ourselves pitted against a formidable adversary, our own mind. Evolved over millions of years, our mind uses many tricks to protect us from the pain it associates with change. The aim of this book is to tip the balance in your favor.

Armed with the understanding and approaches outlined here, you will be able to follow the action in your own mind and your own life. You will be able to push harder in ways you need to and understand why and how your mind resists. Even more important, as you encounter the feelings you have avoided, an amazing phenomenon I will call *catharsis* will detoxify those feelings. It will take away their power to stop you and will give you strength to keep your change process moving ahead.

This book is a product of my passion for precise understanding. Maybe another way to describe my quest is that I am even more interested in what I don't know than what I do. One of my early memories is watching a neighbor riding her tricycle on the sidewalk very fast. I must have been about three because I couldn't yet do that. I was amazed by her speed, but what really caught my attention was wanting to know whether the pedals were going straight up and down as it appeared or around in circles as they normally should.

When I was about eight, my father traveled to New York and brought me back a crystal radio kit. How could the music and voices of radio come out of a wire touching a small stone connected to a long antenna wire? I couldn't resist my curiosity and soon began to read books on electronics and build measurement instruments from Heathkits. By the end of high school, I found there were many more subjects just as complex and fascinating. When I started college at Stanford, I took liberal arts courses aiming towards an English major and expected to dig into the depths of literature.

It took me until the spring of my freshman year to realize that I was much too restless to bury myself in the fine points of obscure works. I needed to be part of the "real world" and interact with people. I had read *Catcher in the Rye* and discussed psychology in my family so when, for no fathomable reason, I found myself waiting till the last minute to do my work, I saw a psychiatrist. With these experiences, the idea of a career as a therapist was not so foreign, but what really made me want to change my major was a transforming moment in my own life.

I had to write a paper on Dostoyevsky's *Crime and Punishment*. I really liked the book and had written a paper on it in high school. My brain refused to come up with an idea. It was 11 p.m. on the night before the twelve-page paper was due. I began to panic. My world was about to come crashing down around me. It felt like an unthinkable, unspeakable disaster. Then, from nowhere, I suddenly felt a wave of serenity. With it came the thought that, even without the paper, in the morning I would wake up and have breakfast. I would still be myself and alive. There would be a mess to clean up, but somehow, even if I flunked out of college I would manage. As I calmed down, an idea came and I wrote the paper.

I had experienced change. It came in a moment and left me feeling like a different person. The experience energized my desire to learn more about how change happens and to help others as well. With my interest in science and desire to get in close, going to medical school and then psychiatry was the clear choice. Even with the practice of therapy as a goal, I wanted to understand the details of anatomy, physiology, and everything about being human. I wanted to participate in people's lives and understand them so I could help them flourish and find their own unique fulfillment. This passion has continued unabated to the present.

You will notice that I am using the word *mind* instead of *brain*. In this age of technology and science, many self-help books are saying that a better understanding of the brain is the key to change. This isn't wrong, but the study of the brain does not include its contents. It doesn't take into account the specific experiences that have shaped our feelings, behavior patterns, aspirations, and values. Mind covers how our thoughts and feelings are organized, how they interact, and how they grow out of our personal history. Some of what we can learn about the mind comes from understanding how it affects the brain and vice versa, but more of it is about how individual experiences shape and influence us. This book will focus on the mind. At times we will look at the brain but when we do, it will be in order to better understand the individual mind.

Why is it so important to understand the mind and its unique contents? This brings me closer to the core of our subject and why it is such a privilege to be a therapist. In every other domain of medicine, treatment choices are determined by placing the patient in a category. A cough might be categorized as pneumonia, and that fact, far more than the individual patient, determines treatment. Other factors like the strain of bacteria or general state of health might play into the choice of which antibiotic, but the patient's individual story is peripheral.

Healing the mind is different. Catharsis, the amazing process mentioned above, happens when we share our humanness with another human and are understood—not categorized but understood. Carl Rogers coined the term *accurate empathy*. That is the essential element in the personal connection that allows healing of the mind. Helping catharsis happen—that is, understanding people in their own unique context—is not only central to the processes of healing and growth but also a great privilege for the therapist.

Teaching was in my blood. With a grandfather who was a missionary and a father who taught at Stanford, after residency it was natural for me to teach and natural to teach the subject of my greatest interest, psychotherapy. Teaching pushed me further to formulate what I was learning in the clearest, most accessible terms possible. The precursor of this book was the handout I developed for my course on psychotherapy for psychiatrists in training.

Perhaps it sounds odd that I refer to "what I was learning." One might think the eight years I spent learning medicine and then psychiatry would have taught me the bulk of what I needed for a career as a therapist. I had devoured what was taught in residency, but therapy is taught mostly as a series of procedures and rules to follow. Concepts help give a rationale to what therapists do but don't really get to the bottom of what is happening. Traditional therapists learn to "make interpretations" based on ideas such as "making the unconscious conscious." Behaviorally oriented therapists learn that erroneous ideas lead to uncomfortable feelings and that helping people correct their thoughts can change their feelings. Neither approach goes far enough to capture the full reality of how therapy works. If becoming more conscious or thinking more rational thoughts is helpful, how exactly does that work and why, then, does lasting change remain so difficult?

In residency at Albert Einstein College of Medicine I was exposed to the study of child development and attachment. Close observation of two-year-olds and their mothers under Eleanor Galenson and Herman Roiphe seemed to point towards the bedrock from which true understanding could come. From that time on, childhood experience, as best we can understand it, has become for me the touchstone of understanding.

After residency, my career soon brought me into territory where my training was of little use. First I was confronted with the emotional consequences of early life sexual trauma. Since the thirties, trauma in general had been relegated to the back wards of veterans hospitals. The field was still in denial about childhood sexual abuse, and what little I had learned was not of much help with my patients. I began to look further afield.

Not too long after that I took a job as director of alcoholism services. My new boss sent me for training at the Smithers Institute, where physicians were taught by members of Alcoholics Anonymous. Recovery appeared to represent a different kind of change. I realized then how little attention my training had paid to problems of action or behavior. I would have to seek understanding from a much broader range of sources.

My own process in coming to the understanding presented here was somewhat of a surprise. During forty years of interest and practice I assumed that someday I would be able to assemble a full picture of how problems develop and can be resolved. As I taught my students, I found myself groping for a new way to conceptualize the work of therapy. I wanted to understand the basic change processes that were taking place and how to encourage or foster them directly, rather than following a procedure and waiting for results to appear. Recognizing that people change in important ways on their own as well as in therapy, and that different schools of therapy seem to accomplish the same results, I believed there must be universal pathways to change. The surprise was that only with the writing of this book did the final pieces come into focus.

Making sense of how people change has been something like what I imagine to have been the experience of trappers of the early American West. At first, they probably observed many things in the woods around them and learned from Indians. Only gradually did they come to see more and to understand cause and effect. With time, their understanding could be put into words and concepts to share with others.

Working with the mind is at least as challenging as the wilderness. There are different parts of the mind and different ways they interact, but the partitions and pathways are not visible. They only become apparent as minds interact with one another. Therapy provides an excellent laboratory in which to observe these interactions, but even there, cause and effect are not obvious. In actual practice, important things happen without our being able to say quite why.

One basic reason is that much of the operation of the mind is beyond the reach of consciousness, allowing only educated guesses about just what is going on. In addition, emotional reactions are inherently nonverbal. Only when we happen to notice them can we try to describe them in words. Much of our internal life goes by as background music outside of our explicit conscious attention and out of reach of language. So it should not be a surprise that really understanding even those limited parts of the mind that relate to our irrational and dysfunctional patterns turns out to be seriously challenging work.

I have borrowed wisdom from many traditions as well as used my own experience. Sifting through concepts from different sources I wanted to pull together the ones that had power and simplicity and could fit together into a cohesive whole. When an idea was awkward or failed to pass the test of time, I would look for a better one. What is presented here has been honed and tested against the best standard I know—Einstein's dictum to "make everything as simple as possible, but not simpler."

The starting point for what I have learned is that childhood is when we first begin to avoid painful feelings. Adult dysfunction most often reflects the style and level of sophistication of the person who first made use of a given pattern. Some patterns are reminiscent of very small children with their simple ways, while others represent the problem-solving skills of a more advanced stage of development. The more specific and accurate our understanding, the better we can relate to the child who first got stuck. Even coping with stresses and

trauma that happen in adulthood can be seen as building upon layers of experience and learning from earlier phases of development,
each layer built on what was before.

To me the idea of an inner child is far more than a gimmick. One of
the very best ways to look at our own change process is as a dialog
between a child who is afraid of change and the adult who knows
change is not so dangerous and will lead to greater happiness. Just
as an understanding of children's development helps us guide our
own children when they are in unfamiliar and scary situations, our
understanding as adults of our inner child's world helps us take a
compassionate yet firm approach to our own life learning.

As you are beginning to glean, the thesis of this book is that emotional and psychological problems, at least those that are not primarily biological, are the result of instinctive childhood needs to
avoid feelings that were once too painful or uncomfortable to face.
Patterns that were first developed to protect us from such daunting
emotions have become embedded in our personality and functioning. Much later, when their origins are no longer obvious, these patterns continue to operate in ways that constrict and limit our lives.
When we try to change, our minds are ready with powerful and subtle layers of resistance to thwart our efforts. As we overcome each
layer of protection and face each layer of feeling, healing by catharsis
will allow us to go on to the next layer—until we are no longer afraid.

The aim of this book is to share with you an understanding that is
broad enough to cover the range of emotional and psychological
problems that cause our human dysfunctions but specific and precise enough to apply to your own unique situation. Once again, it is
my sincere hope that what is presented here will truly be "as simple
as possible but not simpler."

THE CAVE, THE BRIDGE, AND THE VILLAGE

How overwhelming feelings early in life lead to patterns of
avoidance that later cause many of our problems

Unreasonable and self-defeating ways are endemic to humankind. While we have the capacity to imagine being free of them, the truth is that change is hard. This book is an exploration of how these patterns are formed and how change is within our reach. The story has much more detail, but the recurring theme is that our troubles arise from an instinct to avoid painful feelings, whereas the healing and growth that can free us take place only when we face those same feelings.

What makes facing feelings less daunting is that, as adults, we have capabilities and help that were not available when we first learned to shield ourselves. When we first encountered painful feelings, we were young and our ability to cope limited. Drastic and costly measures were all that we could muster to avoid those toxic feelings. Now, as grownups, we have greater understanding, far more strength, and even the ability to choose our team of supporters.

The allegory that follows is a way of describing the process of change. Not everyone will make the journey in quite the same way, but the story captures the important elements.

The Cave, the Bridge, and the Village

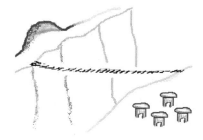

The Cave is dark, with an odor that is slightly unpleasant but familiar. It has been a long time since anyone has visited. The mouth of the Cave opens onto a narrow ledge overlooking the gorge and the torrent below. A short way up the ledge there is the Bridge, just a footbridge, no more than slats hanging from rusting cables. No one has crossed for years. On the other side people move about the Village. They seem far away, perhaps because of the roar of the river. Sometimes we wish someone would come across, but they don't.

On rare occasions, we even think of crossing the Bridge, but it seems too dangerous, too much trouble, too hard. The thought returns from time to time. We push it away. Time passes uneasily.

The Bridge was rickety even long ago when it was thrown across the chasm. It remains the only way to leave the Cave and its narrow ledge. Occasionally someone from the Village sees us looking. They appear friendly. They wave, and we sometimes make a timid gesture back. If it weren't for the Village, we would not think of crossing. In our musings, we wonder, "Could the Villagers understand what it is like on this side?"

One day, the loneliness of the Cave grows. Longing breaks into consciousness. The friendliness of the Villagers tempts us. We start to think that we could venture onto the Bridge. Rising at last, we step onto the first wooden slat. It bends. The second one cracks. We look down into the swirling muddy water far below. We quickly retreat. Not now. Perhaps another time.

Years later, the sun comes up bright, shining on the huts in the Village. Lately the Villagers have been calling out to us. Sometimes we hear their words over the din of the water below. We walk the short distance along the ledge to the Bridge and, again, take the first step. The Villagers see us. They wave. We step again, then again. The wood cracks, we scurry back, but the Cave seems dreary and dark. We try again. We step out gingerly, avoiding the broken boards. There is an excited murmur among the Villagers as they watch. One of them calls out, "It's okay, just step carefully." We take more steps. Suddenly we freeze. We are at the midpoint. The way back is just as forbidding as the way ahead; this is the "point of no return." Terror takes us.

All we see is the water churning below. The noise and fear are engulfing. The Village is infinitely remote and so is the Cave. The voices are gone. What remains is the vast distance down to the water and the Bridge swaying in the wind. Time is meaningless. The wind gusts. In the silent vortex, nothing matters. We feel a glimmer of liberation. It no longer seems to make a difference now if the Bridge collapses. In some indefinable way the terror no longer grips us as it did. We take more steps towards the Village.

At last, we arrive on the other side. The Villagers come to meet us. We feel a wary sense of relief. Exhausted, tears begin. We can't stop them. They have tears, too, and there is laughter. Are they making fun of us? The elder is calm, not smiling too much, looking in our eyes. He doesn't make a fuss. It is as if we had always belonged. They show us an empty hut, a place to put our few belongings. We know that to take up residence in the Village, we will have to go back to make the trip over and over again, each time bringing a few more things. Maybe it will be easier next time.

Now let's look at the component parts of the allegory and how they relate to real life.

The Cave

In adulthood, most of us become at least moderately able to look honestly at ourselves and our lives. As painful as some of our less admirable characteristics may be, we would rather know the truth than to stay in a comfortable fiction that we are perfect or that all of our troubles are due to outside circumstances. The truth is that most of us have at least some areas where our minds produce reactions and patterns that detract from our success and satisfaction. Furthermore, if these patterns were easy to eradicate, we would already have done so. That is how we find ourselves in a Cave, an uncomfortable place that is nonetheless familiar and not so easy to leave.

What is so surprising is that essentially all our mental dysfunctions seem to have the same basic origin. When we trace them back to the source, our dysfunctions are due to the fact that we are constructed from a clear-sighted intelligent and logical mind built on top of an instinct-dominated, mammalian one, the seat of feelings, attachments, connection to our bodies, and much automatic behavior. With the occasional exception of problems that are purely inherited or due to biological conditions, dysfunction is the result of our mammalian mind's commitment to avoiding pain and discomfort. The problem is that its efforts at avoidance such as blocking closeness to keep from being hurt eventually cost us more than the pain we are spared.

Each person's Cave is made of layers of tricks and techniques aimed at keeping us far from feelings we dread. The more layers there are, the less clear is their function and ultimate reason for being. And each person's layers are unique and individual. Difficult feelings and the methods we invent to avoid them are even more variable because they come from different periods of development. Our adult coping reflects the internal and external resources available us at the time we were first challenged.

In its quest to avoid pain and discomfort, our mammalian mind is naturally afraid of change. It is hard enough to construct a Cave for avoiding pain—why would one ever want to change it? Fear of change is yet another reason for staying in the Cave and resisting any temptation to venture outside.

Thus, the human condition is having a mind capable of seeing that change would improve our lives but possessing an inner force, honed over millions of years of evolution, that is firmly dedicated to keeping us locked in dysfunctional sameness.

The Bridge and Village Seen from Afar

Motivation to leave the Cave doesn't come so much from the unpleasantness of living there. That is something we tend to accept even though it is not a nice place. We are used to accepting it. What really gives us the desire to change is hope. It is when we perceive that life could be better that we find the energy and drive to think about making a move.

This perception is represented in the allegory by the sight of the Village across the chasm. Seeing the villagers and occasionally hearing their voices bring a message that a better life awaits. Their apparent happiness and lightness of being tantalize us with hope. But hope has another component. For us really to feel its pull we need possibility. Envisioning a better life when we have no way to get there will not kindle hope. Seen from the vantage point of the Cave, the Bridge represents possibility, a link that can bring us to the Village.

As scary as it may be, the Bridge stands there, a tangible reminder that change is possible. The possibility of crossing, along with the vision of fellowship represented by the Village, keeps tugging on us. Under the influence of hope, the dreariness of the cave grows less tolerable and our readiness to venture out grows stronger.

Paths to the Bridge

In real life, there are four paths that lead to the Bridge. Each one requires undoing a blockage to feeling. When we are able to put aside one of these blockages, we find ourselves on the Bridge; that is, in the midst of an encounter with emotions that once were more than we could handle but are now within our reach. Here are the four paths that lead there.

1. Arriving at simple **willingness** to encounter painful or uncomfortable feelings (Chapter 3).

2. Change in **ideas** that block us from believing that healing and growth are possible or even desirable (Chapter 4).

3. Change in **values** that stand in our way (Chapter 5).

4. Change in habitual **behavior patterns** that steer us away from new experience (Chapters 6, 7, 8).

Each path involves a different kind of blockage to feeling. The complex folded layers that confine us to our individual Cave are made up of these four blockages. As we undo each one, we find ourselves gripped by a feeling that we might only have glimpsed before. For example, one person might have a behavior pattern of refusing to accept compliments. Imagine that person choosing to say "thank you" instead of discounting the compliment. Immediately, the change in behavior leads to an uncomfortable feeling. Now the person is actually on the Bridge.

The Bridge

In the allegory, the Bridge is meant to capture moment by moment the experience of "going through" a dreaded feeling. I consider this to be the most basic emotional healing process in life. It happens all the time, so often that we don't usually notice it, or we may trivialize it by calling it "venting." When a painful feeling is extreme, it causes the heart to pound and skin to go cold. It triggers a primitive "fight or flight" reaction. When we share that feeling with an empathically connected witness, it quickly and dramatically loses its power over us. This is the amazing phenomenon I call *catharsis*. It is the transformation represented by the Bridge.

As each of our dreaded feelings is detoxified, we find ourselves another step closer to full citizenship in the Village, either facing our next layer of blockage or tasting the freedom that has been our goal.

Key Concept: Catharsis

Used in this book to designate the universal healing process by which raw, unprocessed feelings are transformed so as to lose their power over us and give us perspective over them. Catharsis happens when we share feelings in a context of empathic connection and safety. The term was originally coined by Sigmund Freud.

The Village

Humans are fundamentally social beings. Our bodies and brains are wired that way, and of course our minds are fully geared for relationship. In childhood our very lives depend on intensely felt attachments to the people who care for us. In adulthood, we have only to think of the power and intensity of marital arguments to realize that the life-and-death quality of our primary relationships does not end with childhood. In the allegory, the Village represents the all-important pull of attachment to lure us out of the confinement of our Cave and to reward us when we arrive.

As we explore the myriad forms of human dysfunction, we will see that our most toxic emotions and most of our problems grow in some way out of difficulty with significant relationships.

More about Our Problems

While my overall theme is simple, humans come in infinite variety, as do the hang-ups, quirks, foibles, character defects, and dysfunctions that trouble us. During our long development, each of us encounters unique circumstances and challenges. What we learn from each encounter shapes the way we react to the next. Out of these experiences, we gain strengths and abilities, but we may also develop patterns of rigidity and self-limitation as our need to cope forces us into desperate compromises.

The internal and external resources we bring to our difficult encounters are as varied as the situations themselves. Fortunately, despite the uniqueness of each of our experiences in life, humans are built in many of the same ways. As we understand our inner architecture common patterns emerge, and with them clarity about what we must do to heal and grow.

From the earliest age, children are problem solvers. Using the cognitive, emotional, and bodily resources they possess at the time, children adapt to their world by forming patterns that lead towards good feelings and away from bad ones. This is a fine strategy except that, with the limited assets of childhood, we often encounter situations that are beyond our best abilities. We depend on a very few people, and when they don't come through for us or when circumstances work against our vital needs being met, we find ourselves facing hopelessness. This feeling is more than any child can face, so we take desperate measures to avoid the feeling. Even when our best solutions come at a steep price, the alternative—accepting hopelessness—is not an option.

Circumstances such as aloneness, weakness, or disagreement with caregivers upon whom our lives depend lead to adaptations that will eventually work against us. As we grow, the problems we face are no longer the same. As our challenges change, so does our ability to find solutions. Unfortunately, due to human nature our archaic answers tend to remain in place into adulthood, even when they are obviously dysfunctional.

Even when the traumas and stresses we face are contemporary, befalling us in the here-and-now, the difference between disability and resilience may be determined by early experience. In particular, basic optimism and belief in the world, when present, are usually built on a foundation of secure attachment.

Why don't our old, and now harmful, patterns wither away by themselves? The answer is that by keeping dreaded feelings at a distance, we also shield ourselves from awareness that they are no longer dangerous. We develop layer upon layer of avoidance mechanisms to stay as far as possible from feelings that once posed the greatest threat. Each layer of insulation becomes a barrier to change. Even though we have new cognitive and emotional capacities, even though we have the ability to look at things in new ways and try new behaviors, even though we can now exercise choice about the people on whom we depend, a childlike part of our mind continues to act as if the old dangers are as immediate and threatening as they were long ago. Our minds are constructed in such a way as to avoid these threats with power and urgency, even when our rational thinking tells us otherwise.

Finding Our Personal Path to Healing and Growth

Each person's path begins with the perception that life could be better. Whether we call it a problem or an opportunity, the journey starts with the idea that we occupy a Cave with entrenched patterns of reaction that need to change. Our goal is the Bridge where catharsis transforms our dreaded emotions and gives access to the Village. Between Cave and Bridge are the four pathways, each dealing with a different blockage to feeling. Here are some simple rules to start you on your journey.

- **Ask and answers will come.** Once formulated clearly, questions somehow get answered. I often use this principle. For example, when a question is posed, the next few sentences from a patient are very likely to contain the answer. Formulate your questions in as clear language as possible. Set yourself up to find the answer. Be wary of looking only inward, since we all have blind spots. Your quest may lead you to friends, meditation, lectures, books, or to a professional. Insist on answers that are fully satisfying and they will appear. Answers may not come from the expected direction, but they will come.

- **When there is a choice between two blockages, try the easier one first.** There is no need to be heroic. Success comes more often from taking the easiest steps first.

- **Stack all the cards in your favor.** Get help, build a rooting section of people who want you to succeed. Use all the resources available and give yourself credit for your successes.

- **Ask yourself which of the four paths will undo your first blockage:** Becoming willing, changing ideas, changing values or, making changes in behavior patterns. Work on making the needed changes. In the chapters that follow we will take a much more detailed look at each of the four paths.

- **If you get bogged down, scale back the changes you plan to make.** Alcoholics say "one day at a time" because "the rest of your life" is too big to tackle. There are many ways to shrink a mountain to a size that can be climbed.

- **If you really get bogged down...,** keep reading; I'll answer this one later in this chapter.

How These Ideas Fit into the World of Self-Help

Self-help, like psychotherapy, is currently in a state that is both exciting and difficult to navigate. There are so many great ideas and approaches, and each one promises to be the last one you will need to know. Almost every new idea in psychotherapy has spawned a self-help version. Let's look at some of the current approaches to change and how each of them incorporates one or more of the four paths leading to the Bridge and incorporates a process analogous to catharsis to detoxify painful feelings.

- **Cognitive-behavioral therapy** focuses on changing ideas, values, and behavior patterns in order to unblock us. When our inner fear of change resists, persistence aided by workbooks, rating scales, and a support system can help to keep us leaning into the change process. Changes bring out our uncomfortable feelings and catharsis silently heals the emotions we have needed to face. As emotions heal, we experience greater comfort and better functioning.

- **Traditional talk therapy** adopts the goal of achieving insight or understanding. As we pursue the ostensible task of understanding, we are confronted with the four types of blockages. Persistence aided by a patient and confident therapist helps us identify blockages and make changes. As the process of understanding unfolds, we encounter feelings that had been avoided and with catharsis they heal. Undoing blockages and traversing our dreaded feelings leads to new freedom.

- **Positive psychology** aims to change ideas and adopt new, positive behavior patterns. These actions hopefully bring out any difficult feelings we need to experience and traverse. If we persist, the feelings will heal by catharsis and we will be able to maintain a more positive and contented outlook. Imagining where we want to be helps energize us, giving hope and motivating us to overcome our inner reluctance.

- **Mindfulness** helps us "surf the feeling" that is—take a position of perspective on our feelings instead of allowing them to toss us around like crashing waves. Also it helps to know that feelings, like waves, have a beginning and an end. This process is closely analogous to catharsis and is a way to heal painful feelings so we can free our lives. The precise relationship to catharsis is discussed in Chapter 3.

- **Dialectical behavior therapy** uses a toolbox of ideas and techniques as well as experiences to bring overwhelming feelings down to scale. In doing so, like mindfulness, it gives perspective on our feelings, allowing us to surf them successfully till they run out of energy.

- **Emotion-focused therapy** is concentrated on approaching overwhelming feelings with empathy and warmth. This is the same as what I call catharsis.

- **Attachment, imago, and schema therapies** are built around the observation that many dysfunctional reactions, especially in intimate relationships, come from automatic patterns learned early in life. Behavior change again brings out avoided feelings where we can face them. Since patterns come from such early eras of development, the process is different from other forms of voluntary behavior change.

- **Eye movement desensitization and reprocessing (EMDR)** works to heal painful feelings derived from trauma. Its mechanism of action is the subject of controversy, but as we will see in

Chapter 3, it incorporates precisely those elements that are essential for healing by catharsis.

- **Psychoanalysis** creates conditions that bring out strong feelings, especially within the therapeutic relationship. Blockages to feelings are explored and dismantled. With empathy and acceptance, catharsis works to allow painful feelings to heal.

- **Emotional Intelligence (EQ) and resilience** are being taught using a combination of idea change and mindfulness to combat immature, automatic reactions. The end result is, as in catharsis, achieving a greater level of consciousness and perspective on our feelings. As this happens, emotions lose their power to sabotage our effectiveness.

- **Twelve Step groups** create a positive environment to promote hope and motivation for change in ideas, values, and behavior. Sharing in a context of empathic connection helps heal difficult emotions through catharsis.

- **Experiential therapies and body work** focus on bringing out locked emotions in a context of empathy and acceptance. These are the essential elements in cathartic healing.

Only a few of these approaches explicitly identify our inner fear of change. For the most part, when resistance is encountered we are told to persist and follow exactly the steps laid out. If we do so diligently, then the method promises results. These approaches will work if we soldier through them. Unfortunately, what often happens is that our inner reluctance to change and to face feelings finds a way to block or derail our efforts. We may not follow the program in every detail, or we may give up before the end. Perhaps we follow the program but slip back later. We may even follow a program but find hidden ways to sabotage the results and remain stuck.

If You Really Get Bogged Down...

If you really get bogged down, you will need to make friends with an inner child who is deathly afraid of change and afraid of facing the feelings he or she has dreaded and avoided all along. When, as adults, we try to change our now-dysfunctional patterns of avoidance, we find ourselves working against childlike ways that have stayed frozen and have not evolved with time. These patterns are trying to steer us away from pain associated with change.

In upcoming chapters we will see how the mind's efforts at avoidance are primarily based on young ways of perceiving life and young strategies for avoidance. Since these operations take place mostly out of our awareness, for practical purposes it is as if we have a young, inner child who is desperate to spare us from pain and suffering.

I am concerned that the mention of an "inner child" will conjure up thoughts that the author is a new-age romantic. This is not the case. Like any hard-nosed detective, we will be more successful if, based on observations, we can build a picture of the mastermind who is resisting our efforts to clean up our life. As we do so, we will see characteristics that bear the stamp of earlier developmental periods. In our efforts to make changes in spite of resistance from within, our job will be made easier if we are able to picture the motivations and modes of thinking of the young protector within. Not only that, but we will be able to predict and anticipate how our inner mind, unchanged since childhood, will react to our next move. When forward progress is met with backlash, we will be prepared rather than taken by surprise.

There is another huge advantage to the notion of an inner child who has failed to evolve. Approaching him or her with compassion and understanding will be far more effective than trying to force change. As we begin to comprehend this part of our mind, we will find ourselves feeling compassion. Even as our inner child tries to thwart our efforts, we will be able to see her as a committed helper, limited by childlike ways of thinking and perception. She is trying her best, but the tools available to her have not evolved over time because they have been shielded from conscious awareness and contact with contemporary reality.

When we find our efforts at change thwarted from inside we tend to approach the source of our frustration as an enemy. Especially when an automatic reaction is obviously immature, we want to punish the child or even try to eliminate her. Just as with a real child, harshness is absolutely the wrong approach. The child is fighting for survival, and surrender is not an option. She may go underground, but attempts to banish childish reactions are never successful. What does work, as with real children, is understanding, compassion, and a gentle but firm approach. "I know you are afraid, but I'm here to protect you. Come with me and we'll be okay."

This book is intended to help build useful understanding and find resources to lead our inner children into the feeling experiences that they have energetically sought to avoid. We can expect many layers of resistance. Some will be obvious and strong; some will be covert and subtle. As we seek out and choose to face our avoided feelings, catharsis will transform them and remove their power to sabotage our lives. Dread will lose its power and our old, dysfunctional patterns will, at last, become accessible to change. We will gain the freedom to bring our actions into harmony with the adult aims that are dearest to our hearts.

As it turns out, the mind has many ways of avoiding feelings. Every mental system is involved, including how we think, our conscience, our behavior patterns, our most cherished dreams, and even our emotional development. We examine each of these areas in the chapters to come. But in the end, the final common pathway for healing is always the same: catharsis—that is, sharing your uncomfortable feelings in a context of safety and connection.

Will I Need to Be in Therapy?

Of course my bias is towards using a therapist to navigate the pathways and processes presented here, but the truth is that there are far more instances of lasting change taking place in life than in therapy. The books, movies, and other stories we humans find most compelling are those that tell about emotional encounters that change us. As you gain clarity about what you need to do and what feelings you need to face, you will have a better sense of whether you can do it on your own or whether you will need a guide who may be more familiar with the territory.

Which Therapy?

As the descriptions earlier in this chapter make obvious, seeking help in shedding dysfunctional patterns opens up a confusing world of seemingly contradictory theories and therapies. The fact that they are still at war with one another doesn't help. The secret truth is that they are really all talking about the same four pathways leading to the Bridge and one transformative process that takes place on the Bridge. Even though the jargon and concepts are very different, the ways they help people change are essentially the same. In our exploration, we will develop a natural language that can bring disparate theories and therapies under one roof and allow translation between and among seemingly incompatible bodies of wisdom.

Fortunately for the confused consumer, good research shows that the brand of therapy accounts for only a very small part of its effectiveness. Far more important is the relationship you have with your therapist. So which therapy should you choose? You will read here about a few places where one therapy seems to have something special to offer. Other than that, the choice is more a matter of comfort with a given style or therapist. Perhaps it is best to think of a potential therapist as a guide to help you face things that are difficult and scary. You will want to find someone who "gets" you and understands the journey you will be undertaking, someone who will help you want to take emotional risks that seem dangerous but are really not—and feel good that you did.

If you have doubts about a therapy you are already engaged in, Chapter 9 presents a questionnaire based on the concepts presented here and independent of which school your therapist follows. It is intended to help you formulate a sense of how your therapy is helpful and what problems may be hindering your progress. As always, if you have doubts or criticisms of your therapy, you should bring them up. Your therapist is a professional and has handled questions before. He or she should be able to respond to your questions in a way that is helpful to you both.

The Dimension of Development

One aspect of our folded layers of avoidance of feeling is that understanding them depends very much on having a grasp of how children perceive, think, and react at different ages. This developmental perspective is often underemphasized in the fields of therapy and self-help. Throughout this book I will refer to key developmental challenges and the solutions that grow out of the child's abilities and resources at a particular point in development. In my view, understanding our inner child is impossible without putting ourselves in his shoes—and that means having a feel for how the world looks through a child's eyes at a particular point of development. While development will be woven through the chapters that follow, Chapter 8 will give a brief survey of key developmental issues and how they affect our adult coping.

I am careful to say "point of development" rather than "age" because development can happen or fail to happen at any age. I often think of forty-year-olds having temper tantrums. Because we put such a high value on maturity, we tend to feel ashamed of our immaturity. We may have to get over our shame (by catharsis) to be able to talk frankly about parts of ourselves that come from an earlier "immature" time. Getting past our reluctance to admit to immaturity will greatly empower our efforts at change. Even before making us tolerant of and compassionate toward our inner child, accepting the possibility of having immature parts of ourselves helps us recognize and understand how our development may have become frozen. Only when we accept the impact of immaturity on our adult functioning can we unfreeze and pick up the thread of development again.

Some time ago, I was speaking to a colleague about a sullen and defiant fourteen-year-old boy who had been referred for consultation because of marijuana use. My colleague correctly observed that the young man was experiencing "anxiety and depression." He seemed to think those labels would give enough understanding to know what to do next. What he hadn't seen was that the boy had become overwhelmed by the looming challenge of becoming an adult. He had started life with unusual sensitivity and was completely unprepared for the toughness of the adult world. In his fear, he had sought refuge in the soft feeling of marijuana. Now that his parents and others were trying to take away his one means of dealing with life, he was anxious and depressed. His fragile world was under attack. This was not anxiety or depression in a vacuum, but woven into an unfolding life experience. To be relieved of these symptoms, he would have to experience a new, positive way of facing the stresses of growing up. He would have to practice it until it felt good. Only then would he find true relief from anxiety and depression. Without paying attention to the boy's developmental process, it was impossible to understand his distress.

This example shows how contemporary practice often misses the richness provided by an understanding of development. In addition it shows a special and unique type of blockage to feeling. When children become afraid of new experiences and avoid them, development stops. This is non-behavior rather than dysfunctional behavior. Rather than evolving positively unhealthy coping mechanisms, we humans are also capable of avoiding new experiences and putting any aspect of development on semipermanent hold. Even before he discovered marijuana, the boy in the example above was doing just this. He was shying away from the scary challenges of teenage life and gravitating towards like-minded friends. Under these conditions, growth and maturation can come to an absolute halt.

As a clinician, I often see stalled development where others may see illness. When I do, I am happy because development can be restarted at any time, and it is easier to resume development than to unlearn distorted patterns. Fortunately, the process of growing is largely the same whether it is in childhood or much later in adulthood. How do we grow? By trying new behaviors and using catharsis to heal the uncomfortable feelings that are inevitably part of the experience.

The Brain

As indicated in the introduction, while we are currently in the age of the brain, this book is primarily about the contribution of the mind to our problems and to our healing and growth. What is the difference? A simple way to look at it is that the study of the brain covers all the infrastructure, but it does not concern itself with the specific ideas, words, memories associations, and other contents that are stored there. The concept of mind recognizes components and pathways by which meanings interact but is also concerned with the specifics of individual meaning and how meanings affect our lives. These meanings are increasingly known to influence the development, structure, and functioning of the brain and vice versa, which is why treatment choices may involve both biological and psychological interventions.

The dysfunctional patterns that limit our happiness are ultimately expressed in the firing of nerve cells. Nonetheless, those patterns largely grow out of individual meaning. Many of our characteristics are determined by our genetics and brain development, but they also affect the development of our minds. On the other hand, feelings and thoughts triggered by events around us and influenced by past experience have an impact on the brain. The brain develops over many years and keeps on changing as our lives change. Just as muscles grow when we exercise, parts of the brain grow or fade depending on how we use them. It is hard even for researchers to determine what factors underlie a particular characteristic in an individual. Thus, while our focus is the mind, we should remember that the mind is physical and is heavily influenced by the brain.

Which Kind of Intervention?

When people are in some form of emotional trouble, there are, for practical purposes, just two ways to reach into the brain to deliver help. One is to use chemicals (or some other physical means) to influence the firing of nerve cells. The other is to modify the firing of nerve cells through talk. Yes, talk is a very precise and specific way to activate just those neurons that are the source of trouble and to modify their synaptic connections.

Comparing the two, I think of medication as a blunt instrument while talk is a sharp one. Despite efforts to find medications that will have effects on just those few neurons we need to touch, pharmacologic agents usually affect millions of nerve cells, most of which are not involved in the systems we want to change. The impact of medications on these "bystander" neurons is the main source of unpleasant and even dangerous side effects. On the other hand, talk conveys meaning, and meanings light up only small groups of nerve cells, making just those cells and their synapses accessible to change. This is why my bias is towards talk.

In one aspect, medications and talk run into similar problems. Our brain and mind are both fundamentally dedicated to self-regulation—maintaining the status quo in spite of outside influences. We have already seen how psychotherapy and self-help pit us against our own mind's fear of change. With medication, we are trying to alter systems that are often designed to regulate themselves so as to maintain constancy in spite of a variable world. Even if there is a chemical imbalance, built-in mechanisms may come into play to maintain the status quo and counteract our efforts to change the balance. The result is that medications may work for a while and then "poop out." We may be able to increase the dose, but often this means more side effects. For example, powerful pain medications (technically, opioids) are specifically able to turn down the "volume" on our pain system. This is amazingly effective in relieving pain for a few days. However, the brain soon begins to notice the lack of pain signals and adjusts the volume back up. As it does this, we experience heightened pain again. Now we have to take even more medicine to quiet the system. And once the system has adjusted to compensate for the effect of the medication, what happens if you take the drug away? Just as when one child abruptly gets off a teeter-toter, a sudden, violent imbalance ensues. With pain medication, any part of the body that is capable of hurting begins to hurt along with other distressing symptoms. The result is the very uncomfortable experience we call withdrawal.

Which route of intervention is for you? Sometimes one seems better and sometimes a combination is appropriate. On the whole, talk seems to have fewer side effects and more staying power, but there are times when we may be in the grip of a vicious cycle and talk simply isn't powerful or fast enough. Especially with deep depression or manic loss of control over mood, talk may have little immediate effect. Other problems such as schizophrenia and autism may involve disturbed brain architecture or regulatory systems that are not accessible to talk. Then, psychotherapy alone will probably be ineffective, and medication may be a lifesaver.

On the other hand, there are problems, especially those involving the mind and its contents, for which chemicals have little effect. Think of the lasting emotional pain and suffering that can result from being unable to forgive or unable to let go of an impossible goal. People can fall into serious depression and hopelessness when, due to past experience, they interpret events in a dysfunctional way. Not infrequently these emotional impasses take place outside of awareness, so that the good counsel of friends and our own introspection still cannot tell us what is wrong. In these situations, drug treatment can dull the pain a bit, but probing psychotherapy may be the only way to approach the source of our distress.

Sometimes we have a choice, or at least a choice of where to begin. There are times when the pros and cons of the two routes are evenly matched. Psychotherapy may be slower than biological treatments and possibly more costly. But when the problem is situated in the mind, as in the examples in the previous paragraph, psychotherapy may be more able to bring about lasting relief with fewer side effects. In situations like this, the choice is best made collaboratively between patient and professional.

Biological treatments are, by their nature, not the stuff of self-help. Even though I often use medications in my work, I will not try to discuss those treatments here. This book is about the mind, where individual meaning is taken in, stored, and processed. I will discuss patterns and problems that come from the mind's efforts to avoid painful and uncomfortable feelings. These will not include problems that are primarily biological in origin or where treatment is mainly biological.

This book will also not attempt to show the reader whether a problem is best accessed through the biological route or the psychotherapeutic one. That is what licensed professionals are for. What we will do is look into the mind, at how our attempts to avoid feelings can result in a remarkable range of dysfunctional patterns and how facing those feelings is the key to untangling many of the greatest problems we humans experience.

Blaming Parents

An issue that sometimes comes up in talking about mental problems is the tendency of therapists to "blame" parents. You will see in the pages of this book stories of patients such as Andrew, whose anxiety probably had its origins in hernia surgery when he was barely a toddler (see Chapter 2). This and other circumstances were out of his parents' control. His mother had to go back to work when he was seven and his father was diagnosed with heart disease when he was ten. While Andrew's parents had done no wrong and in fact had taken very good care of him, it should not be a surprise that Andrew developed anxiety.

It is true that primary caregivers, most often mothers, are crucial in forming early knowledge of how relationships work. Parenting is critically important, but there are also mismatches. Furthermore during formative developmental periods, crises happen that are no one's fault. In Chapter 2 I introduce the developmental calamity that inevitably occurs when the omnipotent one-year-old turns two and realizes for the first time that "no" means not being the Emperor of the World. Growing up hurts without being anyone's "fault."

Individual humans also have unique responses to what they observe. I once heard the story of a three-year-old who, for no apparent reason, became very upset around Thanksgiving time. The morning after the holiday, the child watched *Sesame Street* and suddenly calmed down when she saw Big Bird. After talking with her, the parents realized that during the previous week she had been listening with horror as they spoke eagerly about eating a big bird at their Thanksgiving meal.

Blaming parents is not only unhelpful but often incomplete or simply wrong. The impact of a particular experience can be influenced by many factors, including inborn temperament, genetics, previous experience, hormonal environment, and the state of brain and/or emotional development at the time. We need to be respectful of the complexity of cause and effect. Furthermore, children's struggles regularly produce skills and strengths as well as dysfunctional patterns. While forming hypotheses is often useful, being judgmental is not. The kinds of change that are the focus of this book are aimed at leaving the past behind and transcending personal history so as to be free in our present life.

How This Book Is Organized

Chapter 2, Avoiding Feelings. The next chapter after this one is about how and why we have problems and find them hard to change. It describes how, from the earliest age, we naturally strive to fend off uncomfortable feelings and how powerful motivational forces go to work to keep those feelings at bay. This leads to development of lasting patterns of avoidance. Over time, long after their original purpose has been forgotten, these patterns can and often do form the basis of our emotional problems and dysfunction.

Chapter 3, Catharsis: Amazing Medicine. This chapter is about what happens on the Bridge. Facing just those feelings we have been avoiding is the way to heal them. When we experience painful feelings in a context of connection with an empathic witness, they heal through a process called catharsis. This chapter will explore the exact nature of catharsis and how to make it happen.

The next five chapters will explore the ways we avoid feelings and how to work around each of them. While chapters 2 and 3 support our understanding and willingness to encounter feelings, the next five are about more indirect pathways to the Bridge: changing ideas, changing values, and changing various kinds of behavior patterns.

Chapter 4, Information and Misinformation. Ideas and thoughts are often products of the hidden part of our mind that is dedicated to keeping us safe from painful feelings. Ideas are crafted to block paths that would lead to feelings. We may deny our anger or minimize the importance of something we don't want to face. We may tell ourselves things like "I'll never succeed" to protect ourselves from trying and failing. But as much as they serve to cover up, ideas are also a means of discovering and clarifying. They can serve as searchlights to open our access even to things we would rather not admit.

Chapter 5, Your Conscience Can Be Wrong. The field of psychotherapy has all but forgotten the importance of the conscience, but it is crucial. Values, attitudes, ideals, and prohibitions are the principles by which we judge our own and others' behavior. These judgments lead to a special category of feelings consisting of pride, shame, and guilt. Strongly embedded in our conscience, our values help us maintain good behavior. But these mental contents can also be part of unhealthy avoidance mechanisms. We sometimes internalize values that steer us away from troublesome feelings that we really need to face. Those who have been traumatized regularly internalize attitudes of low self-worth. In such cases, in order for healing to take place, the dysfunctional value or attitude must first be modified. The key to value change is action. We may need to do the opposite of what our values tell us. In doing so, a kind of "civil disobedience" shows our conscience that its values are not necessarily right.

Chapter 6, Voluntary Behavior Change. Behavior is one of the most powerful and ubiquitous of avoidance mechanisms. We will discuss different behavior patterns from different eras of development and how they allow us to avoid feelings. Once again, healing requires that we do the opposite of what we are used to: voluntarily change our behavior. Behavior patterns come in many types and flavors, often depending on the age at which they are first brought into service. This chapter will focus on how to recognize unhealthy behaviors and how to change them for good.

Chapter 7, Dreams and Quests. Around the age of five, children begin to dream of someday. Their grasp of the dimension of time opens up a new and powerful way of solving problems. They can undo the pain of today by envisioning a someday in which they will become more powerful, more attractive, more desirable, etc. As in the fairy tales they love, they can imagine themselves being able to overcome the limitations and problems that seem to cause their pain. I call these plans quests. When quests become buried they cease to evolve, and when that happens, they can become hidden motivators of dysfunctional behavior. We will explore how to identify and work with these quests.

Chapter 8, Arrested Development. One of the most common ways we avoid painful or uncomfortable feelings is by avoiding the experiences that bring up those feelings. This avoidance of experience can result in arrested development, because development happens when we try new things. Here too, doing the opposite—that is, trying new, healthy, but unfamiliar behaviors—is how we can restart our development and maturation.

Chapter 9, The Future Starts Today. Encouraging words and the Scarsdale Psychotherapy Self Evaluation, (SPSE) a tool for evaluating the effectiveness of therapy regardless of school.

Disclaimer

This book is not intended to substitute for a good evaluation by a competent clinician. Our natural need to push uncomfortable feelings out of consciousness can trip us up. Even with great honesty, our attempts at self-diagnosis are often subject to blind spots related to our need to avoid feelings.

As indicated in the discussion above, even with a clear idea of what the problem is, the question of how best to approach it can be a very serious one. You should consult a licensed professional for help with questions of which treatment is right for you. Distinguishing between mainly psychological problems and those related to biology is what psychiatrists and other professionals are trained to do. This book should not be used for self-diagnosis but to raise questions and explore possible answers.

For this reason, I strongly recommend that you seek an appropriately credentialed professional for help and guidance if you are contemplating your own journey of emotional healing and growth.

A Note about the Case Studies in This Book

The patients described in this book are fictional or composites with many details altered. The aim is to give examples that accurately represent the workings of the human mind.

· 2 ·

AVOIDING FEELINGS

A survey of why and how we shut feelings out and how our
protective castles can become confining prisons

John married Jen a few years after he left the Army. John always felt
proud when she told him how much she loved his strength and sense of
responsibility, but soon after the wedding he became a control freak. John
attempted to run every area of their lives. Focusing most on their finances, he
was constantly irritated with Jen for spending too much money. He lectured
her on how to preserve leftover food and how to drive the car to save gas.
When Jen came up with her own ideas, John would override her with logical
reasons why she was wrong. As time went on, John and Jen grew more and
more unhappy. And the more John worried the unhappier he became. He felt
buried under his burden of responsibility.

John had grown up with alcoholic parents who could barely care for
themselves, let alone a child. Essentially, he raised himself. As he
grew up, he took pride in being more capable and mature than his
friends, but in truth, he was acting out of necessity. What drove him
was a deep fear of being weak or needy. His controlling behavior was
a way of showing that he was in charge and didn't need anyone—but

the reality was that, without knowing it, he yearned for someone to take care of him. Because this need was not provided for in childhood, it grew and became a threat. He learned to fear weakness and neediness, and these ultimately became his demons.

Using behaviors and attitudes as its walls and buttresses, John then had to build a Castle to keep his demons out. He had no idea what he was hiding from, or even that he was hiding. As far as he understood, he was simply trying to make the most of his hard-earned income, and the closest he could come to asking for help was to demand Jen's cooperation. By attacking what he saw as weakness in Jen, John distanced himself from his own weakness. John's Castle had become a Prison that kept him from relating to Jen. Still, he couldn't stop his behaviors or change course. He believed that relaxing his high standards would be a form of failure.

Sometimes Feelings Hurt

But they are also the key to our growth and healing. It's true: You don't have to run from your feelings.

Castles That Become Prisons

The story of a couple like John and Jen could have gone in several directions. John could have developed anxiety attacks or become violent; he might have started drinking heavily. Jen could have had an affair. The marriage could have come apart. Something had to give.

As a child, John had no one to turn to, so it is no wonder he was left with little faith in anyone but himself. In adulthood, help is readily available, but only a really serious crisis could make John reach out. What he needed was simple. He needed to change his controlling behavior, face his needy feelings, and allow the process I call catharsis to heal the old wounds. But simple is not the same as easy, and John had become so dedicated to avoiding his feelings that he might never have escaped. (The sad truth is that many people never do find their way out of their Castles.)

When Jen threatened to leave him, John finally sought therapy. It became
clear that he actually appreciated working with a strong figure—perhaps his
therapist reminded him of his favorite sergeant in the Army. The goals were
for John to learn how to be a more equal partner and, ultimately, for John to
face the need to be taken care of, a need that, at first, he couldn't even begin
to recognize. As he dared to be a patient, he started to see the terrible effect
his controlling had on Jen. Slowly, he came to understand that neediness is
not shameful and that adult life has room for being taken care of. As he went
through the step-by-step process of letting go of his fear of weakness, he had
the opportunity to genuinely feel sadness for his own early deprivation and
grieve for what he had never had.

Why Do We Resist?

Why do so many of us resist facing our true feelings? Avoiding pain
is one of the most basic drives for all living beings. You could say
that the reason we have pain is to point to what should be avoided.
So it is no surprise that the human mind has developed many ways
to avoid pain. The problem is that many of the most effective ways
of avoiding emotional pain come at the expense of truth. Children,
even more than adults, must face many moments when pain is un-
avoidable. They have little control over their environment and have
no choice but to absorb much of the discomfort they encounter. So,
early in life, the need to deny or cover up things that cause emotional
pain is an important part of survival. If these avoidance mechanisms
were not available, then the experience of life might be one of near
constant agony. Especially with painful circumstances that are continuous or repetitive, we develop lasting and remarkably effective
ways of denying and distancing the things that most trouble us.

Thus, it is extremely natural to avoid emotional discomfort. For most
of us, including John, avoidance began at a very young age. As will
later be discussed in detail, small people have big emotions. Their
fragile grasp of the world and their shaky sense of safety can be completely undone by the stress of events that seem minor to adults.
Having a stomach ache or being denied one's way are major events.
Children lack the perspectives of time and scale. There is only one

time, now, and only one measuring stick, the self—and this makes moments seem like eternities and feelings seem limitless. Adding to the distress, children lack the language to describe what is happening, so, in a way, they are alone. Children who face repeated emotional injury gradually build a protective structure, a Castle, to fend off awareness of painful feelings.

John and other patients remind me of the Japanese soldier, Lieutenant Hiroo Onoda.

Lieutenant Hiroo Onoda hid on the remote island of Lubang in the Philippines for almost thirty years because he believed that World War II was still being fought and he had been ordered never to surrender. Like Onoda, emotionally injured children learn the art of camouflage. When their needs and weaknesses are a liability in childhood, they become adept at hiding them from other people and even themselves. They turn privation into a virtue and develop a creed based on self-sufficiency. They don't realize that the war within them can be over. And, just as Lt. Onoda retained the habits he had developed decades earlier to protect himself, adults can hold tightly to the old, no longer useful ways of coping that protected them in childhood.

A young Japanese man, Norio Suzuki, personally took on the mission of coaxing Onoda out from the mountains. However, when Suzuki met the lieutenant and explained that World War II was over, the soldier thought it might be a trick. Suzuki went back to Japan and found Onoda's former commanding officer, Major Taniguchi, who returned with Suzuki to Lubang to relieve Onoda from duty. Finally convinced that the war was over, he could begin to traverse the complex emotions around his lost years and his heroism.

In therapy it takes time and gentle focus by both the therapist and patient to overcome the fierceness guarding each layer of camouflage and misunderstanding. As each layer comes into view and is bathed in the calmer light of another's reality (that is, the therapist's reality), it begins to seem less dire.

Once in therapy, John saw that his need for control was not just about saving money. He began to understand that his exaggerated sense of responsibility and his feelings of shame kept him from enjoying life. Eventually he became aware that he had carried for years a deep sense that he was a child pretending to be a man. Over many sessions, he developed empathy for the child in himself, and he began to admit that he had needs and weaknesses. As he worked through each layer in therapy, his world came to feel less dangerous, and he felt relief from sharing his feelings. (This is a good example of catharsis.)

A quality of our Castles that is further reminiscent of Lieutenant Onoda's experience is their durability. It hardly seems to have crossed the soldier's mind that the war could have been lost. Similarly, we systematically steer clear from the evidence that our Castles no longer protect us. As a result, they remain standing, unaffected by the passage of time.

To summarize, the theme of this chapter and one of the main principles running through this book is that most, if not all, of the dysfunctional patterns that are endemic to humans begin in childhood when we build Castles to distance ourselves from feelings that are too painful or uncomfortable to handle. Because we avoid even knowing that they are there, our Castles can last for years, even decades, long after they have outlived their usefulness; they then become Prisons, the foundation of many problems that plague us as adults. Not only does this simple idea give an explanation of our problems, but it also points the way to healing. To be freed from our Prison, we must face our most dreaded feelings. That is when the process of catharsis comes in to tame even the most terrible emotions.

Key Concept: The Origin of Mental Dysfunction

Our need to avoid painful and uncomfortable feelings leads, mostly outside awareness, to patterns of perception, thought, and action that form the basis of most of our emotional problems. There are other ways to explain what drives us to behave in dysfunctional ways but, for me, this one is the best because it leads naturally to the solution to our problems: the liberating experience of facing our feelings.

Some Feelings That Trigger Avoidance

The defenses against feeling that create our adult Prisons in our adult lives start with some intensely uncomfortable feeling. Such feelings naturally trigger strenuous efforts and the construction of protective Castles to keep them at bay. As small children, they are often feelings beyond our ability to cope. In this section we will examine a number of feelings that commonly trigger our costly efforts at avoidance.

Before proceeding, it may help to take note of a semantic problem. The English language doesn't have words for actions that are purposeful but whose true aim is out of our conscious awareness. When I speak of "efforts" to avoid feelings, even though the words usually imply conscious intent, I don't mean them that way. Rather, I mean actions that are outside of awareness but purposefully driven by our need to avoid feelings. At many points in this book, the language of intentionality will be used to describe operations of the mind that are purposeful but not conscious.

Helplessness and Hopelessness: Primordial, Terrifying

What exactly was the childhood feeling John was trying to avoid? Presumably, it was the pain of needing parental support and receiving none. In addition, probably before memory, there were times when he expressed his need and was rebuked or even punished for bothering parents who were preoccupied with their own chaos. If John expressed his wishes, they would lash out at him. If he stayed quiet, they would ignore him. He had nowhere to turn. The result was one of the most toxic feelings known to humans: helplessness.

For John, and for most of us, helplessness is the most primordial of painful feelings; escaping from helplessness is one of our most basic instincts. We need only see an insect on its back fighting to get on its legs to understand how far back in evolution this instinct goes. Our brains have evolved to make helplessness extremely uncomfortable and capable of triggering massive efforts to escape.

An adult example of how humans struggle with helplessness is the way people respond irrationally to a loved one's being diagnosed with cancer. Even close friends and relatives might completely avoid the topic—even avoiding the very word *cancer*—or they might offer some easy answer or suggestion ("drink carrot juice," "think positive thoughts"). Nothing could be less helpful. Why do we behave like this? We need to distance ourselves from the helplessness we feel in response to our loved one's diagnosis.

Elisabeth Kübler-Ross described in detail how hard it is—and how long it takes—for people to accept the inevitability of their own deaths. Even then, they may continue to keep helplessness at bay by focusing on thoughts such as "death won't be in vain" or "just maybe medical science will find a cure before it's too late."

Elisabeth Kübler-Ross (1926-2004)

Kübler-Ross wrote the book *On Death and Dying*, in which she described five stages that people go through when faced with death: denial, anger, bargaining, depression, and acceptance.

In childhood, helplessness is *much* more terrible. Children are entirely dependent on the older people in their lives for their very survival. Around eight months, when children suddenly become shy of strangers, their reaction suggests that they possess some sense of their vulnerability. To make matters worse, at this early age they lack the cognitive ability to grasp the existence of any social safety net that might come into play if something were to happen to their primary caregivers. The parent says, "Sure, you can hold the baby," and suddenly the eight-month-old's sense of safety evaporates. Unless Mom responds to the desperate cries, what looms is the terrible feeling of helplessness.

The feeling is almost intolerable. Even older children, faced with feelings of helplessness, almost always resort to denial, which equates to hope. If you were to try to tell a child that there is no hope, the child would find a way to evade your logic. Except in the most extreme circumstances, it is essentially impossible for a child to acknowledge helplessness or give up hope.

Faced with helplessness, children and adults are capable of another reaction. We can go into depression. This is complicated because it involves our brain chemistry as well as thought. However, as will be explored later, depression can be the result of an attempt to create hope when hope is lost. By turning against the self, seeing oneself as guilty or unworthy, a depressed person may be following a dark logic that punishment of the unworthy self might bring justice and with it, hope. Another purpose that may run in parallel is turning passive to active. Paradoxically, actively adopting a stance of hopelessness can be a way to preserve hope. How can that be? Hopelessness that is "adopted" is not the same as hopelessness imposed on us by others. If it is voluntary (even if not consciously), then it is under our control and we are not really helpless. If this seems extreme, it is. Extreme measures show how desperate is our human need to preserve hope at any cost.

Hopelessness and helplessness are strongly intertwined. Think of how many cemeteries, places of finality, have the word *hope* in their names. Hope is the antidote to helplessness, and the ability to help oneself triggers hope. The threat of losing hope or losing the ability to take care of oneself is terrifying. Only with a great deal of adult perspective and emotional work can we come even close to contemplating the loss of either or both.

Hopelessness and its sibling helplessness are so toxic that they are among the strongest triggers of childhood strategies to avoid coming anywhere near to feeling them.

Most of the time, the lions that guard our feelings are ancient beasts placed there long ago when the feelings were truly more than we could deal with. Until we begin to approach them, they retain all the fierceness they originally had. Think of the experience of visiting the house you grew up in. Your adult eyes are surprised by how small it is. Your memory has stayed with the giant scale of your childhood. The younger the age at which we have encountered feelings beyond our ability to cope, the larger they loom. As adults, we see a two-year-old's temper tantrum as a brief explosion that will soon pass.

To the two-year-old, it is literally the end of the world. In therapy, when adults inch closer to the ghosts of early life, the scale of their fear is the scale that prevailed when feelings were first encountered and somehow pushed out of consciousness. For this reason, we must have the greatest respect for the power of our need to avoid feelings. That is where the Bridge in the allegory gives some sense of the intensity of our fear at a moment of change.

Key Concept: The Smallest Children Have the Biggest Feelings

The younger you are, the bigger your emotions. When adults experience emotions that are big and intense, the emotions probably come from a young place where catharsis has not yet brought about its healing transformation.

Understanding how the magnitude of feelings is inversely proportional to the age of their origin helps us understand some extreme emotional reactions in adults. This observation is an excellent example of the importance of the developmental dimension mentioned in the introduction. Even more important, having an appreciation of how life is experienced during early years allows a warmer, more empathic understanding as well as some clarity about how to handle extreme and irrational reactions in adults.

Fear of Injury or Death

The fear of physical harm differs greatly between adults and children. As adults, we may dread injury, but we are capable of accepting pain and even choosing to place ourselves in harm's way. On the other hand, with a shaky sense of their bodies and little knowledge of what might happen next, children can be terrified by an injury. Even a small injury can be frightening. Since they cannot judge for themselves, children watch their caregiver's emotional reactions to assess the seriousness of the situation. Using these cues, children will show levels of distress that are in sync with the emotional reaction of the caregiver.

I have seen over and over that children operate as if they know their mission in life is to grow, develop, and survive. While adults and even teenagers can conceive of sacrificing their lives for a cause, smaller children almost never can. For them, death or even failure to develop is unthinkable. Adults may view death as a way of finding relief, but only the most severely traumatized children think that way. Later we will encounter a six-year-old who actually ran out into the night alone to escape bodily harm by an out-of-control parent.

Fear of Not Having Our Way

Another feeling strong enough to trigger the development of avoidance mechanisms is the need for control. Why do we have tantrums when we are two years old? Simple: we aren't getting our own way. This is new to us, and we don't like it. As one-year-olds, we smiled at Mom, Mom smiled back, and all was right in the world. In perfect union with our mothers, we had been Emperors of the World, ready and able to overcome any obstacle. Around the time we are two, however, a terrible change occurs. For no comprehensible reason, All-Accepting Mom starts to tell us "No!"

Of course, this isn't really the first time the child has heard Mom say no. What is different is that the child is beginning to have a greater sense of how things should be. Now, Mom's unwillingness to cooperate seems wrong. How can she do that? What used to be simple unhappiness when our wishes were frustrated now becomes outrage. The more clearly we develop expectations, the more angry we are when they are not met. With our newly developed sense of outrage comes the temper tantrum.

The problem is that our outrage is directed against the very people we need the most. Remember that smaller children have bigger feelings. Even as toddlers we have a tentative sense that our anger might damage or destroy a vital bond. As a result, we feel trapped between our rage and the need for warmth and connection. This is why temper tantrums can get so out of control—we are squeezed by catastrophic feelings from both directions, with no way out.

After a short time, the storm runs its course. With luck, a sympathetic parent is in charge of the situation and offers understanding without giving in. The parent who can sense the moment when the child is ready for comfort, and who then provides it, makes the whole experience less traumatic for the child (and the parent!). The child comes to understand intuitively that you can lose a battle and still be lovable.

On the other hand, the parent may give in, thereby teaching the child that rage is a way to control your environment. Or the parent may be too upset to comfort the child and may instead pull away—in which case the rage has, in fact, broken the connection. In these circumstances, the child may grow up unable to deal effectively with conflict. Knowing how to lose battles gracefully is an important developmental skill. Perhaps you know an adult who still has trouble in this area.

Fear of Loss of Connection

One of the jaws of the temper tantrum experience is also a fundamental trigger for avoidance: the fear of loss of connection. As social animals, we crave connection, and our lives depend on it. Strategies for avoiding feelings of aloneness can themselves be sources of future problems. For example, we can: (1) Pretend that we don't need the person; (2) cling to the person and be willing to sacrifice important personal needs just to maintain the connection; and/or (3) join the enemy by internalizing hurtful or depriving attitudes towards the self, modeling the negative attitudes expressed by the person with whom we yearn to stay connected.

Each of these solutions can become part of the adult personality: (1) Trying not to need anyone can manifest in many ways, such as haughtiness and fear of intimacy; (2) clinging can become obsessive, or we may make self-sacrifice a habit in order to hold onto an unhealthy connection with another person; (3) internalizing someone's hurtful attitudes can result in self-hate and low self-esteem. (We will return to these concepts.)

There is yet another, even more unfortunate strategy. It is believed that some people who suffer from what is called "borderline personality" deal with the dilemma of the temper tantrum by splitting their relationship with Mom into two separate experiences. In order to preserve their good feelings about her, they deny that anything negative could happen between them. When a conflict is inevitable, it belongs to a different child and a different mother. This may seem improbable, but the mind is remarkably capable of keeping conflicting realities apart. Such a splitting of experience remains one of the best explanations of why some people's intimate relationships seem to switch instantly from pure love to pure hate and back, with very little gray area between the two.

Loss and Grief

Who hasn't experienced losses? Emotional losses include not only what we have possessed, but also what we dream of someday having. Losses happen every day, and then there are the ones for which our grief is unbearable. When parents lose a child, not only do they lose the one they loved, but also all the days and possibilities that lay ahead. Like other feelings, sadness and grief heal by going through our feelings. Those feelings can be constant at first, and may seem interminable and limitless. Then, they come in waves. Finally, as we grieve, the feelings begin to be less intense. The healing makes use of the same catharsis as for the other feelings described in this section, but there is a difference. Somehow losses take time to grieve. There is something about the way we become attached to people and things that doesn't allow our losses to heal all at once. It is as if each loss demands a certain quantity of sadness. Like it or not, we must allow our inner doors and windows to stay open as long as the feeling requires our attention. Some losses are forgotten, but others seem never to end, especially those that carried future possibilities. With healing, the ones that remain are reduced to an ache that we continue to carry.

Loss is painful enough that it, too, can trigger avoidance. Others around us can become impatient and want us to "get over it." For ourselves or for others, consciously or quite without thought, we may be tempted to avoid the sadness. The ways we avoid range from putting the thought out of our mind all the way to imagining that someday we will recover or replace what was lost and not have to go through the pain. All the avoidance mechanisms described in coming chapters can be used to run from sadness and grief.

The Special Discomfort of Resisting Impulses

What do you feel when you are faced with a strong impulse? You have an impulse to eat something you had decided not to, or blurt out words you know will get you in trouble. Obeying the impulse is easy and natural, but resisting is not. It is as if, by not following the impulse, you are doing something harmful to yourself. Resisting an impulse causes a distinct discomfort. The problem is that, unlike other feelings, this one is hard to describe. It just feels uncomfortable. In English, we have no word for the uncomfortable feeling of resisting our natural impulses.

Typically we learn impulse control in high school. We are given boring assignments and strong consequences to make sure we complete them. Forcing ourselves to do this drudgery is definitely painful, but it is hard to identify the pain. Even without a word for it, going through this feeling, facing it over and over, we gain a greater ability to do what will benefit us, even when it is distasteful. Since practically every positive activity has a component of drudgery, controlling the impulse to take shortcuts can be an extremely valuable developmental skill.

Controlling impulses brings an uncomfortable feeling. Avoiding this uncomfortable feeling by acting on the impulse, like other instances of avoidance, can be costly and dysfunctional. If we don't want to feel that feeling, then we are doomed to follow our impulse, whether it is a good one or not. Since many of our impulses lead to actions that get us into trouble, being governed by them—being "impulsive"—is a significant problem.

Shame

We have seen that the feeling John most needed to avoid was help-lessness. Early in life, he developed a powerful and remarkable tech-nique for avoiding that feeling. His conscience was brought into ser-vice to keep him as far as possible from neediness or helplessness. To accomplish this, he developed a value system that put self-suf-ficiency at the top of his ideals. From then on, whenever he got too close to the needy feelings that originally got him in trouble, he would experience the emotion of shame. His conscience would gen-erate that feeling as a signal that he was getting too close to danger-ous territory. In this way, he developed a barrier to maintain a safe distance from helplessness (In Chapter 5 this will be called an "in-ternal electric fence"). What is remarkable is that John doesn't even think about helplessness. It is far from his consciousness. The feel-ing John dreads is shame. It would be so terribly shameful to have to ask for help, so he relies only on himself.

In Chapter 5 we will explore in more depth how shame is a very pow-erful motivator. As a preview, unlike the other feelings discussed in this section, shame is a secondary emotion, meaning that it is always the result of comparing the self against a standard. Secondary emo-tions arise from a judgment. The standards or values by which we judge ourselves are the property of the conscience and function pri-marily to keep us in the good graces of the people who are important to us. Different cultures use shame to varying degrees as a way to shape behavior. Even when shame initially comes from without, our instincts operate powerfully to internalize the values of those who are important to us. From then on, shame is generated from within to keep our behavior under control.

Secondary Emotions

Unlike primary emotions (e.g., fear and sadness), which relate directly to experiences, secondary emotions (e.g., pride, shame, and guilt) are generated by judging actions in the light of our personal values or ideals.

The usual way of avoiding shame (and seeking feelings of pride) is to behave in ways that are consistent with our values and ideals. In John's case, in order to avoid shame he had to rely only on himself. He had to shun the warmth and emotional support of Jen and soldier on alone. Ultimately neither of them could cope with this austere regimen. John's elaborate defense against helplessness had become a terrible Prison for both him and Jen.

Why are we taking the trouble to look at feelings that can trigger our avoidance? It is because the way to heal is to counteract our own avoidance and face our feelings. We will need to break into our own Castles, storm our own Prisons. Preparing ourselves for such daring acts, we will need to understand as best we can just how they are constructed.

Understanding Your Castle

Traditional therapy takes it for granted that understanding is essential for change to occur. On the other hand, practitioners of some treatment traditions, especially behaviorism, may still be reluctant to delve into the past. This reluctance has understandable roots in nineteenth century science before Einstein's relativity. In the days when Newtonian physics still reigned, scientists believed they could be objective observers whose presence had no effect on the phenomena they observed. John Watson, the father of behaviorism, thought science should only deal in things that were objective—that is, repeatable, measurable, and predictable. For him, products of the individual mind like thoughts and memories were subjective and therefore did not represent reliable data.

As behaviorism has embraced cognitive science, it has become clear that the way humans react to stimuli depends not only on the nature of the stimulus but also on what each person's unique personal history has taught about the world. This is called constructivism, how we construct meaning from multiple sources, past and present. Increasingly, both traditional and cognitive-behavioral schools of

therapy have embraced the idea that understanding personal meanings, as subjective as it may be, is relevant to making sense of our
unhealthy behavior. Beyond pure intellectual curiosity, seeking to
understand the what, why, and how behind our avoidance will improve our chances of escaping from our Castle in a number of ways.

First, the act of sifting through mental material in order to understand has the very important effect of leading us closer to just those
feelings we have avoided. As we get into the story, we begin to feel
the emotions. A new perspective can surprise our defenses so that
suddenly we are facing feelings we have long avoided. The walls of
the Castle have been breached. We are now inside. The Castle is no
longer blocking emotion and, in keeping with a major theme of this
book, when feelings are accessible, healing will happen.

As we encounter our feelings, we are in a position to learn experien-
tially that our dread was from the past and is no longer appropriate.
As our dread loses its energy, the motivation to avoid the feelings
also fades. We no longer need protection from our feelings. The need
that has fueled the constant maintenance of our Castle has lost its
power. Our Castle is one step closer to being ready to crumble.

Understanding has a second, very important role. It helps our conscious motivation to make voluntary changes in behavior. In Chapter 6 we will see that habitual patterns of behavior like John's pattern of controlling are the most common and powerful tools we have
for avoiding feelings. They are also the source of many of our worst
problems. Much if not most of the time, in order to feel, we must
first make voluntary changes in behavior. Any time we do so, we are
shaking the walls of our Castle. Often we must do this before we can
actually experience the feelings behind the wall. Naturally, our mind
goes to work to block any breach of the castle walls, so our efforts at
behavior change will meet stiff resistance.

John met inner resistance seeking help. He also met resistance to
letting Jen have a role in managing the household. In order to overcome this reluctance, he needed to be motivated to practice acting
in unnatural and uncomfortable ways. The motivation came in large
part from understanding why. The better he understood why he was

so reluctant, the more ready he was to change. At first all he could take in was that Jen had rights, too, and wasn't always wrong. Later he began to see that his need for control came from having "grown up too soon." Intellectually he could see that letting go of control wasn't as dangerous as he had imagined. Along with that came awareness that his "stuckness" was the reluctance of the little John inside who was terrified of trusting anyone, for fear that they would rebuff him like his parents and make him feel helpless and hopeless. At last, his resistance made sense, as did the need to make changes in spite of his inner reluctance.

Thus, seeking to understand our Castle turns out to accomplish more than just understanding. It brings us closer to the feelings we have avoided and bolsters our motivation to make behavior changes that are also needed to bring us closer to feelings. The final common pathway for change is meeting the feelings we have dreaded and experiencing them in a safe context. This is the catharsis mentioned earlier, the basic healing process by which our fears and pain lose their power to distort our lives. As catharsis takes place, in effect, we learn that our feelings are no longer to be dreaded.

Does this make the Castle collapse? Not usually, but now it's only held up by habit. Once we no longer have an enemy, the Castle will be much easier to dismantle and perhaps transform into a manor house, even a Renaissance Chateau.

Your Own Hypothesis

On the way to discovering the ins and outs of your Castle, it will help to develop a hypothesis. Even though it may not turn out to be correct in every way, a beginning idea will help focus your inquiry. A working hypothesis can suggest new questions to ask and new avenues to explore. And, as we have seen, it can even help with motivation. Over time, your understanding will grow and your hypothesis will become more accurate.

In the chapters to come we will explore many of the specific ways we avoid feelings. We will see how values, ideas, behavior patterns, developmental arrest, and even future ambitions can serve as barriers that keep us insulated from our dreaded feelings. For now, the discussion will be limited to a brief outline of how to start building a hypothesis about your own avoidance mechanisms.

Step One

Start with as clear a description as you can of the mental problem that causes you the most suffering. If you are thinking of therapy, this is the issue or symptom that brings you closest to picking up the phone to make a call for help. It usually means some way your reactions are different from others' or from what you would like.

What do I mean by a mental problem? A broad definition would be "a dysfunctional pattern of reaction not caused by biological factors." As indicated earlier, making the distinction between biological and non-biological factors is often not easy. If there is a question, that should be a reason to consult with a professional.

Dysfunctional Pattern of Reaction:

- Dysfunctional means that the pattern causes you some loss or discomfort.

- Pattern means that the reaction didn't happen just once but recurs and can be expected to do so again if nothing changes.

- Reaction can include feelings, thoughts, behaviors, perceptions, and any other products of the mind.

Step Two

Flesh out as much detail as you possibly can. Ask yourself as many questions about the problem as you can think of. If you are not sure of the answer, set the question aside and ask other ones. For John, the inquiry might have gone: "I'm doing my very best to be a good husband, but Jen says my controlling behavior is driving her to divorce. I don't see any other way to keep our household afloat, but I'm at least open to looking at my part in her unhappiness."

Some questions John might ask himself:

- What exactly does she mean by "controlling behavior?"

- What would I feel if I refrained from telling her what to do?

- When did I first start to think about the best way to do things?

- What was happening in our lives at that time?

- Are there times when telling her what to do seems more important or less so?

- Did anyone in my early life act in a way that is similar?

- What do I picture happening if she refuses to do as I say?

Step Three

Ask how the pattern could function to avoid painful feelings. For John, the question would be: "If my showing Jen the right way to do things is partly driven by a need to avoid a feeling, what might the feeling be?" At first, John would have a lot of trouble with this. Perhaps he could admit that not being the one in control is hard for him. That would be a good starting point for psychological curiosity, since it opens up the next question, Why? Why do I feel bad when I'm not the one in control? He knows this has been true as long as he can remember. Now, for the first time, John has a reason to be curious about the past.

Archeologists of Ourselves

Exploring the origin of dysfunctional patterns of reaction is very much like archeology. Archeologists examine the remains of ancient structures to try to understand why they were built and what they meant to the people who built them. We too want to understand what our ancient structures—our Castles—were built for and what they meant to their builders, our younger selves. And, like archeologists, we may have access only to fragments of the ancient structures, which may be greatly changed from the way they originally looked. By thinking of the problem—the dysfunctional pattern of reaction—as the visible remains of our ancient Castle, we can then ask many questions. What motivated us to build it? What did it do for us? When was it built?

Like archeologists, we begin the process of understanding our ancient structures by imagining as many possible explanations as we can. Then we use more systematic investigation to ascertain which explanations make sense and which don't.

The Role of Therapy

Let's look at how two different types of therapy can draw out the feelings that need to heal as well as clues to the original problem, the Castle, and how it became a Prison. Let's imagine John entering into two different kinds of therapy.

> John received a promotion. Soon after starting his new job, he experienced chest pains and shortness of breath. He went to the emergency room, where the physician on call told him that he was not having a heart attack; rather, he was having a panic attack. After some more conversation, the physician suggested that John enter therapy. Reluctantly, John made an appointment.

Let's put John in cognitive-behavioral therapy (CBT) first, then in traditional therapy. We'll see how both approaches lead him toward the feelings he most dreads yet most needs to encounter.

These accounts are idealized and abbreviated.

Cognitive-Behavioral Therapy

> John describes his terrifying panic attack to his cognitive-behavioral therapist, A. K., and says that he is frightened of having another attack. He has no idea what brought on the first attack, so he has become more alert than ever—which is only worsening his anxiety. He feels out of control and at a loss, and he is driving his wife Jen crazy by trying to run her life. He is afraid that his anxiety will cause problems for him in his new job and that it might hurt his marriage, too.
>
> As John tells the story, A. K. listens calmly, so John feels a little better— enough to go on with the session. (John is already experiencing catharsis.) A. K. suggests that they work toward his dealing with anxiety or even panic. He swallows his shock at the idea of facing anxiety he had hoped to eliminate.

First A. K. helps John understand the role of hyperventilation in his panic attack. She explains that because he felt he couldn't get enough air, he breathed more heavily than his body needed (hyperventilation). His body responded (normally) by producing feelings of dizziness, which frightened him, which led to his body releasing adrenalin, which caused his heart to pound—all of which added up to a feeling of impending doom.

A. K. explains that John can learn specific procedures to follow if he feels panic coming on, such as managing his breathing to prevent hyperventilation and finding a quiet place to go in order to calm his fear of being discovered. John makes a commitment to start practicing the skills A. K. tells him about. He finds having a concrete assignment to be reassuring. A. K. and John agree that at the next session they will begin to work with John's fears and worries.

By the next session, John has gotten through six days without a panic attack and feels a little better, but he is still quite tense. A. K. begins to teach John to listen to his inner thoughts. She asks him what most frightens him about having had a panic attack. Little by little, John realizes that he has been thinking that his boss might see him shaking and would surely fire him. A. K. then asks John to talk about his work situation. It turns out that John is highly qualified. Also, he has worked for this boss before, and it is unlikely that the boss would suddenly turn against him.

At the next sessions, John continues to explore his automatic thoughts. He gradually becomes aware that he believes he must be as strong as steel, with no sign of weakness. "If you let your guard down for a moment," he has been telling himself, "something bad will happen and you will be eliminated." A. K. and John discuss the realities of his life. A. K. teaches John to use reality to "talk back" to his unreasonable thoughts.

Eventually, John begins to tell A. K. more about himself. In one session he admits that he feels weaker than he should be. On his way home, he feels intensely ashamed for having revealed this dark concern, even though A. K. listened without judgment. He comforts himself by focusing on his success at dealing with his panic attack.

At the next session, with difficulty, John tells A. K. about the shame he felt. A. K. says she is not surprised and explains that feeling weak may be against some of John's core values. They discuss John's deep belief that weakness is a bad thing. John volunteers a memory from when he was young: John witnessed his father hitting his mother but was too afraid to defend her. He remembers how much he hated being afraid and says that he had vowed never to let it happen again. A. K. and John discuss the reality that everyone has limits and is weak to some extent.

John feels a growing sense of mastery over his panic disorder, and he feels grateful for the help he has received from A. K.. He is no longer ashamed to admit that he needed help, and he feels ready to relax his vigilance long enough to have some fun. Over time, John becomes more tolerant with Jen. They go on vacation together and he's actually able to enjoy himself.

Traditional Talking Psychotherapy

John explains to his therapist, P. F., that he has no idea why, out of the blue, his heart began to pound and he felt sure he was going to die. He explains that he is very worried it might happen again. He says that he wants to prevent another attack but he doesn't know how to do this. P. F. acknowledges that the situation is frightening. John tells P. F. that the ER nurse taught him to breathe into a bag. He says that it seems silly to him, but that she assured him it would work if he had another attack.

P. F. nods and asks John to talk more about his life. John explains that he has a great new job but is afraid of losing it. As John talks to P. F. he realizes that his situation doesn't seem all that dangerous, but he still feels very tense. Eventually John mentions his early life with alcoholic parents. P. F. says it must have been frightening for a small boy. John says he didn't feel scared because he learned to take care of himself. The intent listening of the therapist is reassuring to John.

After three sessions, John tells P. F. that he feels ready to stop therapy. He explains that he used the nurse's technique to stop an oncoming panic attack. Without quite realizing it, John feels proud—the way he did when he was small and pleased his parents. The therapist suggests at least another session to talk about the almost-panic attack and what might happen in the future.

At the next session, John tells P. F. that he had another panic attack and that maybe he does need more help. Little by little over the next weeks, John begins to talk about thoughts that come up during the sessions as well as his dreams. He becomes more comfortable with Paul, but he remains reluctant to express his comfort out loud. One day, during a long silence, John becomes more and more uncomfortable. Finally, he blurts out that he has a picture in his mind of P. F. inviting him to a ball game. He is intensely embarrassed about wanting something from Paul. The therapist sees John's discomfort and asks him to talk about it. John replies that he feels like a weakling to have a thought like that.

P. F. and John talk about why John is so afraid of finding weakness in himself. John recalls his father hitting his mother and his being too afraid to do anything to help her. He remembers how he had hated feeling weak and vowed never to let it happen again. P. F. and John discuss the fact that all humans have limits to their strength.

Over time, Johns becomes more tolerant with Jen. They go on vacation together and he's actually able to enjoy himself.

Both Approaches Work

In both of these idealized therapies, there is a structure. In cognitive therapy John learns to manage anxiety, then he explores his automatic thoughts. In traditional therapy, he is asked to report whatever comes into his mind, and similar automatic thoughts surface. In each therapy he comes to a progressively greater understanding of himself. This understanding helps him stick with the process, but it doesn't cure him. In each case, the structure eventually leads John to face his feelings: fear of weakness and shame at any perceived failure in relation to his value system of absolute strength. Each time he reveals more feeling, catharsis does its work, and the healing allows him to move on to the next layer. The memory he has at the end (of his father hitting his mother) is a therapeutic breakthrough, but it could not have happened without all the emotional work that opened up access to such a deeply significant memory and the feelings that accompany it.

Avoiding Feeling Stops Emotional Development

Not all of therapy is about healing traumatic feelings, as in the previous examples. A good deal of therapy is about growth and maturation; that is, restarting natural processes that for some reason have been arrested. Since growth and development are the result of doing new and unfamiliar things, avoiding them naturally leads to developmental arrest. The common denominator is avoidance—avoidance of painful feelings or avoidance of the discomfort and risk that are part of new experience. Consistent with the common thread of this book, the treatment for failure to develop is also facing feelings. In order to illustrate the developmental aspect of avoiding feelings let's use the example of adolescent development, when growth and maturation are among the most important jobs.

Every day in the life of a teenager is full of intense first-time experiences and feelings. Each of these has a larger-than-life quality because it is so new. Holding hands, trying out for the team or the play, driving a car for the first time—all of these are huge, scary steps into the unknown. And if we want to be seen as "cool," then we won't—can't—admit how scared we feel. Most likely, we won't even admit it to ourselves. It is common these days for adults to say it is good to get out of our "comfort zone," but as teens we hardly even have a comfort zone! Along with skills like talking to a person of the opposite sex, the intense emotional experiences of adolescence lead to emotional growth as well. This is a time when we learn not to be afraid of intimacy, to adopt new values, and to try new behaviors that stretch and extend our definition of ourselves.

For both teens and adults, getting out of our comfort zones means facing uncomfortable feelings. That is exactly where we are transformed. Just as with the healing of avoided emotions, going through uncomfortable feelings leads to a qualitative change in ourselves as well as allowing us to add new skills to our repertoire. Later we will see how this transformation makes use of the same mechanism of catharsis as the healing of painful experiences from the past.

Conversely, what causes areas of immaturity or arrested development is the avoidance of the uncomfortable feelings that accompany new experiences. When we avoid new experiences, we remain stuck with the skills and abilities that we already have and do not extend our range.

Why do we go ahead and face the difficult experiences of growing and maturing? That is what we are built to do. Like other things that are important to the survival of the species, trying new things and mastering new skills is exciting and brings powerful pleasures. These good feelings provide strong motivation to engage with life. On the other hand, there are times when the forces against us seem overwhelming and the support we need is not enough. This is when the only solution may be to put one or more areas of development "on hold."

Developmental arrest can be a positive thing. For example, where the experience of sexuality has been distorted by abuse, rather than developing an unhealthy sexuality it may a good thing to delay development by holding back on new experiences until conditions are more conducive to a positive outcome.

Fear of Growing Up Is Not an Illness

We live in an age of diagnoses and labels, where we treat anything unusual as a "disorder." For example, instead of saying "I feel depressed," Americans have learned to say, "I have depression," invoking the medical model of a condition over which we have no control to be cured by a pill. Another unfortunate consequence of this trend is that arrested emotional development is often mislabeled as psychiatric illness. Teens who don't behave as they are supposed to are too easily labeled as "having" conduct disorder or oppositional defiant disorder. This is troublesome because adolescence, more than any other time, is a period when behavior patterns are fluid and subject to outside influence. Furthermore, for adolescents, being seen and seeing oneself as "normal" is extremely important, while being labeled as ill can do significant harm. We need to be very careful not to confuse developmental issues with illness.

For all young people, growing into adults is stressful. For many, the solution is avoidance of those healthy growing experiences that are also painful and uncomfortable. The temptation to avoid stressful experiences may be too strong to resist, especially when needed emotional support is not available, when a pattern of avoidance has already been established, or when drugs are easily accessible.

As adolescents, we may fear that claiming independence will upset family bonds or that we won't be able to compete in an unforgiving world. To avoid these painful feelings we may stay away from experiences that challenge or frighten us. Doing so undermines part or all of our development. We may feel that we are protecting ourselves, but in fact this is another way of building Castles that will turn into Prisons. Avoidance of new experiences can compromise our own potential success. Avoidance causes us to fall behind, and we may ultimately experience deep shame. Are we suffering from illness? No. The stigma of sickness and the sense of being abnormal that goes with it are quite unnecessary. Developmental deficits don't need to be "cured." We just have to get on with the job of growing. For better or worse, the solution is to find the courage, willingness, and outside support to go through the same uncomfortable feelings that had been avoided. That is the simple secret of emotional growth.

Success and Failure in Teen Development

Under good conditions, when we are teenagers we rise to meet real challenges, even when they have real consequences. Teens with close support from their family, school, community, and friends have a huge advantage. A good support system builds confidence. With confidence we can take a deep breath and move forward.

Scary challenges are a built-in part of the teen years: Competing, achieving, taking emotional risks in new relationships, risking loss of support from parents, facing real dangers, making decisions that count, dealing with rejection. Not everyone gets into the best college; not everyone gets to date the person they want to.

Dealing with each of these challenges demands experience and skills that we don't yet fully possess. We have to accept that we are beginners, learning from others and making mistakes. As described earlier in relation to impulse control, our desire to achieve provides the drive to face the stresses involved in developing broader self-mastery—that is, recognition of and control over our emotions and actions. For example, practicing a sport or doing well in class requires working hard when we feel like quitting. Successful self-mastery brings rewards, but they tend to be in the future. At each step of the way, growing up requires relinquishing the childlike desire to do only what feels good. Self-mastery, a core attribute of adulthood, is achieved by going through truly difficult feelings.

How do younger children react when they try a new skill and don't get immediate results? Often they reject the whole project. Teens begin to find the self-motivation to practice even when progress is slow. Maturity means practicing the patience and self-mastery to keep trying, even when we fail, until success is achieved or we have a true measure of our limitations.

What happens when we opt out of some or all of the challenges that make up adolescence? In certain areas we may remain "immature" into adulthood. How common is this? Very. For example, grownups often exhibit some lack of grace when they fail to meet a desired goal. In golf, hitting the ball into the rough when you really wanted the green is a test of anyone's ability to cope with emotional distress and helplessness. Difficulty with this test could be an indicator of a missing piece of development.

People with a lot of intelligence and resources may not be the most mature. Ask the secretaries of doctors, lawyers, and professors about the maturity of their bosses. Intelligence can and often is used to skirt around difficult challenges and not confront them head-on. Whatever the techniques used, avoidance of uncomfortable feelings takes something away from emotional growth and development.

As our strengths and abilities are tested when we are young, we must find a personal balance between persisting at things that stretch our abilities and turning away from areas of weakness or limitation. How many children dream of becoming a great figure skater or base-ball player or being rich? The majority will need to accept that their dream is, well, a dream. For teens, engagement with the adult world is stressful and success, as measured by adult standards, is rare. Confronting these realities is part of developing a definition of self.

What if we grow up without a support system? What if our parents don't monitor our homework? What if our teachers don't tell our parents that we are missing assignments? A pathway opens for us to avoid what is hard. What if our parents hate their work? Adulthood begins to look like drudgery. It is very tempting to quit trying.

Parents sometimes feel that our adolescent life experience should mimic theirs. "I don't know why you expect any help—no one ever helped me!" The problem is that the hardship these parents succeeded in mastering was due to necessity. It is very different to face hardship that feels manufactured and purposely hurtful. Our experience can never be the same anyway—we are different people in different circumstances. Each of us needs to encounter our own organic adversities, successes, and failures.

The Role of the Parent

How can parents provide needed support without blocking the adolescent's chance to learn from challenges? The answer is that knowing when to offer support and when not to is an art. It requires sensing the degree of stress faced by a teen. Here is a metaphor that describes the roles of parents and teens: Young people can be seen as artists—parents are in charge of the painting's frame while teens own the canvas. At the beginning, the canvas is small and the frame thick. Over time, the frame shrinks away. Another metaphor is that parents provide the guardrails at the side of the road as the teen learns to drive. There is no way to learn without some ungraceful lane changes and perhaps a bent fender, but hopefully flying off a cliff or into a tree can be avoided. Parents are there to prevent irreparable disasters, to provide support for meeting challenges, and, not infrequently, to close off unhealthy pathways to avoidance that can lead teens away from achieving their potential.

For parents, there is no right answer, only their best judgment. One person I worked with was born with a serious handicap. Her parents stood by and let her struggle until she learned to function almost as well as a typical child. This "tough love" was successful in that she went on to have an excellent career and was not held back by her disability. On the other hand, she was scarred by the harshness of the demands that were placed on her. Far into adulthood, deeply buried, was a smoldering resentment against the parents for not being more comforting or helpful, even though their withholding was what allowed her to do well in her life. There was no right course for her parents, only a balance between helping and letting her struggle.

While many parental decisions are matters of judgment, both parents need to agree. One pattern I have found to be almost universal with teens who are in trouble is that one parent is strict and the other is lenient. Each becomes more extreme in order to counteract the other; the strict one tries to make up for the lenient one's weakness and the lenient one tries to soften the strict one's harshness. Guess what the teenager does? He or she ignores both parents and does whatever feels good. Sometimes the teen finds a subculture that is devoted to avoiding anything hard, and that makes evading healthy growth and development even easier.

Avoiding Self-Mastery

In teenage life there is an endless stream of choices, forks in the road, where we can choose to grapple with challenges or avoid them. How do some teens avoid the hard work of practicing self-mastery and other developmental skills? There are a number of highly effective ways to do it. The first is to make a practice of avoiding whatever is difficult. Don't turn in the homework, don't go out for the team, don't try to join the popular group of kids. Experience brings more skill at avoiding and less for adult living.

Teens avoiding self-mastery learn to shrug off angry parents and complaining teachers and calmly watch their failures accumulate while the successful kids forge ahead. Soon the deficit seems so huge that all hope of catching up is lost. At this point, these teens' only goal is to avoid pain. There are two very important tricks that make it relatively easy for young people to ignore the bad feeling of failure. The first is what I call "stress transfer." The second, you will soon learn, is the king of all avoidance techniques.

The Stress Transfer

Teens who are avoiding self-mastery learn to transfer their stress to their parents. By acting irresponsible and passive, as if they don't care about the consequences, they trigger a predictable reaction in the parents. The parents naturally step in and try to keep the teen from doing real damage. The teen responds by being even less responsible. Soon, the parents find that they have taken over the job of keeping the teen on track. Positive behavior becomes their responsibility: "Dad, why didn't you wake me up? You know I don't hear my alarm." The young person's area of responsibility shrinks; soon he or she is only in charge of bad behavior. As the parents try to control the teen, the teen lets go completely. This is terribly exasperating for the parents. They feel responsible for behavior over which they have no control. Imagine how stressful this can become. While the parents bear the stress, the teen feels totally relaxed, no longer having to fight against his or her impulses. Fighting parents is far easier than fighting oneself. The teen is now stress-free and can concentrate fully on bad behavior, while the parents tear their hair out. The stress of growing up has been transferred.

Seeing this pattern gives a perspective on what parents are trying to achieve. They are trying to "sell" adult responsibility to the child. To the parents, the product seems inherently appealing, so they are baffled to see that the child isn't buying. To the young person, responsibility can look more like pain than joy.

Is there a way to prevent young people from being frightened or turned off by responsibility? First, prevention: It helps to start in the pre-teen years to establish accountability for work and achievement. At this stage, kids are less inclined to challenge parents' ideas. Next, as the pre-teen grows into a teen, it is time for rewards and acknowledgment to be less personal and more objective. Achievement should be measured increasingly by objective standards and/or the teen's standards rather than by what pleases the parents. At this age, teens are busy building their own system of values, and they are likely to reject just those things in which parents have the greatest personal investment. Perhaps most important, doing everything possible to help the teen achieve success in any domain will allow rewards to begin to come from outside the family where they are not subject to emotional contamination. Receiving rewards for achievement helps establish the good feeling that makes it worthwhile to endure the difficulty of developing self-mastery.

The positive cycle that once worked in the family—pleasing parents, leading to development of skills and good feeling, leading to greater effort to please parents—with a little modification, is ready to support entry into the world at large. Now the cycle is: Succeed in the world, feel good, and go to the next level.

The best rewards from parents are their genuine pleasure and pride in the young person's achievements. It doesn't work to fake being impressed. Humans are just too sensitive to dishonesty. On the other hand, it is appropriate to look at achievement in relation to the young person's own "personal best" rather than the accomplishments of others. Later in the teens, as young people gain in skill, they will begin to assess themselves in relation to adult performance. The transition to rewards from the outside world is steady and natural. Research suggests that a boss's acknowledgment of an employee's having done a good job at something meaningful is among the most powerful rewards in the workplace. The same goes for parents and teens.

One last thought: Parents need to understand that young people have a hard job to do. It is important not to fight with teens over matters that aren't important to their maturation. For example, parents often try to make teens do household chores that feel more appropriate to younger children. Of course teens fight this to the death. Ideally, when parental expectations feel appropriate to the job of growing—and are not an attempt to kill individuality—teenagers will realize that the best way to escape parental control is actually to take responsibility.

Marijuana: The King of Developmental Arrest

Fourteen-year-old Justin was arrested for possessing a significant amount
of marijuana. Early in his schooling he had been enrolled in classes for
exceptionally bright kids, but his parents had moved to a district where these
programs were not available. Justin became bored and stopped applying
himself. The only subject he studied was the science of cannabis. His parents
saw marijuana as a mild drug and were not that concerned about his use of it.
All his friends smoked, too. Justin explained that he simply "enjoyed smoking
weed." He said it helped him to feel good even when he was doing poorly in
school and his parents were constantly upset with him.

Marijuana is the king of developmental arrest, the most potent of all
arrestors of growth. In Justin's case, it allowed him to sidestep every
challenge and still feel okay. It allowed him to go through each day
without feeling the incredible pressure of knowing that his life was
going nowhere. For him it was truly a wonder drug.

Maturation happens when we do hard things and experience the ac-
companying feelings and challenges that take us furthest from our
comfort zone. These are the experiences that make us grow the most.
Pot eases the way to avoiding these challenges. For some students,
even weekly use can be damaging—anticipation of the approaching weekend makes it easy to devalue classes and homework during
the week. Of course there is the student who gets great grades and
achieves in spite of smoking pot, but I would still ask what effect
cannabis has on more subtle aspects of emotional growth such as
relationships and personal values.

In the summer before his sophomore year, Justin's parents gave him a choice
between a rehabilitation program and military school. He dimly understood
that he would have to face the challenges he had been avoiding for as long as
he could remember. He knew he would have to measure himself against his
non-drug-using peers, and by now the gap was huge.

Justin's assessment was accurate. He really did have to face the
stressors he had successfully avoided. At the same time, he had come
to a point where something had to change, and he still had a few
years before he would have to make his way in the adult world. Soon

Justin would begin the long road towards doing the growing he had bypassed. For now, he chose the easier of the two paths offered by his parents. Next, we turn to some adult patterns of avoidance.

How Castles Become Prisons

Andrew, a managing editor, was in his forties. He had suffered from anxiety for almost as long as he could remember. A series of events in his childhood had left their mark. He had hernia surgery when he was two; his mother went to work when he was seven; and his father was diagnosed with a cardiac condition when he was ten. When Andrew was told that his father could die at any moment he began to experience anxiety. Later he recalled that he was frightened of the possibility of having to be the "man of the family." Soon he became afraid of going to school. His mother made a deal with him that if he ever really was overwhelmed by school and wanted to come home, she would pick him up. He never needed to call her, but his anxiety remained.

With the help of a therapist, Andrew went to college and graduate school despite feeling anxious every day. He married and had three children. Though he handled real-life problems effectively, he always found a reason to be anxious. When his life was going well he invented unlikely calamities and focused his anxiety on them.

Andrew became obsessed with his anxiety and felt that he would do anything to "make it go away." When he developed tension headaches he began to use sedatives to calm his anxiety as well as painkillers for the headaches. He became addicted to both types of medications. His addictions eventually ended his marriage.

It is ironic—but not unusual—that for Andrew, one painful feeling became a means of avoiding another. For him, constant and painful anxiety had become a way of avoiding even more frightening feelings underneath. The irrational and chronic anxiety he lived with every day was a terrible burden; he would have been shocked even to think that it might serve a purpose. Consciously he would have done anything to be rid of it. In fact, he was preoccupied with thoughts of how to escape from this gnawing feeling to the point where he was completely distracted from any thought of the feelings from long ago that made him cling to his mother and be afraid to go to school.

The remnants of those feelings were occasionally visible. For example, after his divorce he was very lonely and felt that he had to find female companionship immediately.

Anxiety remained his avoidance tool; when something made him anxious, he focused on the anxiety rather than its cause. He skipped medical tests because the results might make him anxious. But he always kept his therapy appointments. At the end of each hour, I would say, "I'm sorry, I don't have a cure for your anxiety. I understand it is really hard to bear, but we'll do our best." He would go out and do whatever was necessary to keep his life afloat.

In therapy Andrew started to face his day-to-day anxieties, and, over the years, relying less and less on medication, he greatly improved his ability to face his demon, anxiety. His life improved; he became involved with a woman he liked very much.

> One day, I asked Andrew what his greatest fear was. He said it was the loneliness he would feel if his girlfriend left him. He began to describe exactly what would happen if she left. He would curl up in a fetal position in sheer terror. I asked him to imagine it as if it were happening that moment. (Note that catharsis is taking place.) I asked him what would happen next. Andrew said that he would not be able to move. He would simply stay in that position. His mind would be a whirlwind of terror and turmoil. (Remember the point of no return on the Bridge) He would not be able to think about anything else. "What would happen next?" I asked. I waited for some time and then repeated the question.
>
> "I guess I would begin to feel hungry," he said.
> "Then what?"
> "Then I would get up and look in the refrigerator."

The spell was broken. (Andrew told me later that this was a key moment in his therapy). Andrew had gained the strength to face his fear of loneliness, and his anxiety abated greatly. Andrew was still an anxious person, but he was no longer crippled by anxiety. He dealt with problems by facing rather than avoiding them.

Andrew's story is an excellent example of how surface feelings can distance us from the deeper feelings that need to heal.

How Depression, Too, Can Defend Against Hopelessness

Depression is not the same as sadness or grief. As we allow catharsis to work, sadness and grief related to loss will gradually heal. Depression is more complicated. Unfortunately the word *depression* is used in too many different situations. What I mean by depression is a state in which feelings of unhappiness are out of proportion with what we identify as the causes. To make things more complicated, depression can have a very strong biological component. That is why, for depression in particular, it is a good idea to seek professional evaluation.

What we'll discuss here, however, is the part of or kind of depression that is actually a coping strategy. In a way similar to anxiety, as painful as it is, depression can be a way of avoiding feeling. While the cause of depression may not go back to early life, the way it works as a way of avoiding feelings is reminiscent of the issues affecting children of about three. At that age, one of the biggest problems is feeling anger, even rage, at the very person on whom we depend for survival. A younger child, full of rage towards the loved one, will either split hate and love into two separate experiences or will succumb to a temper tantrum in the hope and trust that the caregiver will be able to handle the intensity and put out the fire. The three-year-old has another option: to side with Mom and turn rage against the self.

Children have some awareness that their parents are supposed to take care of them. When the parents seem to fall short, or even displease, children naturally feel angry. Children are also aware that they may be rebuffed or punished if they express anger or make demands. Even worse, the connection could break. Paradoxically, when parents admit to being inadequate the threat of hopelessness becomes worse. How can you blame someone who admits to doing badly? Admission (without reform) only makes the child feel guilty for blaming the parent. For many children, the only solution is to turn the anger against themselves.

Self-Hatred Can Be a Survival Tool

As painful as it is, turning anger toward the self—that is, hating yourself or things about yourself—actually has benefits. First of all, when a parent is not able or willing to listen to a child's anger, expressing it openly will only make matters worse, leading to unspeakable feelings of hopelessness. With no possibility of being heard, there is no hope of resolution or relief from expressing oneself. On the other hand, when a child turns the anger inward, he or she can imagine a positive resolution: the "guilty party" will somehow be punished or reformed. This way, some hope is restored. Furthermore, being able to channel anger and hatred toward the self may feel better than having no outlet at all.

Hating the self allows hope through punishment as well as a more acceptable path for release of anger, but there is another channel that deals with hopelessness. When the child is threatened by true hopelessness, rather than facing that reality, an alternative is to "adopt" hopelessness. In effect, the child actively promotes a false hopelessness, as opposed to hopelessness being imposed by life. In this way, passive (which feels much worse) is replaced by active. One hint that this mechanism is being used is when the depressed person insists on hopelessness even when it is not realistic. For example, depressed people often tell themselves the situation is much worse than it really is. When given reassurance, they resist. When the feeling of hopelessness is voluntarily embraced, the payoff is that we no longer have a feeling of being "done to" but are now in control. Having control over the situation takes away the worst of hopelessness and may even leave room for the fantasy that some outside force may take pity and resolve the situation favorably.

These two mechanisms are probably originally established during a certain window of mental development. Younger children are believed to experience angry feelings separately from loving, needful feelings, so there is no contradiction when both are present. It is as if they have two different selves—a good self and a bad, angry self—and two different mothers—a good mother and a bad, angry mother. At this stage of development, anger has yet to threaten the precious relationship between the good mother and the good self.

However, with the onset of the "terrible twos," the two images of the mother begin merging into one. Now the mother who can say "No!" is the same wonderful person on whom survival depends. This is when anger at the mother can become too frightening. What if she won't or can't tolerate my anger? What if my anger destroys her or severs our connection? At least some vestige of this dilemma often lasts into adulthood.

We outgrow this dilemma to the extent that we are able to absorb the truth that losing a battle doesn't mean loss of love and connection. When Mom says "No," it is because she feels she must, not because she suddenly hates us. However, for young children a bad event with no one to blame is difficult to conceptualize. Even with adults, emotions often remain locked at a developmental stage where someone must be to blame—if it isn't Mom's fault, it must be mine, and if it isn't my fault, it must be Mom's, and back around again. Until this developmental window is closed, directing blame at ourselves and "adopting" hopelessness remain as patterns for avoiding truly helpless and rageful feelings that are too threatening to allow.

Are children really capable of all this complex logic? They are. It takes place automatically and doesn't even have to be verbal. Think how natural it is for a two-year-old accused of doing something wrong to say that his or her sister did it. The underlying logic is the same but reversed: "It mustn't be my fault so it has to be hers."

When we listen to the automatic thoughts associated with depression, they often contain accusations directed in all sincerity and with true venom at ourselves, even though we are innocent. Not only do we blame ourselves for the original incident/behavior, but we also blame ourselves for being depressed—"Why do I have such low self-esteem? I'm such an idiot." The self-hatred feels so real that it takes a good deal of work to see the fallacies. Eventually you will see how turning blame away from its original target gave the feeling of safety through self-accusation.

The story does not quite end here, however. The depressed person may be insulated from the danger of being overtly angry at others, yet depressed people generally do express anger in a subtle, nonverbal way. The depressed person's self-focus and insensitivity to family and friends is an indirect expression of the rage originally meant for an inadequate or unhelpful caregiver. Perhaps, too, the gratuitous self-blame carries hope that some parent-equivalent will see the unfairness and feel guilty. Or, by suffering in an obviously unjust way, the depressed person may hope to prove to some imaginary judge and jury that it really was the parent who was wrong.

Of course, these are not conscious thoughts. Any suggestion that might be interpreted as accusing the depressed person of willful aggression will be met with anger and dismay. Analyses of unconscious thoughts represent guesses about inner logic that are difficult to prove but should not be discounted, either.

These dynamics can allow the depressed person to feel some deep-down hope and comfort while avoiding the dreaded feelings of anger and helplessness. But the price is very high. Depression is one of the most painful feelings humans endure. Unfortunately, digging through the layers of cover-up and overcoming resistance fueled by fear of hopelessness is, at times, beyond the power of talk. It can be so difficult that medication or hospitalization is required at first.

The irony is that catharsis—in this case, experiencing the dreaded fear of loss of hope in a context of connection and safety—can bring healing. Healing is possible both for the anger and for the fear of loss of connection. When such healing occurs, it allows us to accept that the dreaded hopelessness came from a child's way of seeing reality and is no longer valid. Unfortunately, our instinct to avoid hopelessness can be so strong that we may not gain access to healing. Though once experienced as necessary, these avoidance mechanisms can impose years of suffering and unhappiness. Once again, a Castle has become a dark Prison.

Dissociation: A Special Castle

Dissociation is another natural and automatic way to avoid feelings, yet one that is under-recognized and often misunderstood. In this section, the aim is to take the mystery out of dissociation.

Dissociation

The mind's circuit breaker. An automatic mechanism for splitting off consciousness of circumstances beyond the coping skills of the individual at the time. Anything can be split off, including feelings, physical pain, and memories. The process is usually not voluntary and can last minutes or decades.

My Personal Experience of Dissociation

I have had one episode of dissociation, and it was one of the strangest experiences I have ever had. I had to take an oral exam to become board certified as a psychiatrist. The exam required that I interview a young man in a mental hospital in front of a senior examiner and then discuss the case with the examiner and be judged.

So, there I was, talking to a patient with an older psychiatrist watching, poker faced. I had done many such interviews, but not for an exam. Normally, questions would come into my mind and I would ask them, but this time I found myself thinking, "What would I usually ask next?" The interview probably didn't look or sound odd, and I got through the discussion, but I was not myself. I was more of an outside observer of myself. This feeling of being outside was a good indicator that I was in a state of dissociation.

Relieved to have the exam over with, I returned home and continued my life. I had no idea that I was still not my usual self. Two days later, I felt something "pop," and suddenly I felt normal. Only then did I realize that I had stayed in some unnatural state even after the exam. Unlike the exam itself, there were no clear markers or indications. Only when I felt the contrast with "normal" did I perceive the difference. In a similar way, people who have experienced trauma may have only a hazy sense of something not being quite right. They may see a physician or therapist but often won't be able to give a clear description of what is wrong. As a result, the diagnosis of dissociation is often missed, and inappropriate treatments are given for the wrong condition.

In my case, I had been partially cut off from my feelings. During the exam my intellect ran the show and my feelings had gotten stuck in the back seat. This is the most common kind of dissociation, often experienced by people who have been in a disaster such as an earthquake or a train wreck. When you see them on television, they look zombie-like, doing what they have to, but probably not feeling much. Their minds have automatically created a dissociative barrier to cut off the part of the experience they cannot handle. In its role as circuit breaker, dissociation is keeping them from being overwhelmed. Let's look at how this automatic mechanism for avoiding feelings is a regular part of our response to trauma.

Post-Traumatic Stress Disorder

When a disaster happens, most survivors soon return to their normal state. What we don't see on television is that, for some, the dissociation doesn't end. Susceptibility to dissociation depends on factors such as personal emotional/psychological makeup, genetics, any history of previous trauma (early trauma makes dissociation more likely), the seriousness of the trauma, and its duration. In my opinion, it is when dissociation continues that survivors are subject to post-traumatic stress disorder.

Post-traumatic stress disorder (PTSD) affects a very significant proportion of people who have experienced psychological trauma ranging from early emotional betrayal to frank abuse to war and other life-and-death situations. PTSD consists of three symptoms that usually appear within three months of a traumatic experience. What is often not appreciated fully is that each of these symptoms is closely associated with dissociation. The first symptom is avoidance of reminders of the trauma. Sufferers will go to great lengths to keep away from anything that could trigger recall with feeling. It is not uncommon for survivors to avoid television, keep themselves in a state of incessant activity, or even turn to alcohol and drugs in order to keep the experience behind a curtain of dissociation. Dissociative barriers within the mind do a good job of keeping feelings at a distance, but a reminder can suddenly bring memories back along with terrible feelings. For this reason, survivors instinctively avoid being reminded. While these barriers do protect the survivor from re-experiencing the trauma, they also prevent healing. Feelings remaining out of consciousness cannot heal.

The second symptom consists of partial breakthroughs of the experience into consciousness. Partial failures of dissociation, flashbacks and nightmares, torment the survivor with images, sounds and other fragments of the experience. Unfortunately, even though feelings are painfully aroused at these times, they are still not accessible to healing. Why flashbacks do not lead to healing is not clear, because experiencing feelings usually leads to catharsis. Perhaps what is missing is the context of safety. In any case, flashbacks do not contribute to healing, but they can go on for years without resolution.

The third symptom of PTSD consists of heightened vigilance and active startle reflexes. It is as though the trauma set the mind on high alert and no one ever gave the all-clear signal. Dissociation has kept the feelings out of reach of healing, so they remain unresolved. This obviously interferes with the ability to sleep or to attend to the ordinary business of life. Hyper-arousal also has profound effects on stress hormones, the immune system, and other aspects of normal physiology.

In order for the symptoms of PTSD to abate, the dissociative barrier that walls off feelings must dissolve so that the person can at last face the traumatic emotions in a context of safety. Then, as with other avoided and unprocessed feelings, catharsis can transform the dreaded feelings to the point where they lose their power to cause intense upset. Once this transformation happens there is no longer a need for avoidance, and flashbacks and hypervigilance both can fade into the past.

As mentioned briefly above, trauma has other consequences, such as low self-esteem, which are not part of the syndrome of PTSD. In later chapters we will see that the healing of these aspects of trauma may take longer and be even more challenging. For now, let's look at what it takes for the curtain of dissociation to be drawn aside.

Treating Dissociation

Treating dissociation is challenging because the splitting away from consciousness is truly involuntary. Working with a dissociated patient feels something like holding out food to a wild deer and hoping it will eat out of your hand. Success takes a lot of patience and attention to creating a truly safe environment.

If dissociation were limited to cutting off emotions, dealing with it might be simpler. However, the mind is capable of cutting off or dissociating from anything. People can dissociate from their own identity, from memories (including their entire past!), and from perceiving the realness of the world or even the self.

Just as dissociation occurs outside of voluntary control, its resolution is also largely outside of voluntary control. Patients find it terribly distressing that they can't deliberately regain whatever is missing. Medications are of only minor help. It is only when the right conditions have been created and the person's mind "decides" it is safe that dissociation begins to evaporate and feelings, at last, come into the room where they can be healed.

Dissociation and Hypnosis

Dissociation bears a strong resemblance to hypnosis. Under hypnosis, people can also be stopped from feeling pain or from perceiving their surroundings. Furthermore, people with dissociative symptoms are more easily hypnotized than others. While there is likely a common mechanism, hypnosis is at least somewhat voluntary. People's experiences under hypnosis are subject to control or suggestion, whereas dissociative symptoms are largely not.

Dissociation: Hard to Pin Down

Somehow dissociation is regularly glossed over and not recognized, even when it is causing real suffering. Not long ago, I found that in my own practice, three people I was working with had experienced distressing symptoms of dissociation that had in each case been misdiagnosed. Each had been treated for other conditions with no benefit. I believe there is a good reason why it is so easy to miss.

Our experience of life can be divided into background and foreground. There are many things we take for granted without realizing they are there. Have you looked at a room and suddenly been aware of details you had never noticed before? When I went home after my oral exam, I was not aware that I was still in an abnormal state, because the foreground of my awareness was the same as usual. What I hadn't noticed was that the background was still altered.

Dissociation changes our background perception without touching the foreground. It is like being in a theater when the lights change but the actors and the set don't. The whole atmosphere of the scene changes, though nothing has moved or been said. Our minds are aware of context, but we often don't put words to it. When we encounter a similar background atmosphere, we may have a feeling of familiarity but not be able to express why. Foreground is where we place our focus and what we remember most vividly. Even though quite dramatic, background perceptions can be hard to articulate and are soon lost to conscious memory.

Perhaps also for this reason, dissociation is very often mistaken for something else. One woman discovered that her husband was having an affair. This turned her emotional life upside down, and she began to experience a sense of numbness and unreality about her life. She saw several therapists and was treated for anxiety and depression, but none of them correctly identified what had happened. She had dissociated her feelings. Once we identified the dissociation and created a safe place to talk about the stress, she began to return to her normal state of feeling.

Dissociative Identity Disorder (Multiple Personality)

Much of my experience with dissociation comes from work with people who have suffered from dissociative identity disorder (DID), or multiple personality. While the existence of DID is doubted by some, it can simply be seen as an extreme form of dissociation. DID usually happens when there is trauma in early life and the child's mind splits off one or more parts of the traumatic experience as a survival mechanism. For example, consciousness of repeated molestations might be split off again and again.

Unlike my personal experience, here both memory and emotions are split off. Even more extreme, certain characteristics of the child who experienced the trauma can be split off as well. For example, the part that endured nighttime trauma might have learned to tolerate severe pain, while the daytime child remains less hardened. As time goes on, the split-off part takes on a life of his or her own. Every night when the experience is repeated, the part of the child who can cope reappears and a dissociative barrier blocks the horrors from the consciousness of the child who must go to school the next day. Over time the dissociative barrier evolves to a more or less permanent dividing line between two increasingly distinct personalities.

DID is fairly rare, but a few years after my first encounter I began work with Robert Oxnam, who was at that time the president of the Asia Society of New York. Though I had never mentioned DID and was not looking for it, to my surprise and his, six months into his therapy another part of him appeared. You can read the story in his book, *A Fractured Mind* (New York: Hyperion, 2005).

DID and the Origin of Psychotherapy

Because trauma survivors have taught me so much of what I know about healing, let me tell a little-known story. From 1880 to 1882, Freud's mentor and collaborator, Joseph Breuer, treated a young woman who suffered from classic hysteria with severe symptoms. In addition, according to Earnest Jones's (1961) biography of Freud:

> More interesting, however, was the presence of two distinct states of consciousness: one a fairly normal one, the other that of a naughty and troublesome child. It was a case of double personality.

Joseph Breuer (1842-1925)

A prominent Viennese physician who took the young Freud under his wing and whose patient first suggested the technique of talk therapy.

Sigmund Freud (1856-1939)

Freud founded the field of psychoanalysis and pioneered talk therapy aimed at understanding and resolving the unconscious forces that drive dysfunctional patterns of perception and behavior.

Dr. Breuer attempted to apply the accepted treatment of the time, hypnotic suggestion, where he would tell his patient that on coming out of a hypnotic state, her symptoms would be relieved. This didn't work, but Anna O. (her real name was Bertha Pappenheim) had a better idea. She told Breuer just to listen while she shared the traumatic events that had led up to her symptoms. She called it "chimney sweeping." With these instructions to her doctor, she had invented talk therapy much as it is practiced today.

When he heard about this treatment, Freud was very intrigued and pushed for publication. The case was of particular interest to him because he had sought something more effective than hypnotic suggestion and also because earlier experience had convinced him that hysterical symptoms might be caused by trauma.

Based on her and other patients' recovery, Freud and Breuer developed the concept of catharsis. According to their formulation, when patients recalled traumatic events with feeling, their symptoms were permanently resolved. The symptoms they were referring to were what we now call "conversion" symptoms in which patients experience physical disturbances like blindness or paralysis that do not have a physical cause but are caused by emotional factors.

Bertha Pappenheim had many physical symptoms and suffered severely, but she was improving remarkably under treatment. Sadly, the phenomena of transference and countertransference were not yet understood. Dr. Breuer was not prepared for the powerful feelings that developed in treatment. When his wife complained that she was being neglected for this patient, he broke off the treatment prematurely. His patient, who had been doing very well, responded to this new trauma with a major relapse of symptoms and went on to years of difficult experiences with the psychiatric system of the day. Finally, though, she emerged intact, and she became the first social worker in Germany, working on behalf of disadvantaged and abused women and children.

Alternative explanations have been suggested for the origin and healing of DID symptoms, but the account in Freud's and Jones's writings is consistent with my own experience and that of responsible DID therapists in general. The unfortunate ending of Ms. Pappenheim's treatment with Dr. Breuer highlights how much was not yet appreciated about the intensity of the therapeutic relationship and how to ensure safe handling of transference issues. See further the Scarsdale Psychotherapy Self-Evaluation in Chapter 9.

In the next section we will look into the reasons why people avoid feelings. We will see how our native motivational systems influence us to avoid painful feelings and, often without our awareness, to resist attempts to bring those feelings into consciousness, where they can heal.

Avoidance and our Motivational System

Jeffery, a psychiatrist, had for years planned to write a book about therapy, yet it wasn't until late in his professional life that he finally fired up his computer and went to work. Jeffery recognized that he suffered from avoidance, which he traced to his father, who was the rare full professor at Stanford who never published. Jeffery's father had made many drafts and had publishers lined up, but he never actually finished his book.

> *For many years Jeffery understood that he too was inhibited in this area.*
> *He wanted to write and had plenty of ideas, but actually producing was a*
> *struggle. He did manage to publish one article, then years later another, but*
> *somehow he was more comfortable doing other things. He started a business,*
> *patented an invention, and kept occupied with projects outside his field. He*
> *continued to avoid doing the thing that he felt was his mission in life.*

Yes, that Jeffery is I, and the book I finally began is this book. My experience with avoidance showed me just how powerful a grip the mind has on one's behavior. Even with full consciousness and all my knowledge of psychology, my decisions were heavily influenced from within.

This section focuses on the motivational apparatus that works behind the scenes to steer the direction of our lives.

Adam-1 and Eve-1

When I teach beginning therapists about what makes us do what we do, I start with a slightly modified creation story. You see, God created the earth and all the creatures on it. He was pleased with all the animals and plants, but then decided to make a more advanced animal. He went to the drawing board and designed a creature with a big brain and special thumbs so the creature could do intricate tasks. Then He went to his shop and made Adam-1 and Eve-1. He placed them on earth and watched.

They had curiously blank faces. They stood and looked around but didn't do anything. They didn't even lie down when it got to be night. It got cold, but they didn't put on any clothes. They didn't even eat or drink, and soon they died.

God was distressed. He needed a consultant to help redesign these beings to behave in a way that would allow their species to stay alive and multiply. It occurred to Him that the Internal Revenue Service has special tricks to get beings to do things they wouldn't naturally do such as leaving fields empty when they could grow crops. So He called up the IRS and asked them what to do.

The IRS said, "No problem. Easy. You need to build in incentives. Make them feel good when they do what you want them to and bad when they don't. It's as simple as that."

God went back to the drawing board to produce Adam-2 and Eve-2, and the rest is history.

The Deck Is Stacked

The point of my creation story is that we are not locked into rigid behavior patterns. Humans do have full free will, but the deck is stacked so that we predictably choose to behave in ways that support the survival of our species. Evolution has built in incentives so it is pleasurable to do what we are supposed to do and uncomfortable to do what we are not supposed to.

Recent research has revealed where some of nature's incentives are located. In the nucleus accumbens in the brain, a dose of the neurotransmitter dopamine triggers a good feeling and a desire to do more of whatever caused that feeling. Disincentives are a little less well understood but equally important. Furthermore, much of what influences our decisions and behavior is not pleasure or pain but their anticipation. Anxiety is a feeling that tells us pain could be near. Whether anticipated or actual, our motivational system uses pleasure as an incentive and pain or discomfort as a disincentive. For example, the anticipation of pain influences us not to overuse an injured muscle or joint. The beauty of the system is in its flexibility. It can be overridden if our desire is strong enough or if one competing need is stronger than another. Even with a fractured ankle, we manage to run if our lives are at stake.

The system is so subtle that we perceive our "free will" as entirely free. We imagine that self-determination is a basic fact of human life. That is why many of us are dumbfounded when we see the behavior of alcoholics and addicts. How can people choose to destroy their own lives? Even people with addictions believe that they have free will and freely choose to do what they do. Few of us want to admit how strongly our behavior is controlled by our brain's focus on survival of the species.

Addiction: Motivation Run Amok

Now you are probably wondering, what on earth does addiction have to do with survival of the species? With an understanding of the motivational system, the behavior of addicts begins to make sense. What happens is this: The brain becomes switched into a mode whereby using the substance is equated with species survival. As a result, the power, subtlety, and flexibility of the motivational apparatus, originally set up for survival, begins focusing on making sure the addict gets the drug, even in the face of reason and the attempts of loved ones to return the individual to sanity.

Motivational Apparatus

This is the label I use for the part of our brain/mind that influences us to do what is required for survival of the species. It works mostly out of our conscious awareness and makes use of a number of tools and tricks to steer our choices. It has a profound effect on our lives but does not always steer in directions we might consider healthy.

How can addicts fight their motivational apparatus? They must find a need or desire strong enough to compete with its impressive power. When addicts hit rock bottom and finally see what substances are doing to their lives, it is because they have discovered something more important to them than drugs and alcohol. I knew a woman who realized one day, in a flash, that if her child had awakened during the night with a medical emergency, she would be too drunk to respond. Her love of her child took precedence over her need to drink, and she took action to become clean and sober.

Addiction Interventions work because alcoholics and addicts may be even more strongly attached to family and friends than to substances. Although addicts will do almost anything to avoid having to choose between the two, an intervention narrows the addicted person's choices to two: the addiction or the important people in his or her life. The motivational apparatus then weighs the competing goals and picks the one that is more compelling. When the intervention works as planned, the addict chooses loved ones over the addiction, which is certainly better for the survival of the species.

Intervention

A planned event in which people close to someone suffering from addiction or other compulsive behavior come together in a caring way to confront the person's behavior and invite him or her to accept help.

Our Tricky Brains

So far, we have only looked at the first layer of our motivational apparatus, the one that produces pleasure and pain or discomfort to influence our free will. Let's call this the pleasure/pain layer. Not surprisingly, given the importance of our motivational apparatus over the course of evolution, there are at least two more layers or components.

Why Losing Weight Is Really Hard

A common experience that sheds further light on these deeper layers is dieting. Let's say your brain has determined that you need a certain amount of food reserves (that is, fat) to be sure you don't starve. You, on the other hand, have decided that famine is not likely in the twenty-first century and that you would like to look good on the beach this summer. Your values are now pitted against a motivational system that is focused not on your needs but on the needs of the human race. Let's watch it at work.

The first thing it comes up with is obsessing. You decide to skip lunch and your motivational apparatus barrages you with images of cheeseburgers. Soon you can think of nothing but food. Steadfastly, you resist. You tell your brain that the obsessive thoughts are misguided and that you are not going to starve.

Next your mind tries an even more subtle trick. You find yourself staring at a leftover piece of cake. The edge is ragged, and you think that it really should be neatened up. What if a guest were to come? Tidiness demands that the cake be trimmed. So you reach for a knife to trim the cake. Of course it wouldn't be reasonable to waste the trimmed-off piece, so what do you do? You eat it. But the slice you took was cut at the wrong angle. You need to fix that, too. By now the piece that is left is too small to bother keeping, so you eat the whole thing.

Almost instantly, you feel ashamed at what you have done. What happened to your resolution? You have the thought that it is no longer much use trying so hard. It is only weeks until summer and it is really too late to lose all the weight you want to, so why not forget the whole project and eat whatever you feel like?

This outcome has been precisely and carefully orchestrated by your brain, a cunning and devious adversary with millions of years of practice. It sent you obsessive thoughts, then rationalizations. It used the principle of one small slip leading to another. Then it exaggerated the negatives with its message of "What's the use?" In no time, your once-powerful resolve withered to nothing and you admitted defeat. So although we do have free will, we are also heavily influenced from within, often without realizing why or how.

A Secret Inner Agent of Influence

What happened is that your brain, without your desire or even awareness, had the power to shower your conscious mind with thoughts that deftly influenced you, against your own resolve, to the point of overriding your best intentions. Technically, eating more cake was a free choice, but a powerful influence from a mysterious source had other ideas. This is how our free will can be hijacked.

What is this masterfully clever inner agent? From working with people with addictions, I can tell you that it has two products: thoughts and impulses. The thoughts it produces are no different from any other thoughts that pop into consciousness, except in the agenda they are pushing, which gives them an element of stealth. There are no markers to tell us which thoughts belong to us and which come from this inner agent. Furthermore, it demonstrates great creativity and insight as to the best way to convince us to do its bidding. These thoughts and impulses do not appear to be learned, as they can be quite fresh, unlike any thought we have had before. In Alcoholics Anonymous (AA) the saying is that the disease of alcoholism is "cunning, baffling, and powerful." These adjectives could just as well apply to the agent of our brain that seems dedicated to influencing our behavior in the direction it thinks is best for us.

The same agent is also capable of sending *impulses* into our conscious mind. These are sudden, strong feelings that tell us we need to take a certain action. Our natural tendency is to obey immediately without question. During childhood and especially adolescence we develop some ability to notice our impulses and exercise some control over whether we act or not. This is, of course, called "impulse control." Some people seem to have more and some less. Those who suffer from attention deficit disorder are especially prone to be impulsive. With practice and support, it is possible to strengthen our control over impulses.

The next observation we can make about our inner agent is that it is not restricted to supporting addictions; it uses the same tools to influence our behavior in many other ways. In particular, it is there to make sure we stay far away from uncomfortable feelings. That is why this agent is so central to the theme in this book of avoidance of uncomfortable feelings. In this way, we can see it as a helper of the pleasure/pain system. When anticipated or real pleasure and pain are not enough to put our behavior in line, just as with dieting, our mind digs deeper into its toolkit to come up with thoughts and impulses to further influence our free will.

This influence can clearly work as a survival mechanism. Did you ever jump off a high diving board? Most of us are able to make the decision to climb the ladder with the intention to jump, but when we are out there on the end of the board, we experience strong impulses not to jump. Most of us, but not all, can muster enough free will to override the impulse not to move, especially when we are egged on by others and our social instinct kicks in. Furthermore, observation of people's behavior in the most dire emergencies suggests that when there are multiple dangers, such as being in the upper story of a burning building or when a car crash is inevitable, the brain performs rapid and purposeful calculations about which threat is the most terrible.

So far, I have painted the portrait of a secret inner agent whose job is to use thoughts and impulses to influence our free will to choose the path that it deems best for our survival or the survival of the species. Freud called it the unconscious. Cognitive-behavioral therapists describe "automatic thoughts" that influence our feelings and behavior. Recovering addicts call it "the Disease." For the purposes of this book, I want to give it a new name that will highlight its function and characteristics. From here on, I will call it our "Black Box Motivator."

Engineers use the term *black box* to describe systems that they can only understand by observing what goes in and what comes out. That is true of this agent of the mind. At best, from its input and output, we can guess its intentions. When our guesses are close, there may be a feeling of resonance, but we are never able to observe directly its inner workings and calculations.

I am calling our inner agent a motivator because it seems to have been cleverly designed to do just that. Using only thoughts and impulses, it profoundly influences how we live our lives. Furthermore, it seems intent on motivating us to do what it is programmed to believe we are "supposed to do."

What a marvelous system! As beings, it helps enormously that we can use our thoughtful, inventive minds to come up with crazy ideas about what we would like to do, which give humans incredible playfulness and the ability to invent new ways to adapt to life's conditions. At the same time, our motivational system has powerful brakes to keep us from going too far off the tracks. We may still be able to outsmart our brains, but they are, nonetheless, really trying hard to keep us around.

Knowing what goes in and seeing what comes out, we can form educated guesses about why and where our Black Box Motivator is trying to steer us. Since the Black Box Motivator is very smart, it knows that it is more effective to lead us by small innocuous steps, and it is often unclear where these steps are leading. Understanding this can give us an edge. It is enormously helpful to ask where those steps might take us and even more helpful to ask someone who cares about us and doesn't have our blind spots.

> *When Justin, recovering from addiction for only a few months, had decided it would be nice to see his old friend Jack, the idea seemed like a good one. Jack had been a loyal friend, and he was sure Jack would respect his recovery. He told his 12-step sponsor about the idea and was dismayed that the sponsor felt compelled to say something about "people, places, and things."*

The sponsor had instinctively wondered about Justin's motivation. Could the visit be a step in the direction of trouble?

> *You can guess the rest of the story. Jack was fine, but Fred just happened to drop in, and he was not so fine. Fred urged Justin to have just one beer for "old times" sake. Justin gave in and soon was in the throes of a full-blown relapse. His Black Box Motivator had used a small, seemingly innocent step to steer him where it thought he should go.*

Addiction is so powerful and so counter to good sense that it puts the Black Box Motivator into clear relief. Apart from addiction, this layer of our motivational apparatus may be less obvious, but it is no less active as it operates to support other goals and to produce a wide variety of thoughts and impulses. What they all have in common is that they provide an additional layer of motivation beyond simple pain and pleasure to make sure we do what we are supposed to.

This, then, is a brief introduction to the Black Box Motivator component of our motivational apparatus. It is driven to accomplish the same goals as the pleasure/pain layer but uses well-crafted ideas and impulses to influence our free will towards what it considers necessary for the species.

Key Concept: The "Back Box Motivator"

Not an anatomical structure, but a term invented to capture that part of the mind that produces impulses and thoughts exquisitely designed to be effective in steering conscious free will in directions that the mind presumably (because its operation is not available to consciousness) considers necessary for survival.

The Last Component of Our Motivational System

To round out the picture of our motivational apparatus, let's now look at a third component. It will already be familiar to you as the source of some very important feelings, namely pride, shame, and guilt. I hope you have guessed its name: your conscience.

> *John, the controlling husband discussed earlier in this chapter, internalized a core value that self-sufficiency is good. This became as basic to his conscience as his value of honesty. His mind did this long ago to shield him from the repeated pain of asking for nurturing and love when the answer was "No."*
>
> *On his thirtieth birthday, his need for care and attention welled up. This was, after all, his special day. But his need was in conflict with his values. Working to steer him away from the dreaded neediness, his brain showered him first with feelings of shame, then with automatic thoughts and impulses to deny himself the gifts and attention his family wanted to give him. To his family's dismay, when the cake came out, he became very uncomfortable instead of feeling pleased. His mind filled with thoughts that he really hadn't earned them, and he returned all the gifts.*

Now let's look at all three components and how they work together. Even though it was introduced second, in the diagram I have placed the Black Box Motivator at the bottom of the diagram below because it serves both layers above it, namely the pleasure/pain layer and the conscience.

A Three-Component Motivational System

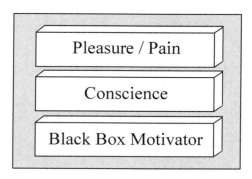

The first layer of our motivational apparatus uses pleasure and pain to influence behavior. The second layer, our Conscience, similarly uses pleasurable and painful feelings to influence us. But instead of ordinary pleasure and pain, it produces feelings of pride, shame, and guilt. Remember, these are secondary feelings that result from a judgment in relation to an internal standard or value.

Where does your conscience obtain its guidance? From the values, attitudes, ideals, and prohibitions we have internalized in the course of our life. Thus our conscience can be seen as a component of the motivational apparatus designed specially to make sure we follow our values.

How do all three components of the motivational apparatus work together? You may notice that the pleasure/pain layer is especially attuned to bodily and biological needs, and the conscience is more focused on our need to fit into our social network. After all, we are both biological and social beings, so it is natural that our motivational apparatus should reflect both sets of needs. Both the pleasure/pain System and the Conscience apply their influence via feelings, conscious positive and negative feelings that operate as incentives. When those feelings fail or need additional help, the Black Box Motivator goes to work to produce thoughts and impulses that are shaped to further influence our free will. Here is a diagram to show how the parts of our motivational apparatus work together.

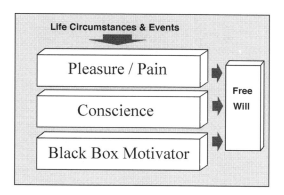

These concepts are consistent with current neuroscience, but they represent a functional picture of how our minds work, not an anatomical one. Using a computer analogy, the three components of the motivational system along with our free will are similar to parts of the operating system, while neuroscience focuses on the underlying hardware. Please note that the computer analogy only goes so far because, unlike computers, our brains grow and develop. Brain hardware is heavily influenced by goings-on in our mind or software while the functioning of our mind is very much shaped by the organization and operation of our physical brain. Putting aside those subtleties, the aim here is to provide the simplest way possible to make sense of human problems and how we can change. Towards this end, an understanding of the functional components of our motivational apparatus helps us to anticipate when our attempts to heal and grow will run into resistance and how to prevail.

We Can Guide Our Lives

If our free will is not really all that free, are our efforts to guide our lives useless? Definitely not. When we make up our minds that change is necessary, we are all capable of foregoing pleasures and overriding feelings of pain. When our conscience objects, we can examine our values and determine if they are unhealthy and wrong. We can identify false feelings of shame or guilt (Chapter 5). When our Black Box Motivator produces automatic thoughts and impulses that steer us towards unhealthy behavior, we can seek support and fight back (Chapter 6).

Let's look again at addiction, representing one of the most powerful examples of a deeply compromised motivational apparatus. How do members of Alcoholics Anonymous fight to reclaim their free will? The first thing they do (the First Step) is to acknowledge the fallacy that we are in full control of ourselves. By showing how the life of an addict has become unmanageable, AA encourages members to look squarely at the reality that their free will has been hijacked by a foreign master. The Second Step says, "We came to believe that a Power greater than ourselves could restore us to sanity." If our mind belongs only half to us and half to some inner force beyond our control, then it makes sense that looking outside ourselves is a way to rebalance the odds in our favor. These steps pave the way to reaching out for help.

It is not incidental that AA calls itself a fellowship. By bonding with fellow group members, recovering alcoholics and addicts access a powerful driver of the motivational apparatus: the need for human connection. The bond of a close-knit group is one of the few forces strong enough to overcome the need to use substances. By pitting one powerful force against another (connection vs. addiction), AA opens a pathway to recapture free will when it has gone the farthest astray.

This section concludes a survey of how and why avoidance of feelings can be seen as the source of the irrational problems that become lodged in our mind and cause us so much suffering and dysfunction. Now, in this chapter as at the end of each of the following ones, we will turn to practical ideas about how to retake control of our lives by facing the feelings we have avoided.

Next Steps: How to Avoid Avoidance

The overarching theme of this book is that emotional healing and growth are the result of going through the feelings we work the hardest to avoid. Because most of our avoidance is habitual and not voluntary, encountering our dreaded feelings is not an easy task. It is as though we are trying to study a very shy and rare species of jungle animal. We must be observant, put ourselves in the right place at the right time, be quiet, and be confident. When we finally do meet this rare beast made of our hidden feelings, the experience will be brief but unforgettable and life changing. Here are some tips on how to entice the beast from hiding.

Build a Safe Place. Unprocessed feelings naturally come to the surface when we feel out of harm's way, so we must create a safe place for ourselves (therapy is one place designed for just that).

Tune in to Your Inner Self. Tuning in to your inner self is something like spending time in the woods. The more you linger, the more you notice details that you once passed over. With experience, you learn what things mean and what to expect.

Another way of looking at it is that your readiness to listen will invite out the child within who has been waiting for someone to show interest. As mentioned earlier, formulating a question almost always leads to an answer. To John: "Why do you suppose you felt so unworthy on your birthday?" It is impossible to predict by what route the answer will come, but it will, and usually sooner than you might imagine.

Step back from action and listen to your thoughts, feelings, dreams, and fantasies—anything that comes from or to your mind. Do so in a warm and accepting spirit. When you notice something that surprises you or feels notable, ask yourself what it means. (Doing this in explicit words will force you to be precise and specific.) Then open your mind and be ready for the answer to come to you, perhaps in a form you couldn't have predicted. Of course it helps to have a therapist-partner who is equally interested but who doesn't have your blind spots. Even so, you are the one in the driver's seat.

Change Your Unhealthy Behavior. This will be discussed in detail in Chapter 6. For now, let me just say that unhealthy behavior is by far the most common and most potent means we have for avoiding feelings. Clearing out unhealthy behavior patterns is not only good for us, but it also uncovers a treasure trove of uncomfortable feelings— exactly the ones we need to go through to heal and grow.

Seek Intimacy. I know a therapist who suggests that couples in treatment seek ever-greater intimacy by sharing emotions and experiences more and more deeply. He has them chart their scores every day. The result is that the couples' uncomfortable feelings come flooding forth. Intimacy is hard. Deep sharing uncovers all kinds of unfinished business. After a few months the couples reach a crisis point. If they stick with the process, they come to healing and growth—and then they find themselves able to engage in even greater intimacy. When you try hard to share your inner feelings and thoughts within the context of a relationship, things get intense. I would recommend working with a therapist to make sure what comes out is handled in a positive and productive way.

Enter Individual or Group Therapy. Therapy, particularly the unstructured and the experiential kinds, is designed to have the same effect that intimacy has for a couple. Therapy is structured to bring out the unfinished business of childhood, and the relationship with the therapist will naturally create a level of intimacy that fosters the uncovering of real, here-and-now feelings. Irvin Yalom has eloquently documented in his book *The Theory and Practice of Group Psychotherapy* (2005) how the group modality is particularly well suited to ambush our feelings. Group dynamics are complex enough that our defenses are soon caught off guard and we find ourselves face to face with feelings we would normally sidestep.

Irvin Yalom (1931-)

Yalom, therapist and author of *The Theory and Practice of Group Psychotherapy*, a classic description of the therapeutic process, is Emeritus Professor of Psychiatry at Stanford University and writes both fiction and nonfiction.

Facing uncomfortable feelings is so hard that no one does it for pleasure. The readiness to undergo the kind of journey we are discussing comes from awareness that we are imprisoned as well as hope that there might be a way out. Such motivation is precious. It can lead to acts of great courage and unimagined improvement in life. When we have the motivation, it is important not to lose momentum or waste it on ill-designed attempts to change.

This is why a good therapist can be critical. Training and experience do much to help therapists recognize Prisons and help people understand how change is possible. If you are going to undergo an arduous and costly procedure, you need someone to help you evaluate the pros and cons of each move so that you can decide for yourself if the result will be worth the effort and stress. This is all the more true when your mind is flooding you with automatic thoughts telling you that nothing will help, or it will be too hard, or that the status quo is really not that bad. Amid the confusion and complexity, a therapist can help you to see how thoughts you had not questioned are actually reinforcing unhealthy beliefs and values and keeping feelings out of the reach of healing.

Onward

The actual work of letting go of avoidance will be addressed further in the chapters to come. Most of the time the work consists of voluntarily fighting unhealthy patterns of thought and behavior. In Joseph Conrad's *Lord Jim*, the character Stein says, "You must immerse yourself in the destructive element." By this he means we must face the things we most want to avoid. And when we finally do, catharsis will bring about healing and growth.

References

Conrad, Joseph. *Lord Jim*, Classics LTD, 2013.

Jones, Ernest. *The Life and Work of Sigmund Freud*, Edited and abridged by Lionel Trilling and Steven Marcus, Anchor Books, 1961.

Yalom, Irvin D., and Molyn Leszcz. *The Theory and Practice of Group Psychotherapy*, 5th ed., New York: Basic Books, 2005.

CATHARSIS: AMAZING MEDICINE

How facing feelings allows them to heal.

A particular concern is eating at you. It distracts you at work and interrupts your sleep. Finally, you tell someone you trust about what is going on. The person you speak to doesn't scream or run from the room or stop loving you. And the thing that has been costing you sleep suddenly loses its grip. You have experienced catharsis.

Catharsis is the most basic form of emotional healing. It happens every day in ordinary life and is the backbone of talk therapy. Like the common cold, it has mostly been neglected by science—until recently. Some therapists call catharsis "venting," inaccurately trivializing one of the most remarkable phenomena of emotional life. Sharing feelings is much more than letting off steam! In this chapter we will explore catharsis in depth.

Catharsis: Simple and Powerful

Imagine a medicine that is extremely powerful yet has no maximum dose or dangerous side effects. You don't have to have a medical degree to dispense this medicine, and it costs nothing. In fact, you may actually feel richer after giving it to someone. The medicine, of course, is catharsis, which could be defined as the healing that takes place when feelings are shared with an empathically attuned and safe other.

Putting Catharsis to Work

Let's explore how you can use catharsis to solve most of the problems in your intimate relationships. Let's say you and the person you love get into an argument that seems impossible to resolve. Your loved one spouts familiar phrases: "You always," "You never," "Why don't you," "Can't you see what you're doing?"—and maybe even "I can't stand you." You feel compelled to defend yourself or at least correct the obvious errors. Unfortunately, arguing back doesn't seem to help—your partner is braced and ready to counter your best points. You are getting nowhere, so you escalate. You are tempted to go after your partner's deepest vulnerability. The argument only intensifies. You both feel misunderstood, wrongly accused, and hurt. Nothing is going to be settled. Even if you manage to cool off, nothing has been learned and there has been no resolution.

Getting to Full Understanding

Ultimately I want to convince you that your partner's bitter accusations are as precious as gold and jewels. For the moment, I'll settle for something more modest.

Picture an imaginary bucket or container you can fill with your partner's words. I want you to collect as much of this valuable content as you can. When your container is full, grab another one. And another. If your partner becomes quiet, ask for more.

Here's the thing: When your partner kept saying "you" this and "you" that, your partner was not actually talking about you! This may seem hard to understand, but your partner was really trying to get you to listen. Underneath the accusations was a desire to be understood. When she realized that you couldn't or wouldn't understand—or that you didn't even seem to try—your partner began to throw accusations. That is when the real fight took shape. Now neither of you can back down. But stop! You don't even have to remember how it began to turn this ugly process around. By this time, you have both lost track of how it began anyway, so you may as well start where you are. As I suggested above, reach for your bucket and gather content. But don't just collect words; take an interest in what is being said. Your partner is telling you about her wants, needs, and experiences. Not only that, but your partner is telling you with feeling.

What We Want

- What do women want? They want to be understood.
- What do men want? They want to be understood.
- What does understanding give? Healing by catharsis.

Telling with Feeling

Telling with feeling is the key to catharsis—That's what I mean about gold and jewels. As soon as you begin to hear what your partner is communicating, you will begin to understand where she is "coming from." You will begin to be empathically attuned. Whether you intend to or not, you will start to feel what your partner is telling you. Being able to share feelings with an empathically attuned other is the essence of catharsis. This is what heals the most painful feelings. Instead of fighting, you will be helping your partner to resolve the emotions that are causing pain—and without even making concessions! As you go deeper into understanding your partner's concerns, her pain will likely vanish. In minutes, you will be able to take care of a large part of the problem the two of you were having.

What comes next? Your partner will feel so much better for having been heard and understood that she will probably be ready to really listen to you as well. With your understanding of how catharsis works, you will wisely stay away from "you" statements and talk directly and accurately about your own feelings and observations ("I" statements). Without accusations from you, it will be easier for your partner to hear you. As you report accurately your feelings and point of view, your partner will become empathically attuned and feel closer to you. Now you, too, will begin to feel much better.

"I" Statements

Not only does sharing your feelings make you feel better through catharsis, it is also the best way to communicate without inviting an argument. You are the expert on your feelings and perceptions, and they are what they are. What you say about your own emotions and point of view is inarguable. Even better, it is much less threatening for the other person. Think about the difference between someone telling you what they insist is truth versus telling you their personal opinion or feeling. It is easy to listen to another's views and feelings as long as you don't feel they are expecting you to change yours. As soon as you say, "Here's what I am feeling..." or "This is how I see it..." your words lose all their threat but none of their content.

When you have each shared your feelings and arrived at a broad and deep understanding of each other's point of view, a remarkable thing will happen: Neither of you will care much about the outcome of the original argument. What seemed passionately important will seem less so, and you will likely be able to come to an easy resolution of your issues.

If the Problem Can't Be Solved

Of course, it's possible that the problem may not be resolved so easily, but the bucket method will still help you to learn more about your partner. You may realize that he won't accept your understanding because he has some other agenda. Or maybe he is afraid of true understanding and wants to distract you from his secret vulnerability. If catharsis is not achieved, it may mean that your partner isn't ready yet to change. You might be asking your partner to face something deeper and more uncomfortable than either of you realized.

The Greatest Source of Misunderstanding

How can you tell that you have gotten to full understanding? It will be when you understand each other's motivations. Unfortunately, this is where the greatest errors are made.

What happens is this: We observe actions more or less objectively, but we can only guess at the other person's true motivations. We often make assumptions about motivation. We are quite sure we know just why the other person acted even when we are way off base. Our assumptions about others' motivations are the main source of strong feelings and the main reason for harmful misunderstanding. Most of the time, our emotional reactions to others are really reactions to what we imagine is going on in our partner's mind. "She's trying to provoke me." "He's just lazy and doesn't want to help."

The problem is that our firm beliefs about the other person's motives are usually based on patterns experienced in childhood. Typically the flare-up happened because something you did reminded your partner of an interaction with significant others from long ago. This is not the conscious kind of remembering but an automatic, non-verbal reaction triggered by some resemblance between the present and the past. Not surprisingly, without even thinking, your partner takes it for granted that your motivations are identical to those of figures from his past.

The bucket method encourages you to actually listen until you understand your partner's motivations. As reality becomes clearer, you won't feel so defensive and will have an easier time understanding that the reaction was not really about you. With the presence of mind and wisdom not to take the accusations personally, your non-defensive expression of interest will be evidence of your innocence. Your accepting manner will be in sharp contrast to the early life figures who never examined their own behavior or admitted wrongdoing or hurtful motives. Perhaps you will surprise your partner into seeing that his assumptions have more to do with his personal history than with you.

When True Feelings Are Suppressed

In a misguided attempt to keep peace, your partner may be reluctant to expose his real feelings. For example, he may not openly want to question your motives. Unfortunately, many people are afraid to express strong feelings. Honest feedback is important in sorting out a relationship. Hopefully, using the bucket method and asking questions will encourage a more honest and open exchange. Learning to listen to your own feelings and share them is probably the single most important skill in improving relationships. As you both get better at doing so, your appreciation for each other will increase steadily. This is almost universally true, but there is one exception, which I will describe in Chapter 8, when we discuss narcissism.

Catharsis, the amazing medicine that actually calmed things down in your discussion, was simply the sharing of feelings in an open and caring context. Now let's look at just how powerful catharsis can be in healing even the most extreme feelings.

Catharsis in Action

Annie came to the hospital when marriage counseling stirred up suicidal feelings. She was a small, brunette woman who stared steadfastly at the floor. She spoke in a monotone. As I inquired about her background, she became more and more uncomfortable.

Annie had grown up the eldest child of a psychotic mother. Her father abandoned her and her brother when Annie was eight. While trying to protect her younger sibling, Annie had endured her mother's rages and punishments for imaginary sins. School authorities noticed that something was wrong, but when they questioned Annie about what was going on at home, she lied.

Eventually, Annie began to act out and was placed in a home for troubled teens. She experienced a turnaround there, becoming the star student, eventually getting a steady job. Later she started a family of her own. Annie did well as an adult until marital problems reminded her of the compromises she had made for the sake of survival. It was then that she became suicidal.

Interviewing her in the presence of a group of trainees, I asked Annie one more question about her early life, and she bolted out of the interview room, back to the ward. I knew the nurses would be there to help her so I didn't follow. To my surprise, she soon slipped back into the room as if nothing had happened and sat down to continue the interview.

Her courage and determination were striking. One day Annie came to the emergency room and asked to speak to me. I located a private room where we could talk. As soon as I had closed the door, she reached into her purse and pulled out a pistol. "You're going to listen to me," she commanded in a suddenly fierce voice. As calmly as I could, I replied that I had a family and would have trouble listening while the gun was pointed directly at me. She turned the pistol away from my face. That small gesture told me we had a genuine connection and that she was more interested in talking than hurting anyone. She began to tell me about her trauma.

While the gun turned out to be an air pistol (dangerous enough!), her brandishing of it was an indication of how much she needed to talk and how many times she had felt ignored in the past. Over the ensuing months, feeling gradually safer, she began to show more flashes of the volcanic rage she held inside. At the time, I was only instinctively aware of the benefit of our sessions. I had a sense that each time she exposed a bit more of her emotion, some kind of healing took place, so I tried to create a safe place for her to reveal more layers of her story.

It took four more years of twice-a-week meetings before she began revealing specifics of the horrific abuse she had suffered as a child. When she spoke of the details and I listened empathetically, something remarkable happened. Despite the terrible nature of the abuse, as she experienced her feelings, each part of the trauma healed to the point where it no longer held the same power. Feelings that had been too intense and too painful to go near now became speakable. Pain that had been too sharp to endure had been reduced to a dull ache. Surprisingly, once her feelings emerged, the healing took place in the course of a few hours. Annie left each session worn out, shaken, but feeling better. Not only was the healing rapid, but it was permanent. Her feelings would never be the same.

Over the next few years, we went through her most terrible experiences in detail until there were no more memories to process. We
were done.

Sharing Feelings with an Empathic Witness = Catharsis

My residency program in psychiatry had emphasized psychoanalysis, not trauma, so when I began working with Annie, I had little
training to fall back on. I did, however, possess the complete works
of Freud. Looking there for help, I found that his earliest papers were
about trauma. This is where I first read the story of Anna O. in Freud
and Breuer's paper. To my relief and fascination, the experience they
reported was exactly like mine. In 1893, they wrote:

> We found to our great surprise at first, that each individual hysterical
> symptom immediately and permanently disappeared when we had succeeded
> in bringing clearly to light the memory of the event by which it was provoked
> and in arousing its accompanying affect...

And likewise with my patient, bringing the facts to light along with
the feelings led to what Freud called catharsis. When patients shared
emotional events with me, one of two things would happen. When I
could feel their pain or distress, healing would occur, and they would
leave the session feeling worn out but not so troubled.

On the other hand, if the patient's description was abstract or
intellectual, I couldn't feel much and catharsis would not happen.
One man told me, "I often have trouble with relationships. I can't
seem to get close and when my girlfriend pursues me, I distance."
His understanding was no doubt accurate, but it didn't convey any
feeling. I asked him to tell me about the most recent occurrence. I
knew that speaking about a single incident would lead him to be
specific and concrete. He said, "When she looked in my eyes, I felt
terror. I just wanted to run away." This time, the specifics brought the
feelings into the room and it was hard not to experience empathy.
When that happened, I now knew from experience that healing was
taking place.

Empathy Happens

Empathy is not the same as being solicitous or nice. It is a natural human reaction that has evolved to support our functioning as social beings. Empathy happens when one person expresses feelings in detail and the other hears.

Catharsis Heals Pain, Big and Small

As my practice continued to reveal, when feelings entered the room and there was empathy, catharsis was there, too. And the healing I had come to rely on in cases of severe trauma worked exactly the same when the emotion was less dramatic. I came to understand that the same mechanism works for any painful feeling. It is present in every therapy session and in everyday life as well. Sharing feelings leads to healing. The action of catharsis is lifelong and universal.

While catharsis itself is not hard work, getting close to painful memories is. For example, Annie's rage at her parents was so immense and so intense that it took many therapy sessions to reduce her mountain of feeling to a hill that we could finally climb. Each time a chunk of feeling was exposed, it was healed.

Transforming Painful Feelings

Let me review three broadly accepted treatments aimed at transforming the feelings of trauma so that their overwhelming intensity becomes less threatening.

Talk Therapy. The oldest treatment option is traditional talk therapy, which remains much as originally practiced by Freud in the late nineteenth century and much as I experienced it in working with my patients. Patient and therapist take on the task of understanding, and in doing so, they encounter painful experiences and feelings. This exploration brings emotion into the room and, as I see it, allows healing by catharsis to take place. While feeling is encouraged by all the therapies derived from Freud's original talking cure, only a few contemporary schools, such as Diane Fosha's accelerated experiential-dynamic psychotherapy (AEDP) explicitly identify the core healing process as a meeting of the patient's feelings and the therapist's empathy.

Diana Fosha (1952-)

Fosha developed accelerated experiential-dynamic psychotherapy and is the author of *The Transforming Power of Affect*.

Exposure Therapy. When behaviorists realized that the "desensitization" treatment they had espoused for years lacked effectiveness, they looked closer. Desensitization treatment invited patients to experience painful feelings and then practice relaxation techniques to diminish the pain. Unfortunately, the relaxation gave patients an opening to slip away from intense feeling. It was avoidance rather than healing. When this happened, there was no change. So behaviorists developed exposure therapy. Exposure therapy seeks to overcome the patient's natural avoidance of feeling by showering them with vivid pictures and sounds chosen to bring back recall of the traumatic experience. Under these conditions, it is hard not to feel. When successful, the patient's defenses are breached, feeling comes into the room, and healing takes place.

Eye Movement Desensitization and Reprocessing. In this treatment modality, also known by the acronym EMDR, the patient is encouraged to focus on the emotional aspects of an experience. He is then asked to "hold the feeling" while simultaneously paying attention to a side-to-side stimulus such as the therapist's waving finger or clicking sounds. The stimulus lasts about ten seconds; this brief time is sufficient for healing of the feelings that have come to the surface. Exactly how EMDR works is controversial, but the key elements are the same as those seen in talk therapy and exposure therapy: recalling events and experiencing associated feelings in the presence of a witness.

Some people believe that the alternating stimulus does something unique in the brain. However, since other treatments that simply bring out feelings produce similar results, it seems to me more likely that side-to-side stimulation serves mainly to distract the intellect and prevent distancing from feelings. Whatever the mechanism, EMDR works.

In my experience, exposure therapy, EMDR, and talk therapy all produce the same results, but EMDR sheds additional light on the process. EMDR divides the therapeutic work into segments lasting a few minutes allowing us to see that the healing action is very rapid. Each chunk of feeling can be transformed in a few seconds. Experiencing your feeling in a context of safety for just ten seconds is all that is needed for significant healing to take place. Of course, the healing only applies to what is consciously felt at the time. Every trauma has a myriad of different facets and layers, so treatment usually takes multiple sessions, not counting the considerable time it might take to bring the feelings into the room.

Whatever the Therapy, Catharsis Is Key

In all three treatment methods, feeling is brought into the room and healing happens. Simply put, all these methods lead to catharsis. And we use catharsis every day to cope with painful feelings. When we are upset, we naturally share our feelings with an empathic other. This is so much a part of life that we hardly pay attention to the underlying process. Consider this story I heard from a friend:

> *An irate passenger at an airport was jumping up and down and screaming loudly. A security officer began to jump up and down and scream along with him. After a few minutes the officer said, "Boy, this is hard work. Do you want to go get some coffee?" The man went willingly.*

By acting the same as the passenger, the officer had (nonverbally) created the conditions for catharsis. The man communicated his feeling, the officer displayed empathic understanding, and the man's pain was healed. Rapidly, and predictably, his anger abated and he was ready to go for coffee.

Crying in The Shower

Trauma survivors sometimes ask me if they can heal their pain by crying alone in the shower. In general, the answer is no, but the question raises important issues. In working with people who have been traumatized, I have felt intuitively that the presence of an attuned other is an essential part of what makes treatment work—and patients usually agree. However, the professional literature seems to downplay the importance of the other person. Is the presence of another person really necessary for the healing of traumatic feelings? The story of how EMDR was invented highlights this question. Francine Shapiro discovered EMDR when she was walking alone in the woods, thinking about a personally troubling matter. While holding the feeling in her consciousness she moved her eyes from side to side and was surprised to feel relief. Based on this experience she went on to develop her treatment technique. If EMDR worked for her while she was alone, then is an empathic witness really necessary for the healing of trauma?

Francine Shapiro (1948-)

Shapiro is best known for her invention of eye movement desensitization and reprocessing, EMDR. She is a licensed clinical psychologist, Senior Research Fellow at the Mental Research Institute in Palo Alto, California, and Executive Director of the EMDR Institute.

I puzzled over this question for some time. Finally, I began to explore how children first acquire the ability to heal feelings by catharsis. Eventually that exploration led to an answer. In the first year of life, children have little capacity to regulate their emotions. When they cry, their distress is total. We try to fix the problem, and when we can't, all we can do is to hold them and speak in a soothing voice. That works to some extent, but around nine months of age, something new happens. In *The Interpersonal World of the Infant*, Daniel Stern points out that at nine months, baby and mother begin to engage in two-way emotional communication. (Please note that I am using the word *mother* to represent the primary caregiver, whoever that might be.) When the baby communicates feelings in one form and the mother bounces back the feeling in another, the baby "knows" she has been understood. Using Stern's example, when the baby makes a cooing sound and the mother comes right back with a shimmy of delight, both feel a surge of pleasure and connection.

Daniel N. Stern (1934-2012)

Stern was a psychiatrist and psychoanalytic theorist specializing in infant development. His recent book on how therapy works is *The Present Moment in Psychotherapy and Everyday Life.*

This emotional communication back and forth allows for a new level of regulation of the baby's emotions. Think of a toddler who falls down. The first thing the child does, even before reacting, is to make eye contact with the mother. If she smiles, the child will likely get up and go on playing. If the mother shows distress, then the child will almost certainly cry. In this way mothers help regulate their children's emotional states. They can calm their babies with just a look.

Two elements seem to be required. One is understanding—that is, the baby needs to feel that the mother is tuned in. Second, the mother's larger view of the situation must be transferred to her baby. It is not the intellectual content of the mother's understanding but her calm and steady manner that helps comfort her offspring. As in other examples of catharsis, the relationship is not symmetrical but is one in which the person experiencing the distress makes use of the other's sense of perspective and ability to tune in without being overwhelmed.

Clearly the actual presence of the mother is necessary for the toddler. If catharsis is basically the same as the soothing mother–child interaction, then how could Francine Shapiro have experienced healing while alone? The answer comes from another facet of child development. At one year of age, children need the physical presence of the mother in order to feel calm and safe, and they are acutely distressed when she leaves the room. As children grow older they begin to acquire "object constancy," that is, the ability to tolerate their mother's absence. Many developmentalists believe this maturational step is the result of the child gaining an internal image or sense of mother's presence.

Object Constancy

Margaret Mahler developed the idea that, around age three, children develop a more substantial ability to tolerate separation from their mother by internalizing a representation of her. Object in this context means the opposite of subject, that is—the other person.

An Internalized Sense of Safety and Connection

Imagine how valuable it is to carry a feeling of connection to Mom, even when she is off in another room. As children grow through their twos and beyond they can play alone but frequently have to make eye contact or return to their mother as if to check in. As the feeling begins to be built-in, it becomes available to help with difficult times like going to sleep. On the other hand, it doesn't take much—a fall or a mild scolding—for the feeling to disappear. More about that soon, but first what happens to this internal feeling of being connected and safe as we become adults?

Erik Erikson coined the term "basic trust" to describe a feeling of safety and predictability about the world that comes from reliable parenting and gives those who possess it a basic sense of optimism that everything will turn out okay in the end. If we look deeply at this basic trust in adults, I believe we will find the internalized sense of connection that helped us when we were young. Even when physically alone, we may be able to sense this built-in feeling of not being emotionally alone. Have you noticed that when you are alone, you may carry on a silent dialogue with someone important to you? This is an indication that when you are physically alone, you are very likely not psychologically alone. Though we tend to take it for granted, this feeling is really crucial to our ability to keep calm as we go through difficult passages in life.

Erik Erikson (1902-1988)

A Danish-born American psychoanalyst who taught, treated patients, and studied child development. He coined the phrase "identity crisis" and he described developmental stages through the life cycle.

People who have been severely traumatized early in life, or whose early experiences were not safe or predictable, are likely to be much more vulnerable to feelings of aloneness. When we see catastrophic emotional reactions to the threat of abandonment in adults (one of the hallmarks of what is termed "borderline personality"), the root is probably difficulty in gaining access to this deep feeling of safety and connection. We could think of the feeling as a memory of the safety of being held in Mother's arms, but it isn't really a memory. It is more a state of being that all is right with the world. When we gain access to that state, tension leaves us and we feel "centered" and whole.

The Internal Rechargeable Battery Pack of Connection

Even those of us who have a fairly solid sense of what has been termed, "basic trust," experience the need to connect often with the safe and reliable people in our lives. When we do so, I believe we are reinforcing and strengthening our internalized sense of connection. For this reason I like to refer to it as our internal rechargeable battery pack of connection.

The key to Francine Shapiro's healing of her painful feelings seems to me most likely to have been that she was able to heal through an internal context of connection. Like most basically healthy adults, she was probably carrying her own internal rechargeable battery pack of connection, so she didn't need the immediate presence of another. The eye movement did something to help her gain access to her inner connectedness and safety. In doing so she met the conditions for catharsis: awareness of her painful feelings in a context of safety and connection. In this case, catharsis could do its work without the physical presence of another person. Does this mean, then, that tears in the shower can be healing? Yes, it does, but we will see

in the next section that this does not apply to the most severe traumas, especially early ones.

Trauma Therapy and Feeling Alone

If we normally possess an internalized sense of connectedness, why
would an empathic witness be needed for the healing of trauma? The
answer is that severe stress can, and regularly does, disrupt the internal sense of connection. This has been noted by various observers
of child development. For example, Margaret Mahler (1975) noted
that children can handle separation under conditions of comfort
and safety but cannot do so while under stress. She concluded that
adverse conditions disrupt the internalized mother, making her unavailable to comfort the child. At traumatic moments in early life,
this is just what happens.

Margaret Schöenberger Mahler (1897-1985)
Mahler, a Hungarian physician and psychoanalyst, studied separation and
individuation and described how children go through various stages of
development on the way to acquiring a sense of identity.

During a traumatic event, a child's internal sense of connection is
not just weakened but obliterated by terror and pain, resulting in a
feeling of utter aloneness. When the traumatic event is recalled in
therapy, an integral part of the memory is that feeling of total isolation. At the moment of recall, when the trauma is being re-experienced as if it were happening all over again, the survivor is also
re-experiencing the aloneness. I have informally tested this a number of times by asking patients who were in the midst of recalling
childhood trauma, "Do you feel completely alone?" They have in-
variably answered yes, even though I was only a few feet away and
emotionally present. In cases of severe early trauma, for healing to
take place, the state of aloneness that is re-experienced as part of
the memory needs to be counteracted by the actual physical presence of an empathically attuned other. Only then are the conditions
of catharsis met, allowing healing to take place.

Catharsis in Slow Motion

Let us follow the process of catharsis in slow motion as it relates to childhood trauma. As explained in Chapter 2, post traumatic stress disorder (PTSD) is a reaction to stress that appears within a few weeks of the trauma, in which survivors experience three groups of symptoms: (1) avoidance of reminders of the trauma, (2) breakthrough into consciousness of dissociated (meaning mentally walled-off) parts of the experience (flashbacks), and (3) hypervigilance, as if the danger were still present. The underlying mechanism in PTSD is that the whole experience—or parts of it, such as the emotions—have been distanced through dissociation, where the mind sets up barriers to distance parts of the experience, especially feelings and/or memory.

When PTSD arises from childhood trauma, the dread of recall is magnified by the giant scale of the original childhood experience. This occurs because the original fears and memory have remained unchanged since they were originally split off. Remember, smaller children have bigger feelings. As long as memories or parts of memories are walled off from our consciousness, they retain their original power and don't soften or fade. I call this the "freezer effect" because even after decades, the original intensity and flavor of the experience remain unchanged. When we avoid feelings from an early age, our ability to keep them from consciousness is so effective that they are also inaccessible to modification, change, or healing.

Key Concept: "What Isn't Conscious Doesn't Change"

When feelings, experiences, plans, and intentions from childhood are pushed out of consciousness, they can no longer be influenced by reality. If and when they come back into consciousness, only then are they subject to adult perspective, modification, and healing.

In therapy (and sometimes spontaneously), the re-experiencing of early trauma often starts with isolated sensory impressions. Like a collage, fragments of images, smells, sounds, and sensations arrive as if they are happening in real time, right now, raw and unprocessed. Feelings, too, are unprocessed. As the facts of an experience come into focus, feelings often come with them. Bessel van der Kolk, a researcher and clinician focused on trauma emphasizes that sometimes the trauma experience is locked up in the body. It is as if recall is tied to a certain body position or movement and until the survivor is able consciously to gain access to the exact bodily sensation, the emotions and pain remain inaccessible.

Bessel van der Kolk:

A pioneering researcher, clinician, and teacher specializing in trauma and PTSD since the 1970s. Recently published *The Body Keeps the Score: Brain, Mind, and Body in the Healing of Trauma.*

In effect the original experience is being relived as if it were happening for the first time, except we are peripherally aware of being in a safe place with a safe person. The experience is equivalent to the point of no return on the Bridge (See Chapter 1), where emotions and memories have total immediacy. For a moment we are alone, our consciousness swirling with utter distress. But as the feelings are shared with an attuned witness, they undergo the transformation that is catharsis. As we hold the feelings and impressions for a few seconds, balanced between aloneness and connection, they begin to lose their ability to be so upsetting.

Like the toddler who has fallen and whose mother responds with a comforting smile, we start to absorb a sense of calm and perspective. The empathic connection makes it possible to see the trauma through the eyes (or, perhaps more accurately, the mind) of the other. Again, it is the calm, more than words or ideas, that conveys a sense of safety and draws us out of the immediacy of the experience. As we see ourselves and our pain through the eyes of the other (whether internal or external), we gain a consciousness of our own experience and with it a sense of perspective. This is catharsis in slow motion.

As we process facet after facet of the experience, we gain greater distance. Sensory impressions are less jumbled and fall into place as a coherent series of events. It is not long before we begin to feel better and experience a natural desire to weave the past into a meaningful narrative, a story.

Is Building a Story Necessary?

Some people think that putting events into a story and/or gaining a conceptual grasp of what happened is what brings about the healing. I don't agree, because I have seen healing take place many times with the barest exchange of words. As I have said before, it seems to me that the essence of catharsis is experiencing feelings in a context of empathic connection with someone who is not overwhelmed by the experience. All it takes is for the witness to listen, to be relatively unperturbed, and occasionally to give some indication of being tuned in. While the narrative is not the agent of healing, both patient and therapist find satisfaction in reconstructing the story.

What about Adult Trauma?

Trauma can strike at any age. Traumas of later life include experiences like war, rape, natural disasters, and the full gamut of experiences that go beyond our immediate ability to cope. The healing of these memories still comes down to catharsis. Just as with ordinary painful feelings, healing is most likely to happen when the pain is brought into consciousness in a context of safety and connection. From the previous discussion, we can see that those who don't have as strong an internal rechargeable battery pack of connection are likely to have more trouble healing. It has also been documented that survivors who have a greater capacity for dissociation, often acquired through childhood trauma, are more likely to distance painful feelings, preventing them from healing.

Ilene was involved in a terrible automobile accident but was not badly hurt. Her children were safe, but her husband was severely injured and was taken to intensive care. After several hours of anxious waiting outside the ICU, the nurse came out to report that he was going to make it. Ilene suddenly began to sob. She had held herself together during the ordeal, but when the tide

> turned, she could, at last, reconnect with her feelings. Then, at that moment,
> the nurse said, "Don't cry!" and she stopped.

For the next ten years, out of her awareness, she held her tears back. It was only in the safety of therapy that she was again able to experience the feelings that had been suppressed for so long. Only then could they heal. You will not be surprised to learn that Ilene had also been traumatized as a child. The commanding voice of the nurse brought her right back to her childhood where she first learned to cut off her feelings.

Catharsis Is Not Just for Trauma

> Cassie, a teenager, came for her initial evaluation looking angry and
> uncomfortable. I encouraged her to talk about her discomfort at that moment.
> As she did so, catharsis quickly took place. In no time, her discomfort was
> transformed. She was no longer uncomfortable and was eager to talk about
> her life and problems.
>
> At one point, Cassie's conversation became ragged; she slowed down, misused
> a few words, and lost track of her sentences. It seemed clear to me that she
> was approaching a topic about which she felt uncomfortable. I thought it
> might be shame. This was not a time to force the conversation; my task was
> to help her talk about the feeling, or at least to acknowledge her discomfort.
> I said to her, "It looks like this is hard to talk about. Do you feel ashamed of
> something?" As she felt her discomfort being acknowledged and understood,
> the shame she felt about giving in to emotion abated through catharsis, and
> the session went on. Cassie then told me tearily about her parents' divorce
> and how much she wanted a normal family for the upcoming holiday. Again,
> as she brought her feelings into the room, healing took place.

It's important to remember that catharsis is not just for trauma but is also part of any therapy. A great deal of the therapist's job is creating optimal conditions for catharsis and letting it happen. These instances of catharsis are so much part of the fabric of therapy that they are often not recognized for what they are: small miracles.

Becoming more and more aware of catharsis and other change processes has quietly transformed my work as a therapist. My original training was to follow a set of rules or principles and wait for the patient to get better. Now I seek actively to make healing happen. And when a patient shares new material with feeling, I know something of real value has been accomplished.

What Catharsis Is Not

The word *catharsis* has one unfortunate connotation. It has sometimes been associated with uncontrolled expressions of strong feeling such as "scream therapy." It is true that we may experience some sense of release when we express strong feelings, but release does not always lead to healing. I described earlier how the conscious source of feelings may not be the authentic original one. Sharing "derivative" feelings can give temporary relief but does not accomplish permanent healing. True catharsis, in the sense I mean it here, occurs when we experience and share the authentic feeling, whether current or held somewhere in the mind, unprocessed since it was first experienced. When the raw, unprocessed feeling comes into consciousness along with the original circumstances, in a context of connection, then permanent healing does happen. On the other hand, the same feeling connected with inauthentic events or circumstances does not lead to healing or even to permanent change. Here is an example:

> Matthew was showered with material luxuries as a child, but his mother did little to fulfill her role as a parent. He carried a deep resentment far into adulthood but felt too guilty to acknowledge his real feeling. Without being aware of the connection, he often found himself enraged at service people and others who acted irresponsibly. Although their performance was genuinely substandard, his anger was out of proportion. The primary source of his anger was far back in his history. When he would "let them have it," he felt some immediate relief, but there was no long-term healing. Each time he encountered irresponsibility, he would go through the same cycle. He didn't experience catharsis until in therapy he was able to connect his feeling with the times when his mother was more interested in her social life than her son.

Matthew's anger at negligent service people was derivative. The circumstances were similar enough to trigger his feelings, but the here-and-now circumstances served as a more "acceptable" but inauthentic context for his old buried feelings. Healing of the old emotions is possible but works only when we experience awareness of their true source.

One patient called it "time stamping," meaning associating present feelings with their authentic roots. He experienced powerful tears when he saw a movie scene where a man was trapped and crushed in a construction accident. Later, he recalled how asthma made him feel trapped and helpless. As soon as he made the connection, he felt healing of the original pain and was no longer troubled by the movie scene. In a similar way, recall of specific positive moments allowed him to take ownership of the successes and strengths he had but that he sometimes forgot.

Attempts to bring about healing by inciting rage for its own sake, or by misdirecting it at someone or something different from its original source, may give a brief feeling of relief, but it does not produce lasting benefit and may do harm.

Acting Out

Another source of misunderstanding about catharsis is that the word can be associated with "acting out" feelings as opposed to communicating them. Hitting someone when we are angry is acting out the feeling; it does not lead to catharsis. Worse than that, it can have unfortunate, even dangerous side effects. In general, acting out feelings, especially derivative ones, allows us to avoid actually experiencing the emotion and benefiting from catharsis.

Even words, when their purpose is to hurt, can be a form of acting out. How can we tell the difference? Usually it is more a matter of feeling than definition. Our social sense tells us when words are used more to hurt than to communicate. In contrast, when they give the other person an empathic understanding, even strong words can serve as communication. My favorite example of a healthy communication of angry feeling is when we get too close to a dog chewing a bone. The dog will growl, communicating that we are too close. We instinctively back off and nothing bad happens. If we fail to heed the communication, the dog may bite. In this example, growling is a communication, while biting is what I would call acting out. Perhaps the distinction is that communication goes just as far as necessary to let the other person know what our feelings are and how strongly we feel them, but no more. This might include raising one's voice, repetition, even some body movement, but not injury or even intimidating gestures.

When we move directly to action, we actually bypass the stage of feeling the emotion and fail to communicate what we are feeling. As a result, the conditions for catharsis are not met and the action is at best a Band-Aid solution. It may feel good to punch a wall or even hurt someone, but the relief doesn't last or change anything in the long run.

Key Concept: Acting Out

Another phrase coined by Freud, who pictured releasing the energy of a feeling without actually experiencing or sharing the feeling itself. He saw acting out as blocking the process of catharsis.

The Greek Notion of Catharsis

Perhaps the original Greek meaning of catharsis, feeling good after you see a powerful play or film, is a bit different from what Freud meant. We do feel good, and may react especially strongly when the drama reminds us of our own unfinished business, but once again, the actors are proxies; even powerful feelings on stage or screen are "derivative" and do not permanently resolve our personal problems.

Mindfulness: A Possible Challenge to Catharsis

Recently there has been a lot of interest in "mindfulness" as a way of coping with painful feelings.

"Surf the Feeling"

My favorite way of explaining mindfulness is to think of surfing a wave of feeling. Think of the difference between riding on top of a wave and being swallowed up and tossed about by one. In achieving mindfulness we experience the energy of the feeling, but from on top, so we are not overcome by its turbulence. We feel the energy and may even be exhilarated by its power, but we know that it is temporary. We ride it out until it gradually washes away. We are no longer subject to its destructiveness. Is mindfulness an alternative to catharsis or in some way related to it?

Mindfulness comes from the tradition of Buddhism. To oversimplify, the word is an English translation of the Sanskrit word, *smrti*. As of this writing, Wikipedia defines mindfulness as "the calm awareness of one's body functions, feelings, content of consciousness, or consciousness itself." This calm state of observation and perspective sounds very much like the feeling of perspective that comes with catharsis. The main difference is that mindfulness is thought of as a solitary pursuit.

We have already seen that under safe, nontraumatic circumstances, catharsis can happen without the physical presence of another person. Could it be that mindfulness is really the same as catharsis, except that the sense of calm and safety comes from within? Does mindfulness make use of the internal rechargeable battery pack of connection that we all possess? *Smrti*, the calm awareness that is central to mindfulness, is strikingly reminiscent of how it feels to be in touch with the internalized other. I think it is very likely that mindfulness is, in essence, the cultivation of awareness of the inner context of connection with its feeling of serenity and perspective.

It is my contention that in order to achieve this calm, to surf above our feelings, we must access our internal rechargeable battery pack of connection. In seeking mindfulness we are actually working to put ourselves in a state of mind that we first learned from moments of connection and safety long ago. As this universal safe feeling washes into our consciousness, we come to the same simultaneous balancing of feelings of distress with feelings of safety that are at the heart of the experience of catharsis.

My View

Given the striking similarity, I am ready to propose the theory that mindfulness and catharsis are really two ways of approaching the same experience. If this similarity is valid, then it is no surprise to us as students of catharsis that mindfulness brings a natural serenity in the face of life's troubles. Furthermore, whereas mindfulness has sometimes been questioned as promoting detachment from life, it seems more likely that mindfulness actually represents cultivation of a greater attachment or connection.

In recent years, while working on new course material, I became more familiar with the writings of Peter Fonagy and Daniel J. Siegel. While I had been interested in catharsis as the basic healing process in therapy, these writers had also been seeking a more universal understanding of therapy. They, too, found a basic transformation at the heart of how psychotherapy works. They see therapy as a way to foster mindfulness, which they see as responsible for healing.

For them, the starting point is not the sharing of feeling between therapist and patient, but in leading the patient to a state of mindfulness. Each came to the conclusion that therapy works by helping people to gain self-perspective, especially awareness of the workings of their own minds. Fonagy named this process "mentalization," defined as "seeing yourself from the outside and others from the inside." Siegel adopted the term "Mindsight," which he defines similarly as "a kind of focused attention that allows us to see the internal workings of our own minds." Each description bears a very close resemblance to *smrti*, mindfulness. For these authors, helping patients to see themselves and their own mental processes from outside is the key to therapy.

Peter Fonagy (1952-)

Freud Memorial Professor of Psychoanalysis at University College, London, Fonagy has focused on the integration of research and theory, particularly in relation to early attachment and psychotherapy.

Daniel J. Siegel (1957-)

Siegel, Clinical Professor of Psychiatry at the UCLA School of Medicine, is the author of *The Mindful Brain: Reflection* and *Attunement in the Cultivation of Well-Being and The Mindful Therapist: A Clinician's Guide to Mindsight and Neural Integration*.

The Role of the Therapist

While I had been working on cultivating my patients' ability to bring feelings into the room, these two respected and influential therapists had come to a conclusion that seemed the opposite of mine. Where I had become convinced that catharsis was primarily a product of empathic connection, Fonagy and Siegel were championing the view that a more philosophical understanding helps the patient to develop a new perspective on events of the mind, which, in turn, is at the root of healing.

Although we seemed to disagree, or at least approach healing from different directions, we agreed in practice. Fonagy's mentalizing and Siegel's Mindsight were exactly what I spent a good deal of time and energy doing with my patients. I regularly invite patients to notice the workings of their own minds—that is, I am as dedicated a mentalizer as anyone. If emotion were at the core of healing, then why did my instinct, like theirs, push me to seek understanding? This commonality only heightened my sense of curiosity about the true role of self-observation and insight in psychotherapy.

Gaining Perspective or Emotional Sharing?

As I pondered this puzzle, I thought again of how a toddler falls and then makes eye contact with his mother or caregiver. His face and eyes are clearly communicative. If he had words, he would express surprise and shock more than pain: "Did you see what just happened?" Along with those feelings, he would ask, "Mommy, am I okay?" Then his mother would smile in a way that said "Oh, my! I understand your worry. It is distressing to fall down, but it really wasn't a bad fall and you are okay." The toddler feels better and soon forgets the distress of a moment before.

In other words, there is actually a two-way exchange of information. Here are the steps: (1) The toddler tells his mother what he is feeling. (2) Mother observes and has an empathic understanding. (3) She makes her own assessment of what has happened: "It was not a big fall and no damage was done." (4) She communicates both her empathy and her assessment to the child by facial expression and perhaps a verbalization. (5) The toddler takes in her response and adopts her perspective as his own. In this way, the mother regulates the toddler's emotions, keeping them in a range that he can manage.

Now picture an adult version of the same interchange. Say the doctor's office calls to tell you that you must have another test because of an abnormal result. You become frightened and your mind races as you imagine what might lie ahead. You confide in a person you really trust that you are scared. She has the wisdom not to attempt to reassure you; instead, she just listens and, perhaps without words, communicates both understanding and an assessment that there is nothing to do but get the second test. Almost instantly you feel better, even though the facts have not changed. What she doesn't say or show is as powerful as any words. Said differently, you communicate your feelings and she communicates very little. The fact that she stays composed and listens without losing control tells you she is not overwhelmed. That is the extent to which she puts things in perspective for you.

Even if our intellect has a realistic grasp of the situation, recall of events can awaken very young feelings of terror, the kind experienced at the center of the Bridge. We are instantly back to a place where we are alone and trying to cope with unthinkable dread. Once we share the fear, it joins the ranks of things that sometimes happen in life. The act of sharing with another human being automatically brings a sense of perspective as we adopt a more mature point of view. This leaves us with an important question: Was it the perspective that made you feel better, as in mentalization or Mindsight, or was it something more fundamental about the human interaction of sharing and being understood?

Two Elements Common to Both Catharsis and Mindfulness

Let's step back for a moment to review. First, recall that intellectual explanations and reassurance are not the essential ingredients of the healing transformation of catharsis. In fact, many instances of catharsis work with neither words nor analysis. Rather, catharsis is an emotional interchange in which one person shares painful feelings associated with the event that caused them, giving the other person an empathic understanding of the feelings. The empathic connection awakens a mental state of connection and safety that transforms the acute feelings of distress.

In both mindfulness and catharsis, the state of calm perspective and safety is essential. It is my view that this comes from gaining access to the deep, internalized memory of early connection with Mother, or the primary caregiver. In other words, we access our internal rechargeable battery pack of connection. It makes no difference whether this safe and connected feeling is evoked by the practice of mindfulness meditation or by the presence of an empathic other. The experience is the same and has the same healing effect.

Another element is just as critical. Our feelings of distress must come up to the level of consciousness. In Chapter 4 we will discuss the realm of implicit knowledge, the background hum, where we are vaguely aware but not consciously focused on our feelings or inner experience. The practice of mindfulness emphasizes gaining awareness of our inner processes and feelings which means bringing them from the implicit world to the sharp focus of our explicit consciousness. The same thing happens in catharsis, but through a slightly different route.

For catharsis to accomplish its transformation, feelings have to come to the foreground of our attention. As long as they remain in the background, felt in some vague way but not consciously noticed, they are not accessible to healing. A therapist, friend, or loved one, listening to our distress, wants to hear the details so as to be able to feel what we feel. We want them to understand and they want to understand. The need to communicate forces our feeling to full conscious awareness. Furthermore, when someone points out a feeling, —"Wow, you look sad today"—it is instantly brought to the foreground of our consciousness. The comment makes us notice our own feeling and makes it "real." Only with conscious awareness and attentive focus do our feelings become accessible to healing. Thus, our communication serves two purposes: It brings our own feeling to consciousness, and it allows the other person to experience empathy. As our opposing states of distress and calm meld together, we heal. Catharsis happens at the intersection of terror and safety.

Mindfulness accomplishes the same thing. In a state of attentive awareness, we encounter our terror juxtaposed with a feeling of calm and perspective similar to the state of mind that comes from empathic connection. Again there is a moment of intersection of terror and safety. Thus, the practice of mindfulness and the experience of sharing feelings with a friend or therapist bring about the same two essential elements: the achievement of full consciousness of our painful feelings and the emotional state of safety and connection. In therapy, seeking insight and understanding serve both functions at once. The quest for insight brings our feelings to consciousness and, through sharing, establishes an empathic connection that resonates with our deepest internalized experience of safety.

The Healing Moment

Recalling the middle of the Bridge, the point of no return, there is a fleeting moment when two emotional states exist simultaneously. One is the primal state of terror. It is characterized by physical reactions, such as the heart pounding, along with perceptual changes, including loss of awareness of time or surroundings. The other emotional state is the context of connection and safety, harking back to early experiences of Mother. Paradoxically, at the moment of healing we feel both utterly alone and comforted by the state of mind of connectedness. Simultaneously we feel the original distress and the calming context of connection. Even while we are in pain, we have a wordless awareness of the other person's calm mind or of our own internalized other. We are conscious of a greater, more universal understanding.

In addition, we have seen that in really traumatic situations, ones in which the physical presence of another person is required for healing, aloneness is a major component of the experience. In those cases, the empathic other gives something else besides calmness and perspective. The actual presence of a safe person has the effect of undoing the aloneness, the isolation that has heretofore been an integral part of the experience.

The Healing Agent

This explanation still doesn't identify whether the healing agent is information or purely emotion. What, exactly, allows catharsis to bring about permanent change? The answer is that in the brain, everything is information—that is, emotions, like all mental contents, exist as the activation of collections of neurons called neural networks. Sensory impressions, behavior, knowledge, and feelings are all represented in the brain by the activation of groups of nerve cells.

According to current thinking, the healing of traumatic memories can be thought of as a welding together of two previously unassociated neural networks. One group represents the traumatic experience and another represents the feeling of safety and connection.

When both networks are simultaneously activated, they become connected through strengthening of the synapses linking them. This new association takes place when we experience both danger and safety, aloneness and connection, at the same moment.

Neural Network

A grouping of nerve cells in the brain that function as a unit and that store and together represent a specific chunk of mental information.

Catharsis, the healing of painful feelings, has four aspects: First, it is an emotional event in which the soothing of relationship reaches the site of distress. Second, it is an informational event in which the other person's more mature assessment and perspective on the situation modifies our instinctive fear or dread. Third, it is an attentional event. The act of focusing on our feelings, either directly or indirectly by communicating, brings the feeling into the foreground of awareness where healing is possible. Fourth, it is a biological event in which nerve cells firing simultaneously cause a strengthening in the chemistry of synapses that join neural networks.

If we must decide what comes first, it is the communication of emotional information from patient to therapist or witness, which awakens conscious attention to the feeling. Next comes a communication from witness to patient. As that packet of information is received in the patient's brain, the healing transformation of catharsis takes place. Similarly in mindfulness, first comes the awareness of a distressing feeling, then the soothing state of mind.

Neurophysiology of Trauma

Recent work in the neurophysiology of trauma tells us more. The memory of danger is permanently etched in our minds via a deep brain structure called the amygdala. This is the core of an early warning system that alerts the rest of our brain to potential dangers. The amygdala compares incoming sensory impressions to stored memories of past experience. According to Joseph LeDoux (1996), "Unconscious fear memories established through the amygdala appear to be indelibly burned into the brain. They are probably with us for life." They can't be erased, which makes sense because we would never want to forget knowledge that could save us from danger. The amygdala uses these memories as templates to judge the potential danger of any current situation. (It also uses memories of positive experiences to judge potential pleasures.)

The triggering of the amygdala happens very fast and outside of consciousness. Have you ever had a close call and felt your hair stand on end before you realized how close it was? The physiological reaction is the end result of a chain of events starting with the amygdala recognizing possible danger. When memories of dangerous experiences are triggered, we go into what has been called fight-or-flight mode. Our hearts pound, we sweat, and our nerves go on high alert. Evolution has made sure that this system is not afraid of false alarms. It is better to trigger a false alarm than to miss a real one. This is what happens when trauma survivors are reminded of their experiences, even if they don't consciously remember the trauma and even when the current trigger is not really threatening.

Amygdala

Almond-shaped groups of nerve cells located deep within the medial temporal lobes of our brains, one in each hemisphere. They are specialized for detecting potential dangers and pleasures.

How can catharsis permanently remove such deeply rooted reactivity? It can't. Even though the essence of catharsis is that we no longer experience the physiological fight-or-flight reaction, the amygdala still remembers. Research has shown that healing does not stop recognition of danger but inhibits the spread of the alarm signal. The prefrontal cortex, the part of the brain that makes more thoughtful judgments, sends inhibitory signals that arrest the chain reaction that would otherwise end with feelings of the heart pounding and a sense of dread. Think of someone seeing a wisp of smoke and pulling the handle on a fire alarm; that's comparable to the initial panic response. Think then of firefighters arriving on the scene and performing a thorough inspection to determine that there is no danger;

that is comparable to the slower and more thoughtful prefrontal cortex sending an inhibitory signal to the primitive parts of the brain to turn off the fight-or-flight reaction.

There is much yet to learn about the neurophysiology of these interactions and how the perception of another's calm has such amazing power, but the fact that this happens has deep roots in our biology as social beings. Nor did it start with humans. Just as we humans look to our mothers for reassurance, baby rhesus monkeys cling to their mothers when frightened and presumably feel better. One of the powerful tools that evolution has given us is the ability to heal each other's pain.

Putting It All Together

To summarize, in my view, Buddhist mindfulness, Fonagy's mentalization, Siegel's Mindsight, and Freud's catharsis are all terms for the same healing exchange. This is an exchange in which conscious awareness and empathic connection with another being, whether internalized or external, makes it possible for us to face distress and receive the other's calm presence and perspective. In doing so, we are able to emerge from the isolated and timeless state of terror that engulfs us when our brains perceive that danger is at hand. Furthermore, once this exchange has taken place, our reactivity to the original trigger is permanently transformed. As we cross the point of no return on the Bridge, our experience is brought out of the primitive realm of solitary, unspeakable horror and joins forever the stream of events that make up shared life.

While catharsis is the core element in the healing action of therapy, the intellectual content of insight or understanding has additional benefits. Besides bringing feelings to consciousness and conveying a broader perspective, words add an important dimension to our experience. Words don't shift or flow. They are steady and, once said, lasting. Where our worst fears and dread exist in a swirling realm without words, connecting those feelings to words gives us a sense of solidity and reliability. We will explore this aspect in more depth in the next chapter on information and ideas.

Next Steps: Putting Catharsis to Work

Catharsis is universal and happens with every human encounter. In the healing of trauma and painful experiences in general, it is the crucial element. The following are some thoughts about how to put catharsis to work with your own difficult experiences and feelings. Most of them apply equally to early life trauma and to experiences from later life as well.

Sharing painful events and feelings with an empathetic other is the road to healing, but you may feel reluctant to re-experience painful incidents. How can you overcome your reluctance?

Believe That Healing Is Possible. I hope the examples in this book help you to see that healing, even of the deepest wounds, is possible. You can't change the past, but you can heal your feelings about it. And remember that the fear you have of your memories is the fear you felt as a child or in an adult situation that was more than you could handle. Now you are in a safe place and have more resources. Most important, you no longer have to face your terror in isolation.

Remember That Facing Your Feeling Is the Road to Catharsis. Extreme fear, horror, anger, etc., are frightening and painful to experience when you are powerless and alone. But you are no longer powerless and alone, and when your memories return with feeling, cathartic healing can take place. You will then be relieved of the pain and stress that you have carried in solitude.

Know that You Are Not at Fault. If you are a survivor of early trauma, there is another factor that can increase your reluctance to remember: a sense of guilt or responsibility. When adults fail to take responsibility for their actions, it is natural for children to do so instead. Also, abuse may be the only way you received attention or anything that felt like love (and your body may have responded involuntarily to sexual abuse). Under these circumstances, it may be easy to wonder if you somehow brought on the abuse. However, the truth is simple: as embodied in the law, children are not responsible. Children don't possess the judgment and self-control that make adults accountable. That is why children are not responsible for their feelings or actions. You were not at fault and you are not at fault for what happened early in your life.

Accept That Your Mind Will Resist Remembering. You may tell yourself that nothing so bad really happened. You may tell yourself that you are imagining things in order to get attention. However, if your feelings and reactions are different from other people's it is for a reason. Real psychological damage usually comes from real causes.

You may fear that, once started, your tears will never stop. They will—and if you allow catharsis to do its miracle work, you will have less reason for tears than ever before.

You may think that so much time has passed that the experience doesn't matter anymore. But the experience is still with you and in you, and it will continue to affect your life for as long as it remains out of full consciousness and unaddressed. The saying "time heals all wounds" doesn't apply to feelings that have been walled off. Here, the principle "out of mind; out of reach" applies, meaning that what is out of consciousness does not change or heal.

You may doubt your recall, thinking that things couldn't have happened quite the way you remember. This may be true. Memory is imperfect; however, some aspects of an event are more likely to be retained accurately and others less so. Research shows that children are more prone to misremember the order in which things happened and perhaps who was there. Adults may also purposely confuse or mislead them. On the other hand, the raw images, smells, and physical sensations that appear in your dreams or spontaneous thoughts are more likely to originate from real experiences. Your safest stance is to have an open mind.

Accept That Digging Won't Work. What if you only remember a small part or only suspect that something is "down there." Don't dig. You cannot and should not try to force memories. Sometimes thinking about aspects that carry some emotional charge will help to bring up others. However, the experience should not feel forced. What does work is to create a place where re-experiencing painful emotions feels safe. When your insides perceive that you are safe, what you need to remember will come back. I like to say that memories are "self-propelled."

While digging doesn't work, techniques such as exposure to graphic images or descriptions are designed to force recall. This can be effective, but may be dangerous in that pushing by therapists can reenact a component of many traumas in which the survivor has been made to feel powerless. Exposure or any treatment with a coercive aspect should only be done in a supportive, fully voluntary, and positive context. Retraumatization is the word for forced recall under unsafe (non empathic) conditions, and it can add to the damage sustained in the original trauma.

Listen to Your Inner Thoughts. Once you are ready to let go of your fear of feeling, it is very useful to pay attention to the thoughts, images, sensations, and emotions that come into your consciousness. These spontaneous products of the mind can lead to recall of what has been distanced.

Understand That Accessing Feelings Is Not an Intellectual Job. Your intellect will tend to make you analyze rather than feel your feelings. It will keep you away from specifics, as in, "Well, yes, I was angry on many occasions." Here, by abstracting multiple occasions into one description, the feelings are distanced, and the intellect actually prevents healing. On the other hand, think about how novelists describe situations. Their concrete words and specific facts not only give you a vivid picture but also bring feelings with them. Both for novelists and for you, details bring feelings into the room where they need to be. A therapist should help you to notice when your intellect is getting in the way and help you get back to your feelings.

Be Patient. When memories start to return, sometimes they come in a flood. At other times they emerge a little at a time. Either way, recall tends to start with isolated images and/or sensory impressions or feelings. Don't worry that, at first, these are disconnected and may not make sense. Be patient, let them be what they are, and work with the feeling part. Whatever needs to come will eventually do so. As I said above, memories are self-propelled.

There Is More to Trauma

In this book so far I have described the immediate feelings of distress that go with recall of trauma. But, as discussed briefly in Chapter 2, people who have suffered trauma may also experience "secondary feelings" of shame, guilt, and unworthiness. These feelings come from a conscience that is trying to protect you by adopting the values and attitudes of those who hurt you. Sharing these secondary feelings is part of therapy, but, because these feelings are based on judgments and the values underlying them, simply sharing will not change them. The values that underlie negative judgments must change as well as the feelings. Chapter 5 focuses on how trauma and other circumstances can cause you to acquire values and attitudes that are not appropriate or healthy and how it is possible, with hard work, to change them.

Looking beyond Trauma

Trauma has served to sharpen our understanding of catharsis and how painful feelings can heal through sharing. However, most of the dysfunctional patterns that plague us humans are less obvious and more convoluted than simple reactions to traumatic events. Chapter 4, about information and ideas, discusses the how and why of seeking to understand your own inner workings. Since the chapter is about ideas, it will also be the place where we look at how ideas can be part of avoiding feelings and how new ways of thinking can be the key to understanding our Castles and unlocking the feelings they guard.

References

Allen, J.G., P. Fonagy and A.W. Bateman. *Mentalizing in Clinical Practice*. Arlington, VA: American Psychiatric Publishing, 2008.

Le Doux, Joseph. *The Emotional Brain*. New York: Touchstone, 1996: 252.

M.S. Mahler, F. Pine and A. Bergman. "The Fourth Subphase: Con-solidation of Individuality and the Beginnings of Emotional Object Constancy." In *The Psychological Birth of the Human Infant*. New York, Basic Books, 1975: 109-120.

D.J. Siegel. *Mindsight: The New Science of Personal Transformation*. New York: Bantam Books, 2011.

D.N. Stern. *The Interpersonal World of the Infant: A View from Psy-choanalysis and Developmental Psychology*. New York: Basic Books, 1985: 173.

Bessel van der Kolk. *The Body Keeps the Score: Brain, Mind, and Body in the Healing of Trauma*. New York: Viking Adult, 2014.

· **4** ·

INFORMATION AND MISINFORMATION

How we use thoughts and ideas to shut out
feelings and how knowledge can save us.

So far we have seen that the transformations at the heart of healing and growth require that we consciously experience catharsis; that is, that we feel our most dreaded feelings in a context of safety and connection. We have also seen that powerful forces in our own mind work to keep us in a comfort zone far away from those feelings. In the interest of avoidance, our Black Box Motivator crafts thoughts exquisitely calculated to steer us away from anything that will bring our dreaded feelings into consciousness. But all is not lost. We— that is, our conscious self—can use a higher level of understanding to outsmart our own Black Box Motivator.

To put this chapter in perspective, the inner forces that are trying to keep us from our feelings and from the transforming power of catharsis utilize three main tools. First, our Black Box Motivator produces thoughts (the subject of this chapter) that serve to get us off the track of our feelings. In the next chapter (Chapter 5) we will see that our conscience can also be put to work to reinforce the status quo. Then, Chapter 6 will discuss how habitual behavior patterns are some of the most powerful feeling-avoidance tools in our mind's arsenal.

How can we sift through the multitude of ideas that come into consciousness so as to recognize which are "ours" and which come from our Black Box Motivator's dysfunctional efforts to avoid feelings? The first step in meeting this challenge is to develop a new and overarching set of ideas about what we really want and what we don't want. Our efforts at healing and growth start with thinking about how to understand and override our own motivational system so as to face things our mind doesn't want to face. This involves information and misinformation.

Now, let's explore how we can use our own mind to understand how ideas lead us away from uncomfortable feelings and how understanding can help us accept those feelings in a way that allows us to heal and grow.

Ideas That Hold Back Feelings

When ideas block access to our feelings, the best way to get closer to the feelings is to pit ideas against ideas. Using insight, we can expose the mental tricks that hide the feelings we dread. In the movie *Good Will Hunting*, the protagonist, Will (Matt Damon), carries the idea that his abusive father was right to punish him and that he is an undeserving and bad person. When his therapist (Robin Williams) tells him, "It's not your fault" and keeps repeating the words until Will actually hears them, the therapist is challenging an idea that has kept Will from facing his pain and anger. As long as Will considers himself at fault, he doesn't have to feel badly about the life that has been taken from him. That's what he deserved. Suddenly, as the idea of his unworthiness is challenged, he realizes how much he has lost and tears start to flow.

Good Will Hunting (1997)

Directed by Gus Van Sant and written by Matt Damon and Ben Affleck, who won Oscars for Best Screenplay. Will Hunting, played by Damon, is a math genius, unable to get over his abusive childhood and make full use of his gifts. To stay out of jail, he agrees to go into therapy.

Will's tears tell us that his feelings are active and fully conscious. As is familiar now, once the feelings were there in the room, catharsis could begin to transform them. Catharsis is wonderful, even simple, but the twists and turns required to access deep feelings are far from simple. They can involve many layers. The movie character, Will, needed not only an empathic therapist but a lot of trust building and finally a forceful challenge to the idea barrier that kept him from feeling.

Most of the traditional defenses that are taught in beginning psychology classes consist of ways to twist ideas so that they hide the truth and keep us from feeling. Will Hunting's defense could be called rationalization in that he created (or accepted from his father) an explanation that rationalized his self-directed abuse. Idea defenses are products of the Black Box Motivator, working as intended to shield us from painful feelings. The following are some additional examples.

Denial

When we think or say the opposite of what is true, it is called denial. Denial has many flavors besides outright negation of what is true. Minimization is admitting the truth but denying its importance. We admit to something but tell ourselves that its significance is so minor as to be negligible. Blaming the wrong person in order to deny our own responsibility is another form of denial. What all these actions have in common is that they distort our perception of reality. We often describe the use of these defenses as if it were willful, but it is not. The person who denies is actually the victim of his or her own self-deception. The cost is not only truth but also the loss of the chance to confront feelings and experience healing. The result is an intellectual Castle that has become a Prison.

If denial were actually conscious and willful, then it would represent an entirely different and even more costly distortion. Lying is a way of protecting against painful feelings, but one that is even more damaging in that it places a barrier between the self and others and powerfully blocks empathy. Frequently lying is a characteristic of serious personality pathology.

Projection

Attributing to others what we can't face in ourselves is known as projection. Hate is a common example in which negative characteristics are projected onto others and despised. This distortion of reality is very alienating to others. Paranoid ideas are examples of projection where there is a loss of contact with reality. This defense tends to arise from very early or primitive developmental eras when distinctions between self and others are yet to be clearly delineated.

Displacement

When feelings that were originally generated in relation to one person are redirected onto someone else we call this displacement. Typically the person who is spared is someone so important to the individual that safety requires transferring the feeling towards another person who is less important or safer. In another twist, feelings unresolved in early life can be displaced onto someone in contemporary life, such as a spouse or boss or therapist. These were mentioned in the last chapter as *derivative* feelings. Although they are real they probably don't quite fit the circumstances. Unfortunately, catharsis doesn't work for displaced feelings. Until the feeling is experienced in its original context, healing does not take place.

Fantasy

Based on imagination, fantasy is a kind of defense that is less destructive than many. Imaginary solutions to emotional problems can often be constructed so as to avoid any dangerous clash with reality. In Chapter 7 we will look extensively at fantasies of future good fortune or success that take away the pain of today. Fantasy play is another way of using imagination to deal with today's pain without sacrificing reality. But when fantasy becomes confused with reality, the results can be dangerous.

Automatic Thoughts

Cognitive therapists have identified a number of typical distortions that work to justify unhealthy actions. Indirectly, these too are aimed at avoidance of painful feelings. Typically a behavior pattern blocks a feeling and automatic thoughts hold the unhealthy behavior pattern in place. Thus, there are two layers of defense working to keep us from feeling.

For example, catastrophization, the opposite of minimization, makes the situation seem so bad that there is no need to face the task of fixing it. "I did so badly on that test that I might as well drop out of school for good." The feeling being avoided might be a fear of failure, or even of success. The behavior being discouraged is perseverance in school. The Black Box Motivator uses exaggeratedly negative thoughts to talk the individual's free will into quitting. In general, catastrophization supports avoidance of an activity that might lead to uncomfortable feeling.

Overgeneralization, refers to the art of taking one example and using it to prove a general rule. "Doctor, I tried what you suggested and it didn't work, so I'd better quit while I'm ahead." Once again, the object is to avoid a behavior that could lead to uncomfortable feelings.

Each of these distorted ideas represents a blind spot. As long as we follow our distorted thinking and rationalizations, we are unlikely to change our unawareness or dysfunctional behavior. And as long as the behavior patterns remain, we are not likely to encounter our dreaded feelings. Each layer serves to cover up something we would probably do better to face.

Ideas Are Mercurial

When we become aware of new facts, our ideas change instantly and effortlessly. This is why it is apt to call ideas "mercurial." Occasionally, new facts will come into view and suddenly trigger a major change. When the reality that Will Hunting was not at fault finally got through, his reaction was immediate and dramatic. Once his mind was opened, he saw instantly that the new fact presented was true and the emotions came flooding in.

But, when ideas represent part of an avoidance mechanism, we can become very attached to them and cling to them in spite of new evidence. Against the evidence, Will Hunting held onto the idea for years that he was to blame for his problems. Even when it was pointed out, he seemed actively to fend off acknowledgment of his error. Only with extensive groundwork and a very safe therapist could he respond to the therapist's energetic assertion that his plight was not his "fault."

Before we can let go of distorted ideas, especially when they serve an emotional need, we must first become aware that they are incorrect. Since we are quite practiced at maintaining our blindness in spite of reality, it often takes another person to open our eyes. This is one of the places where therapists and other outsiders come in. They usually don't have the same blind spots we do, so for them it is not so difficult to see our distortions. The hard part is for us to come around to accept the new vision. We may have to hear truth stated in many ways before we can open our eyes. When we do, the result is an "aha" moment when we suddenly see what we have been avoiding and experience blocked feelings in a new and poignant way.

Ideas That Block Acceptance and Forgiveness

Acceptance of what we can't alter and forgiveness for transgressions are two important healing processes that involve both feelings and ideas. Very often, when we have trouble with acceptance or forgiveness, it is because we are secretly harboring the belief that someone or something should change first. Most of the time, this secret hope is held on a level where we are unaware of its presence and wonder why we are having so much trouble letting go.

In order to come to acceptance, we must first relinquish the hope that the problem might be undone or fixed. For forgiveness, we must give up hope that forgiveness might not be needed, for example because the wrong was not willful or someone else was to blame. Until these hopeful thoughts are put to rest, the emotional giving up that is the essence of acceptance and forgiveness cannot happen.

What is surprising about both acceptance and forgiveness is that the blockage at the level of ideas is often not in our awareness. We may think that we are having trouble dealing with feelings, when in fact we are still stuck on the part that has to do with information. In the case of acceptance, it may be because we are waiting and hoping that something will change so that we won't have to go through the painful process of acknowledging a bad outcome. In the case of forgiveness, we may also be hoping that we won't have to forgive. Perhaps the guilty party will reform, or maybe punishment will take care of it, or maybe nothing bad really happened in the first place. As long as these hopeful thoughts are in play, then why go through the painful process of admitting hopelessness and of letting go?

But what happens when we are not aware of the fact that we are waiting for a problem to be fixed or the guilty party to ask for forgiveness? Think of the not-uncommon example of a parent who was abusive or neglectful. As adults, we recognize (intellectually) that the past is the past. "It's been so many years, and time heals everything." So we don't allow ourselves to acknowledge that we are still angry or still waiting for our needs to be met. Instead, we find ourselves enraged by every contemporary instance of neglect or abuse, but not the instances from our own past. It may take a lot of work to bring to light the hopeful but unrealistic thoughts that are preventing us from doing the hard work of making peace with reality on its own terms. Until it becomes clear that there is no other option, the mind will have a great deal of trouble facing the hopelessness of an irreparable loss or an unacknowledged wrong. And by now it won't come as a surprise to you that the mind will actively resist such clarity.

When we face the conclusion that no other option exists, then we begin to feel the pain of the loss or misdeed. It is that pain, having come at last to the surface, that allows catharsis to take place, bringing permanent healing in the form of acceptance or forgiveness.

Are You Blocked from Acceptance or Forgiveness?

How do we explore the unconscious hopes and wishes that block resolution of feelings left over from unfortunate events? The process is the same as for other thoughts stored away. Curiosity, openness, and a readiness to face our feelings are the keys. In spite of our natural drive to avoid facing feelings, it is our own wish to be understood, and belief that such a thing can happen, that will eventually propel our secret thoughts to the surface.

Two Minds and Two Kinds Of Knowing

Looking carefully at just how catharsis transforms our feelings, I have emphasized the need for conscious awareness. Even the toddler's distressed look after falling down tells us that she is consciously aware that something possibly bad has just happened. Then and only then can the soothing presence of an empathic witness bring calm and perspective. Now it is time to look in more detail at what actually constitutes *conscious awareness*. Furthermore, it is time to examine the vast and less clear realm of what we know without conscious awareness. Not only will this be of direct importance for catharsis, but it will also help us to recognize and override our own avoidant thoughts and impulses.

While conscious thought has been the subject of much observation and philosophy since civilization began, the study of unconscious thought is relatively new. Though unconscious thought is mentioned much earlier, in the 1890s, Freud championed the idea of the unconscious mind as a major player in our daily lives. Recently there has been a resurgence of interest and experiment. Daniel Kahneman, in *Thinking, Fast and Slow* (2011) details recent work confirming that much of our thinking takes place outside of consciousness. Kahneman suggests that it is to save time and energy that we base many decisions on the results of a quick, unconscious assessment. I have placed more emphasis on the way the mind, in the form of the Black Box Motivator, works behind the scenes to guide our behavior in order to avoid anticipated pain and to make sure we do what we are "supposed to do."

Daniel Kahneman (1934-)

Khaneman is an Israeli-American Psychologist who won the Nobel Prize in Economic Science in 2006 for his work on the psychology of decision-making, including nonconscious influences.

Whether it is to save energy or to guide our free will, unconscious thinking uses shortcuts for us to arrive at judgments. A few salient features of the present situation are matched with previous experience. Using the assumption that the present must be "just like" something from the past, a decision is made. The resemblances are often quite flimsy and can result in unreliable judgments as well as savvy intuitions. We could compare this to courts deciding guilt or innocence based only on circumstantial evidence. In one experiment, first done by Todorov et. al (2005), subjects were asked without explanation to look briefly at photos of faces and to rate them for "likability" and "competence." The pictures were actually of political candidates. The researchers found that the raters were in good agreement among themselves and that in two thirds of cases, actual election results were in line with the ratings, especially for competence. The suggested conclusion is that, without realizing it, we tend to make important decisions based on very little relevant data. Kahneman's book has been influential among decision makers, who are urged to go slower and to be more thoughtful in pondering major decisions. Perhaps more important is the advice to work on being more aware of our own mental processes and how they influence our perceptions and decisions so as to avoid uncomfortable feelings.

The mindfulness movement has emphasized that we can learn to be more aware of our own mental processes and that greater awareness brings with it resilience, serenity, and empathy. Training programs such as Khabat-Zinn's Mindfulness Based Stress Reduction (MBSR) have been devised to teach this skill. I have already suggested that the sense of perspective that mindfulness practitioners seek is likely to be the same as the perspective that results from catharsis. In the case of mindfulness, rather than seeking to connect with an empathic other, meditation is focused on directing our attention. Going back thousands of years, practitioners of meditation have learned to be aware of their bodies, minds, and surroundings in increasing breadth. As we consciously direct our attention to expand our awareness, we gain a sense of perspective as well. The key here is in directing our attention. But mindfulness is only one of several ways to gain awareness of what was previously not in the foreground of our mind.

Khabat-Zinn, Jon (1944-)

Prominent teacher and proponent of mindfulness meditation and the integration of Zen into American medicine. Developed the Mindfulness-Based Stress Reduction program (MBSR).

All three traditions—psychoanalysis, cognitive-behavioral therapy and mindfulness—would have us move what was in the background into the foreground of our conscious awareness. If it is this easy to use focused attention to move thoughts and feelings from one domain to the other, then are unconscious thoughts really that different from conscious ones?

What started out as a simple distinction between what is conscious and what is not becomes more complicated as we recognize the ability to move mental contents between the two compartments. As we become consciously aware of a certain impression, we can see that before it caught our attention, we did nonetheless have a vague sense of it. That feeling of uneasiness at the end of the day was there even before our attention brought it into focus. So, rather than trying to divide our mental contents into conscious and nonconscious, let's try a different distinction. We'll use the words *explicit* and *implicit*. Explicit refers to what is in our conscious awareness, the focus of our attention. Perhaps an operational definition would be that which is immediately available to express in words. This doesn't mean that everything explicit is in words. A "look" in fashion or a "move" in sports might be the focus of our attention but might require some effort to translate into words.

Implicit, in contrast, refers to impressions that belong to the background of our consciousness. Impressions may be vaguely conscious or not at all conscious. *Contextual* is another word for implicit, one that emphasizes the part of our environment that is not in focus. Feelings, an atmosphere, a vague sense, an intuition, a hunch, or even a belief that we "take for granted," all these, until they become explicitly conscious, are implicit. Because implicit mental contents have profound effects on our daily life, decisions, and emotions, it is desirable to cultivate a curiosity about what is going on in the background. When we turn our attention to this background activity it is no longer implicit. What was implicit becomes explicit, and with this move into conscious focus come the important possibilities. What is explicit can be subjected to logical evaluation and becomes available for emotional healing.

When it comes to memory, the distinction between explicit and implicit is sharper. Remarkably, the two kinds of memory are not processed by the same parts of our brain. Explicit memory refers to facts and other pieces of information that we might want to recall: what we did or what someone said, or what was in a book. In contrast, implicit memory stores information we don't think of searching for, like how to drink from a glass or what to say when someone says hello. Implicit memories are also called "procedural." They might include knowledge of how to drive a car but would not include remembering the location of the radio controls on a particular car.

Brain research has shown that the explicit type of memory requires a specific brain structure, the hippocampus, for successful storage. In contrast, implicit memory processing is spread more widely through the brain. The result is that for explicit memory, damage to this small brain structure can prevent new information from being stored. Information that was learned prior to the disruption remains accessible, but new facts are not registered. During alcoholic blackouts (periods of loss of memory but not necessarily loss of consciousness), the hippocampus stops functioning and memories are not recorded. Some kinds of dementia also affect the storage of explicit memories while leaving implicit memory untouched.

Hippocampus

A seahorse-shaped brain structure involved in moving explicit memories from short-term to long-term storage. Injury to the hippocampus can destroy the brain's ability to form new explicit long-term memories.

Here is an example that highlights the difference between explicit and implicit memory.

Linda, once a respected lawyer, resided on the dementia unit in a nursing home. She could process information and even do calculations but could not remember recent events. While she did not know where she was, she could remember her former address. She also had no trouble with implicit knowledge like knowing how to brush her teeth or cut up her food. When her son came to visit she recognized him, but ten minutes after he left she could not recall the last time her son had been there. And, although she couldn't learn new information, she could keep score in the Scrabble game that her fellow residents were playing. At first she asked constantly when she could go home. Months later, still without knowing exactly where she was, she seemed to settle down and accept her new home. It seemed likely that she had gained implicit knowledge of where she now lived.

The Implicit Realm Is a Great Hiding Place for Feelings

Keeping information implicit prevents us from seeing the contradictions and errors in our perceptions. Even more important, when feelings become explicit, we experience them as more "real" and immediate. When emotions come into our conscious awareness, they move from a vague sense to a sharp affect that takes hold of our emotional apparatus. We react physically, our faces showing our feelings. Tears come and painful emotions hurt. They can hurt so much that our Black Box Motivator anticipates their coming to awareness and blocks us from acknowledging what is in the background.

Working against our tendency to keep uncomfortable knowledge and feelings in the implicit realm, therapists insist on putting feelings into words. When a therapist puts an observation into words, our awareness can move instantly from implicit to explicit. Say you tell the therapist about something you struggled with when you were young, and the therapist observes, "You really had a tough childhood." Suddenly you feel tears. Something you already knew implicitly just became "real." The therapist has directed your attention so as to bring the knowledge into the realm of the explicit. Through this exchange, your feeling is shared. The therapist has led the way, first sensing your implicit feeling, then naming it explicitly and helping you to shift your own awareness of the feeling from implicit to explicit. It doesn't matter who gets there first. What is important is that the feeling is consciously shared. Then the requirements for catharsis are met and healing can take place.

Implicit Is Often Wrong

John suddenly feels a flush of anger at Jen. Once again, she has left the light on. Last month, he had emphasized that their electric bill was too high. Jen seemed to understand and said she would be careful. Now he could see it was only lip service. She really didn't care about the bills or the stress he felt at work in trying to keep up.

Jen had the intention of turning off the lights. But she was exhausted and underneath that, though she wasn't really aware of it, she resented John's badgering her about every detail of their life. Besides, she was going out to the car to bring in heavy grocery bags and wouldn't have hands free for the light switch. She didn't want to trip in the dark.

> *As she walked in, John made a sarcastic remark. Jen blew up, pointing out*
> *that she didn't waste anywhere near the cost of the gas for his daily trip to the*
> *coffee shop. The exchange left them both feeling hurt and discouraged for the*
> *rest of the day.*

The most common and painful clashes in marriages happen because of our reliance on automatic, implicit assessments of situations. John came to an immediate but incorrect conclusion that Jen's behavior could only have been explained by an attitude of selfish disregard for his feelings. He had no doubt that his assessment was correct. But his implicit thinking was actually guided by early experience with his father, who chose alcohol over his responsibilities as a parent.

Before his thoughts or feelings could become explicit, without thinking, John made his sarcastic remark. Before she had any explicit awareness of what was happening, Jen hotly defended herself with a counterattack. If they had been able to have a slower, more conscious conversation, one in which their true thoughts and feelings could come into explicit awareness, they would have discovered not only what really happened but also the feelings and needs that were behind their words. Deep down, John was looking for the helper he had longed for. Jen was hoping to have some recognition of her efforts and the difficulty of her life.

This small example illustrates what happens in the majority of marital arguments. They start with instant information processing in the implicit realm. These lead to automatic strategies invented by children to solve problems of long ago. Since the thinking is based on faulty conclusions and instinctive approaches to no-longer-relevant family issues, it is not surprising that these strategies are not productive.

The example also highlights what a different exchange could take place, either at the time or afterwards, in which both parties could connect and share their own experience while coming to understand the other's. Such a conversation would be healing for the individuals and bonding for the couple.

Implicit Thinking Uses a Different Kind of Logic

Having promoted the idea of paying attention to implicit thoughts, it is helpful to realize that they do have a logic to them, though it is not the same as the formal logic we use for thinking in words. Let's go back to the experiment looking at how voters choose their candidates. The implicit thought might be, "In the photo, the candidate looks competent, therefore I'll choose him as my representative." In formal logic, we can see the fallacy. People's looks don't necessarily reflect their true personal qualities, nor their beliefs, nor who contributed to their campaigns. But in the world of implicit reasoning, the choice makes perfect sense. A competent appearance has associations to competence and brings up positive feelings and confidence. The special logic of implicit thought follows three simple principles: (1) Relationships between mental percepts are limited to just two types, like and opposite; (2) feelings are black and white; (3) the concept of absence or zero has no meaning.

The implicit world is organized around associations. "Things" (meaning any mental contents including images, feelings, words, sensations, or movements) can be associated in only two ways: They are either positively associated as "likes" or associated as opposites. Sweet, for example, might be associated with soft and with sugar, but opposite to bitter. Associations can be strong or weak, but subtle distinctions such as the differences between identical, similar, and reminiscent are absent. By contrast, using explicit logic we might see George on the street and remark, "Oh, that's George." Or we might say, "That looks like George but isn't him." Or, "He reminds me of George." The distinctions are important in explicit thought, and each of the three sentences has a very different meaning. In the implicit world, there is no such subtlety, only a group of associations including the image, the name George and all that is associated with each. In addition, there might be a negative association: George once insulted me and I associate him with dislike, badness, and anger.

Implicit logic may seem simplistic, but it is very powerful. In an instant, the image of George conjured up a myriad of associations and prepared us to deal quickly with any interaction that might ensue. We couldn't appreciate poetry without implicit logic and association. As Khaneman points out, each system has advantages and disadvantages, and we often combine them, usually without realizing that we are doing so. Every day, our quick and easy ability to grasp metaphors, based on the implicit logic of association, helps us quickly understand each other. Metaphors bring to light subtle comparisons, then, when words have transferred it into the explicit realm, we can test to see if the comparison is logically correct.

In the implicit world, feelings are black or white. Imagine that your doctor's office calls to say you will need to repeat a test. Your mind will tend to track one way or the other. You will either imagine that there is nothing to worry about, or you will begin to imagine some terrible illness invading your body. People may oscillate back and forth between the two, but we generally can't handle shades of gray in between. Now imagine that the test is repeated and the doctor says there is a 17% chance that the results will indicate a fatal illness. The explicit mind has some grasp of that statistic, but the emotional mind can only seize upon black or white. Either you are sure to die, or it could never happen to you. Again, you might oscillate back and forth, and feelings may be stronger or weaker, but they will be of one color or the other at a given time.

Mixed feelings do exist in the implicit realm, but they tend to consist of multiple sets of associations that operate separately. On the other hand, a new and distinctive set of perceptions, if repeated, could form a set of associations in itself. The doctor, reciting the research showing a 17% chance of a lethal outcome to one patient after another, might experience it as a familiar percept that has taken on its own set of associations. When he utters the words, they have explicit meaning and a familiar set of associations as well. To the doctor, the meaning of "17% mortality" is a unique mix of denotation and connotation, very different from the meaning to his patient.

Finally, if you try to convince a child that monsters don't exist, you will confront the implicit world's lack of the concept of absence or zero. For children the idea doesn't have any meaning though they can grasp the idea that the monster might be somewhere far away. Similarly, even for adults, death is hard to grasp emotionally. It is easier to think that a person has "passed away" than to wrap our minds around the thought that the person might simply be gone. The explicit logic is simple, but the implicit mind can't easily follow.

We Often Think Both Ways at Once

Though it may violate strict logic, combining the two forms of thinking is typically human. We may think we are being perfectly "logical" without being aware of the intrusion of implicit logic. On the other hand, the more poetic connotative meanings enrich the bare denotative sense of our words. Let me share a dramatic example of this kind of mixed logic. I recall an interview of a veteran of the Vietnam War who had lost a limb in combat. The interviewer asked him if he thought the war was a "just" one. The young man replied, "Of course. Look what I have sacrificed for it." Using explicit logic, the statement made no sense. His loss of limb had no bearing on the rightness of the war. But the emotional logic was completely understandable. Coping with his injury, he had worked hard to defeat feelings of bitterness and hopelessness. His loss of limb had become associated with positive feelings about his sacrifice. It was emotionally obvious that the idea of losing a leg fighting an unjust war would simply be too painful (and unhealthy) to allow.

We often use mixed logic to override or cover up important feelings. A common example is neediness. John said, "I learned in the Army to fend for myself. I don't really need anyone." It was true that he had been trained in survival techniques and could survive, but his associations to survival in combat crowded out any awareness of the lifelong yearning to be taken care of that was making him resentful of Jen. As a therapist, I often find myself trying to pull the two components apart so my patient can face the unhealed childhood feelings while acknowledging adult reality. As mentioned before, a good way to do this is to suggest a split between a young self or inner child and the adult self. When a person is able to embrace this split, then it is much easier for the adult to take the inner child by the hand

and help him or her face (meaning bring into explicit awareness) the troublesome feelings and heal them through catharsis.

Using Words to Plant a Stake in the Ground

Turning to the explicit world, let's look at a special quality of words. Words have staying power. Once you have uttered a phrase you can't take it back. An observation like "I really did have a hard time when I was a kid," plants a kind of stake in the ground. You can never stuff those thoughts all the way back into the implicit box. To use another favorite metaphor, words are like the pitons or "protection" that rock climbers use. Once hammered into the rock, these metal spikes hold the ropes that keep the climber from falling while allowing free movement forward. In a similar way, words record a point in your progress that will remain in place.

Sometimes I use words to ease a patient into awareness of a feeling that he has warded off. First I might apply a more abstract expression: "John, it seems like you might be experiencing a wish for help." If the more intellectual expression works to soften his emotional reaction, he may at least be able to ponder the idea. Now the feeling has been named. It has been brought into the light, and will be harder for John to push it into the background. If a reaction of shame comes to consciousness, if it is not too intense we will be able to do some healing. Later I might use a stronger, more emotional word. "There is that neediness that makes you feel so ashamed." Again shame comes to consciousness, where another layer can be detoxified by catharsis. Finally, "Right now, you are feeling a longing for someone to be there for you." Hopefully, by this time John will be past the shame and able to acknowledge the feeling. He will leave that session feeling better and being more free.

Different words and images resonate differently with each individual. Sometimes it takes ten different ways of saying something before one strikes us and lodges in our consciousness. Not infrequently, something read in a book or heard in another context will "click" even though our therapist has said the same thing many times before. One patient was backsliding into negative thoughts and the rationalizations that supported them. She was a staunch liberal, so I suggested that we label positive thoughts as "blue" and negative ones as "red." This shorthand helped us to identify—and remember—which thoughts would help her grow and which would do the opposite. The bit of humor cut through her feelings of shame and made it easier to acknowledge the red thoughts that came from her Black Box Motivator.

It is no surprise that AA has slogans. Addiction is so powerful that strong words are not only needed, but required. Slogans are a way of using words to strengthen the effect and lasting power of ideas aimed at supporting behavior change. Sure, the slogans may be corny, but they are genuinely helpful in battling a force as entrenched as addiction.

One of my favorite words when talking about emotional growth is *backlash*. I use it to refer to the negative thoughts, impulses, and feelings that come flooding out of our Black Box Motivator when we make positive changes to a longstanding dysfunctional pattern. I tell my patients when they embark on healthy change not to be surprised by backlash from within, "trying" to reestablish the old status quo.

Insight = Explicit = Healing and Growth

In summary, the implicit realm is where feelings originate, while the explicit realm is where healing and growth take place. When feelings stay implicit, they are distanced from awareness. Also distanced are mental contents, such as early life problems and the yearnings that once promised to solve them. These remain fixed and unresponsive to the passage of time. Thus, keeping feelings, ideas, and values implicit, that is, out of conscious awareness, is one of the basic principles of avoidance. As long as feelings and information remain implicit, we don't consciously notice them and can't communicate them to others. When therapists call our attention to implicit contents, they become explicit and bring feelings with them. When feelings come into the room by whatever route, explicit words allow us to articulate the feelings so our witness can understand accurately and feel empathically with us. Those are the conditions for catharsis, which removes the negative power from our feelings and opens us up for yet more understanding and more feeling. In addition to their role in communication, words put a stake in the ground, allowing us to measure our progress and stop ourselves from backsliding.

Due to the mind's immense capacity to form new associations and attach new meanings, the distinction between what is implicit and what is explicit is often clouded. Furthermore, our ability to direct our attention to the implicit and to articulate it in words again blurs the distinction. Nonetheless, awareness of the differences and of the interaction between both realms is very helpful as we work to outsmart our own avoidance.

Can Insight Heal You?

For much of the history of psychotherapy, insight has been synonymous with change. For a while, practitioners of behaviorism eschewed insight and said that positive and negative reinforcements could determine our choices and help us change dysfunctional behavior patterns. Cognitive-behavioral therapy brought back the importance of understanding individual meanings, arguing that for humans, becoming aware of and changing our dysfunctional thoughts (seen here as coming from our Black Box Motivator) was the key to change. Currently most therapies place a great deal of emphasis on observing and understanding various aspects of inner mental life.

Insight

Understanding of our own psyche. When put into words, insight can help us to understand and change our conscious and unconscious thoughts, feelings, motives, values, and goals.

Does this mean that understanding or insight can heal you? I have argued that insight leads to healing but is not in itself the agent of change. Rather, the position taken in this book is that achieving insight has the following five effects.

1. Seeking insight indirectly leads us into contact with feelings we have been avoiding. As long as we are attentive to steer clear of too much abstract analysis, understanding the intimate details of life inevitably leads to feelings. We find ourselves surprised by emotions when we thought we were seeking knowledge.

2. Self exploration with an empathic but non-judgmental and accepting witness naturally brings feeling laden material into explicit consciousness where catharsis or mindfulness can do its transformative work.

3. Insight shows us how our mind uses thoughts to hide and avoid dreaded feelings. As we become aware of our own mind's tricks, we can often overcome them and gain access to feelings that had previously been inaccessible. Then catharsis can do its work.

4. Insight allows us to put into words the values by which our conscience judges us and our world. As we become explicitly aware of our values, we gain the ability to evaluate where they come from, which ones are healthy, and which ones need to be let go of or modified. In Chapter 5, we will see how knowledge of our values, healthy and unhealthy, will be instrumental in finding the motivation and the means to change the ones that are dysfunctional.

5. Insight leads us to identifying and understanding behavior patterns that serve to block us from feeling. In Chapter 6, we will look at how insight can give us motivation and clarity in identifying behavior patterns that need to change before we will be able to access deeper layers.

Tools for Inner Exploration

At last we have enough background to bring into focus how we can formulate ideas about ourselves and our Castles. As we have seen, developing a working hypothesis about what feelings we are avoiding and how we avoid them will not remove our dysfunctional patterns, but it will help us get closer to what we need to face next. Fortunately, a complete understanding, which would be very hard to achieve, isn't necessary. We might want to know more, but knowing what is in the next layer will be good enough.

What would really help is a roadmap to our next encounter with feeling. Whatever our starting point, having a clear idea, a working hypothesis, will make our observations sharper and suggest new questions we hadn't thought of before. Besides, we can always modify or even scrap our hypothesis if it turns out wrong. Calling our map a "working hypothesis" will remind us to maintain a proper attitude of skepticism. But where should we start?

Curiosity Leads to Questions

We humans are naturally curious about ourselves and others. As social beings, we are exquisitely attuned to subtle departures from what we might expect. Even though we may have important blind spots due to our avoidance of feelings, we may still be aware of dysfunctional behaviors or uncomfortable feelings or feelings that don't seem appropriate to the circumstances. These are good starting points because each leads to a question, "Why?" Here are some keys to using questions:

- An important key to getting results with questions is *persistence* to get to the bottom of things. Simply labeling a feeling or behavior is not enough. "It's my insecurity" doesn't tell enough. The follow-up question is, "Why do I feel insecure when there is no good reason to feel that way?"

- The next key is *patience*, holding the question open as long as it takes. Finding the answer may take a very long time. Some manifestations of our problems are easy to identify on the surface, but others may only make sense after years of exploration. Think of those detectives who don't forget their cold case files. Every once in a while a clue pops up, and if we still have the question in mind, it will fit into place.

- There may be more than one answer or one motivation for a feeling or behavior. Sometimes we can only guess which one is the most important. In general, if we hold a hypothesis for a while, we will gradually get a feeling for which answers are the important ones.

- Answers should *resonate*. We will discuss testing your ideas later, but answers that are purely intellectual are likely to be wrong and won't help bring out feelings anyway. So expect that true answers should stir up feelings and give you a deep sense of rightness.

- Seeking *full satisfaction* is another key. When we read mystery novels we expect the author to tie up all the loose ends; if not, we feel unsatisfied. We should have the same attitude towards our own hypotheses. Until everything makes sense, we should remain unsatisfied.

Look for Avoidance Mechanisms

A theme in this book is that there are only a few basic groups of avoidance mechanisms. This makes it easier to be on the alert for them:

- Conscious avoidance of uncomfortable feelings. We may be aware of things we don't want to think about or acknowledge.

- Thoughts and ideas, as described in this chapter, when they block or distort or contradict the knowledge we are avoiding are called defenses. When they support behaviors that keep us from feeling, they may be called automatic thoughts.

- The values, attitudes, ideals, and prohibitions, that form the templates our conscience uses to form judgments can be used to influence free will. John's strong value of self-sufficiency is there to keep him from seeking support where, in his early years, he found only pain (Chapter 5).

- Behavior patterns that keep us from feeling or that support other avoidance mechanisms, for example, seeking substitutes for love may keep us from taking the risk of finding out that we really are lovable (Chapter 6).

- Dissociation, some forms of depression, obsessiveness, and anxiety can function as avoidance mechanisms (Chapter 6).

- Secret quests that seek to solve today's problems through future achievements can become frozen and out of touch with reality (Chapter 7).

- Developmental deficits or immaturity are the result of avoiding new behaviors in order to eliminate the risk of pain (Chapter 8).

Look for What Feelings Are Being Avoided

We may be able to guess what feelings we dread the most. Perhaps it is the situations we most avoid, or maybe there are times when the feeling spills out in spite of our efforts. John's exaggerated emphasis on self-sufficiency was a tip-off. Shakespeare said, "The lady doth protest too much."

Trauma can happen at any age and is often a source of avoided feelings. Hypervigilance, memory gaps, loss of feeling, avoidance of things that might be reminders of trauma, and flashbacks of traumatic events can be signs that something is being avoided. Constant activity and substance use can also serve to keep feelings at bay.

Try to Recognize Your Young Feelings and Reactions

Most of our avoidance mechanism can be traced to a particular era in our early development. In Chapter 8 we will look in much more detail at the characteristics of problems that bear the stamp of certain periods of development and how they are manifested in our adult lives. The following are some highlights. Note that these are possibilities and should be applied with great caution and skepticism. It is easy for adult characteristics or symptoms to look like something quite different from what they turn out to be.

- Extreme fragility of boundaries, fear of being taken over by others, and a tenuous grip on reality may signal difficulty with very early formation of a distinct, robust sense of self in the first two years of life.

- Adult temper tantrums, narcissism, and difficulty not getting one's way may indicate a problem with not having learned to "lose battles" gracefully. This issue can hark back to age two, when children develop a strong will and test it against the people they can't afford to lose.

- Seeing all people as pure two-dimensional beings, either all good or all bad. Perception of the same person can shift instantly from one category to the other, but only one at a time. This can be a sign of difficulty resolving the power struggles around age two.

- Problems around abandonment or aloneness can signal trauma or problems in early attachment. Substitutes for love such as drugs, self-mutilation, compulsive sex, and thrill seeking may be indicators of relationship problems in early life, especially in the first four years.

- Depression and exaggerated self-criticism can be related to attempts to connect with an important other, starting with the development of a functioning conscience around age three.

- Overemphasis on rules and "right and wrong" may be indicators of attempts to control a difficult environment by hoping to influence others to "do the right thing." This suggests problems at age four or older when children focus on rules.

- Secret quests that are fraught with passion and guilt can be the result of five-year-olds and older children's future solutions to present problems. The hallmark is seeking something quite specific with intense passion and never quite succeeding.

- Seeing oneself as not grown up, unconsciously waiting for some sort of "rite of passage" to be completed before accepting adulthood. Can be due to deficit or trauma in older childhood or adolescence.

- Missing the acquisitions of adolescence: A clear sense of self and values, impulse control, and relationships based on appreciation of the uniqueness of the individual.

These characteristics may be only partial or they may reflect a small part of the person's functioning. Seeing reactions that seem younger than the adult in whom they are manifested should be a reason for curiosity and compassion. We have such strong values around being "grown up" that we often experience shame about areas of immaturity. For this reason, young characteristics should be approached very gently and with warmth.

Recognize Reenactment in Important Relationships

One of the most common and powerful mechanisms for avoiding feelings is reenactment. We have a strong tendency to repeat unfinished business from the past, usually without any awareness that we are doing so. Why? This tendency comes from the unknowable depths of the mind, so it is hard to tell, but there are a number of possible reasons. Having things done to us when we are helpless is extremely painful. This regularly happens to children, and the drive to repeat the same situation but by choice is one motivation. Another is the hope of a happy outcome this time. Perhaps another is to see the ones really at fault admit their guilt or change. It is likely in most cases that all four motivations are operating at once. Here are some of the ways we set up reenactments in our relationships.

Blind Spots In childhood, we tend to take our parents' behavior as the norm. In adulthood, we may not be appropriately shocked by the same kinds of bad behavior from a new person we meet. We find normal what others would find unacceptable. In fact, bad behavior may feel safer simply because it is known. As a result, in selecting someone with whom we feel comfortable, we may miss the signs that we are making an unfortunate choice. (This all may occur outside of our conscious awareness.)

Trying to Fix the Unfixable The second way we reenact is to choose a mate, consciously or unconsciously, in order to solve unresolved issues from early life. In effect, we set things up to give ourselves a second chance at problems that we could not surmount in our early years. If we had a fantasy plan to reform our father, say, we might choose someone with a good heart, who also has the characteristics we wished to change in our father. Some people even marry someone with an addiction in the sad belief that their love and kindness will reform the other person. An important principle is that the closer the situation is to the original we are seeking to fix, the closer we feel to being able finally to resolve the old problem. Unfortunately, the closer the situation is to a repeat of the original, the more likely it also is to be impossible to fix, and the more certain we are to fail. This pattern brings us close to a popular definition of insanity: "repeating the same, unsuccessful solutions to problems and expecting a different outcome."

Provoking Familiar Behavior In the third pathway, we provoke exactly the behavior that most dismays us. This is an important pathway, because it is the most repairable. Becoming aware of how we provoke the other person is the beginning of the road to change. As we will see in the next section, John and Jen give us a perfect example of this third path. Given no recognition for her efforts, in the end she begins to give up on helping John and leaves him to fend for himself. In this way, John's controlling ultimately provokes Jen into behavior that looks to him just like what he experienced from his parents and had hoped to avoid in marrying her.

Seeing the Past in the Present Finally, we misinterpret what we see in the present as being "just like" what we have experienced in the past. This applies especially to the assumptions we make about the other person's motives, which are among of the hardest things to know and easiest to get wrong about our loved ones.

Consider Possible Biological Factors

This area is controversial. Well trained professionals range from the extreme view that practically all emotional problems should be approached biologically to the opposite extreme that all our troubles can be talked out. What is stated here should be taken with thoughtful circumspection. Psychiatrists are trained to discern biological causes of emotional problems, and questions should be referred to properly licensed professionals.

Furthermore, a large portion of our personal makeup is inherited. Our genetic makeup is not likely to change, so much of the way we react is not changeable. This book is about those aspects of the mind that are subject to change. A few syndromes or constellations of symptoms seem to have a strong biological basis and can be thought of as illness. The following are a few of the most important tip-offs that might lead you to consult a psychiatrist.

- Loss of contact with reality suggests likelihood of a biologically based problem.

- Consistent difficulty with interpersonal closeness can be a sign of autism.

- Periods of mood instability characterized by depression, irritability, excessive emotionality, or over-energized behavior. It is very hard to tell the difference, especially with regard to depression, between the kinds that are mostly psychological and the kinds that are primarily biological.

- Anxiety: Some people are genetically predisposed to be anxious. Help with coping skills can still be beneficial even if the cause may not be all psychological.

- Addiction: There is a strong biological component to what I think of as a "disease of the free will." Approaches need to be individualized and can involve biological treatments, but in my experience, the most successes come from having a great support system and an emphasis on emotional health.

- Attention deficit disorder: Characterized by difficulty focusing and organizing, impulsiveness, restlessness, procrastination, creativity, inconsistency, and doing much better with things that engage the individual's interest and passion.

Look for One Organizing Theme

Emotional problems have a way of organizing themselves in our mind around a single theme or problem. I am not sure why this is, or whether it is always true, but it is a good assumption to start with. John gives us a good example of an underlying theme. His problems are organized around the issue of his need for support and help. Understanding that issue helps make sense of many surface facts. Let's look at them:

John's controlling behavior attempts to satisfy his need for Jen to give him support but exposes his difficulty trusting that she really is on his side.

His feelings of pride about being self-sufficient and shame when he fails come from values that have become part of his conscience. They discourage him from seeking support because his early experience with his father showed him that expressing his needs only brought pain.

Behavior patterns of doing everything on his own and not accepting help reinforce his values and act to prevent disappointment (his Castle) but also keep him from receiving support or help (his Prison).

His success in the Army is due to the interesting way that military service is both a very strong, though not obvious, source of support that paradoxically encourages self-sufficiency and strength.

He experiences a promotion with anxiety that he can't understand. The anxiety is because a promotion brings increased need for support and help as well as internal demands that he should be able to perform without help or support.

Test Your Hypotheses

Any hypothesis should, as mentioned earlier, resonate; that is, it should generate a feeling reaction and a sense that it is on target. Even if correct, until there is some resonance, the hypothesis will be of questionable usefulness.

Hypotheses that involve characteristics of a certain developmental era can sometimes be tested and conviction strengthened when known history seems validating.

Correct hypotheses should lead to further discovery, emotional healing, and improved functioning. If not they should be questioned.

Consultation with another person or professional who will not have the same blind spots is very important. It is too easy for us to talk ourselves into things that, in the end, strengthen our Prisons. When we are stuck then an outsider can be of great help.

Be Ready to Go Back to the Drawing Board

Skepticism is a good attitude to have. It is very easy for us to talk ourselves into erroneous conclusions. The "medical student syndrome" is occurs when a little knowledge leaves us thinking we have every illness on the Internet. Please be ready to question and let go of hypotheses that are not producing real improvement in life.

A Special Note about Reenactment in Therapy

Reenactment in therapy is called transference. Especially in long-term and intensive therapy it is a natural occurrence. As in marriage, there tends to be a honeymoon period. Then, when the phenomenon does appear, it will very likely not be apparent—even the therapist may not notice at first. Transference doesn't feel like a phenomenon, it feels like life. Feelings towards a therapist are based on real characteristics or events interpreted through implicit logic. Helping patients become consciously aware of what is happening is a delicate operation, since the one who is challenging the patient's perception is also the object of the strong feelings.

In one sad example, a patient fought with her therapist because she found his office cold. She asked him to raise the temperature but he insisted on his right to control the thermostat. Most likely, each was reacting to the imagined motivations of the other. Perhaps he thought she was intent on usurping control and rationalized that she needed to experience an unbending stance in order to become aware of her need. She was re-experiencing the willful neglect that was part of her early life. Before either one had a chance to explore the underlying assumptions, the angry patient quit therapy. Both lost the opportunity to examine and heal the smoldering issues left over from their respective pasts.

Do therapists have transference? Yes, they do, and it can be just as difficult for them to see as it is for their patients. That is why it is recommended that therapists experience their own therapy before doing intensive work with others, so they can resolve their own blind spots. Even then, therapists should be open to the possibility that their own unrecognized reactions can interfere with progress.

A therapist who accurately recognizes his or her own transference-based reactions can also recognize the patient's and use both as an authentic guide to unfinished business from the past. In fact, the distortions imprinted on each of us from early experiences are so basic and so specific that their expression in transference may represent a more accurate record of the past than our conscious, explicit memories.

Not only does transference help in understanding our blind spots and dysfunctional patterns, but it provides a pathway to healing. When unfinished business from the past is replayed in current life, strong feelings come to the surface. It is at the moment when the patient becomes consciously aware that their feelings are really about the past, not about the therapist, that catharsis can happen. At these moments when the therapeutic relationship can provide the context of safety and connection, permanent healing of the still active feelings related to the past can take place.

Along with transference, Freud discovered early in his career that resolving problems that reveal themselves through transference is every bit as therapeutic as resolving feelings that come up in association with memories of early life. Because this principle is so important, let me paraphrase it once again: Resolving problems in a therapeutic relationship is fully equivalent to resolving them in relation to figures from the past. Because reenactment is so often at the bottom of dysfunctional patterns, understanding, experiencing, and resolving problems in the therapeutic relationship is one of the most important pathways we have to healing and growth.

Key Concept

Resolving today's problems in the therapeutic relationship is as healing as repairing problems through direct recall of the past.

But They're Still Guesses

It's okay to use the tools I have outlined to inquire about how and why things happened in one's past. But we always have to remember that people are very complex and that our hypotheses can be subject to blind spots. The solution is to keep an open mind, to be skeptical of our hypotheses, and not to be afraid to seek the opinion of others. It is vital to keep testing our ideas as we gain more information. Stagnation in your healing and growth is a strong sign that a trip back to the drawing board is needed; progress in therapy and in life is the best indicator that your hypothesis is on the right track.

Persistence and Onion Layers

One final principle pertaining to understanding ourselves: Expect to find more than one layer. You finally make the breakthrough for which you were hoping. You expect liberation only to find that there is something still standing in the way. There is a new layer of blockage. Maybe it is another layer of the same old thing, or maybe it is something new. Each layer needs to be approached the same way as the previous one. You may be disappointed, but there was no way to know what layers were yet to be found. You may find progress too slow; even worse, you may make progress and then backslide. You may want to throw up your hands in despair and quit. Don't. Persistence will be rewarded. Often, the only way to know about a layer of avoidance of feeling is to clear out the ones that come before.

Frequently, we have more layers of feelings and avoidance than we imagined. Perhaps we missed something and it's time to take another look. Perhaps it's simply time to deal with another layer. Even when emotional healing has taken away most of the need for misinformation and cover-up, habit can still keep old ways in place. Force of habit shouldn't be too hard to dislodge, but it may, nevertheless, require a push.

Because of layering of avoidance mechanisms, it doesn't matter so much where we start our journey. There will be work to do no matter where we are, and over time it will lead to other layers. The process is like an onion; we peel off a layer and there's another layer. But, at some point, we arrive at the center. Therapy is not interminable. There is an endpoint, after we have addressed all the layers. From then on, as it is for all humans, our job is to continue growing.

Next Steps: Ways Of Getting To Know Yourself

The variety of issues that bring people to therapy is so vast that no single path to self-knowledge could work for everyone. Still, using the principles underlying this book, here are some basic questions that can serve as a starting point:

What, exactly, is troubling you? This is the source of your motivation and energy, so you can't underestimate the importance of asking yourself just what is making you think that something in yourself needs to change. Or maybe you'll find out that what you really want is to change someone else. I'm assuming that you have already done all you can to shape your world to your needs and are ready to accept that the only thing left is to change you, but you might have a secret wish or plan that you haven't acknowledged yet.

What do you want most? Did you really think hard about what you are looking for? The more you know about your deepest desires and wishes, the more helpful your hypothesis will be. Try to be open and so honest with yourself that you could admit anything, even if it is shocking and troublesome.

What about you is standing in your way? Therapy is about changing you. Even when others are part of the problem, knowing how you want them to change is important knowledge about you. Changing others is futile unless they really want it, but at least you can evaluate what might be possible and what you will need to accept as it is. Therapy can help you change yourself so as to unblock the route to your deepest feelings and desires.

What if my greatest wish is a childish one? Great! If you are aware that your wish is childish, you are already way ahead. Your job now is to make friends with the child within you. Your inner child has desires for good reasons. If you approach him or her with love, interest, and respect, you will gain your inner child's trust and you will learn a great deal more. Children don't necessarily need to have their way. They need your adult wisdom and sometimes firmness, but they also need to be listened to, whatever it is they have on their mind. Don't scold or shame, just listen. Later you may need to take charge, but not yet.

Is there a biological component to the problem? As noted above, sometimes biology plays a big part in emotional problems, ranging from inborn temperament to ADHD to regulation of moods to addiction and psychosis. If you suspect a biological cause, it is a good idea to get professional help in evaluating and approaching that part of the problem. I have put this question in fifth place because I wanted you to have maximum clarity about what is going on in your mind before you ask the question about biology. It is too easy to generalize: "I am depressed, so it must be a chemical imbalance." Most of the time, the picture is more complex than that.

Are you simply afraid to feel something? Is there a feeling or a memory with feelings attached to it that is so painful or uncomfortable that you are avoiding it? As indicated in Chapter 1, any feeling can be dealt with when you have someone there who understands with you. The feeling won't go away by itself; it will wait until you are ready to address it. Most importantly, you will almost certainly feel better after you face the feeling and go through it.

Are blocks to feeling causing trouble? As discussed previously and in the chapters to come, there are a few patterns that comprise just about every way your feelings can be blocked. At any one time you are probably only dealing with one of these patterns, though they may form multiple layers. When that is the case, you will most likely have to tackle only one layer at a time, so you should focus on the one at hand.

Is an idea or thought holding you back? The present chapter focuses on how thoughts like "it's my fault" or "maybe I can teach the other person a lesson or change them" can stand in the way of acceptance and the changes you need to make. Ideas are one of the main aids in the avoidance of feeling, even when we hardly admit to ourselves that we carry them.

Remember that the patterns of your relationships, including the one with your therapist, can bear an imprint of unfinished business from the past. These valuable sources of information can hold important clues to the issues you need to tackle, especially since the patterns were probably developed in the first place to help you avoid feelings that you were not ready to deal with.

Are values standing in your way? Chapter 5 deals with values, attitudes, ideals, and prohibitions and how they can sometimes be unhealthy or just plain wrong. If you believe you are unworthy or are stopped by "shoulds and oughts," if shame or guilt are the feelings that stop you, then you need to take a very hard look at the values you have internalized and ask yourself if they are the values you would want others to follow. Are they ones that really help you be a better person? Your conscience is like a boss. Some bosses give only criticism and are never satisfied. Is yours one of those?

Are behavior patterns standing in the way of feeling? Chapter 6 focuses on the great variety of patterns of perception and behavior that we use to avoid feeling. They range from relationship patterns to constant activity to compulsive behaviors to automatic reactions that are not in our immediate control. That chapter will also address how to change your dysfunctional patterns.

From some deep place in your mind, are you on a quest? In Chapter 7 we will examine one of the most powerful problem-solving methods invented by children, what I call "Someday Plans." By about age 5, children begin to be able to imagine the distant future where things can be better and today's problems solved. When these plans are buried, the hallmark of their presence is that you keep trying to achieve something but never quite succeed. It seems like you are thwarted by bad luck, but repetition of the pattern suggests it is something deep in your mind that is sabotaging success. Changing this pattern requires pursuing deep understanding of the quest you are on and why somewhere inside you don't feel you should be allowed to succeed.

Was arrested development one of your coping mechanisms? When feelings are too much for a child to handle, one of the most common responses is to stop trying out new behaviors. When you do this, development stops as well. You are protected but also prevented from growing. Fortunately, the developmental trail can be resumed at any age. Now it's time to stretch beyond your comfort zone. This kind of blockage is the subject of Chapter 8.

The Right Stance for Understanding

Knowing about your own mind is different from learning science or math or even philosophy. Here, your intellect is not your best tool and may actually betray you because it often serves to distance you from feelings. Your curiosity and intuition are much more reliable. I picture throwing a net in the water to see what is there. You will need an attitude of openness to anything you may find. The more spontaneously a thought pops into your consciousness, the more authentic it probably is. Remember those automatic thoughts that come in dreams and idle moments. They may be aimed at steering you away from change, but they also tell a lot about the things that are troubling you.

Don't forget to be skeptical. Your best understanding may not stand the test of time. If you (and your therapist) are open to being wrong, then you will be ready to go back to the drawing board when necessary. Your life should be improving, or at least you should be making measurable progress in removing blockages so as to improve your life. If you feel stuck, then you and your therapist should reevaluate your understanding. Skepticism is the best protection you have against wasting your energy and getting nowhere.

References

Kahneman, Daniel. *Thinking Fast and Slow*. New York: Farrar, Straus and Giroux, 2011.

Todorov, A., A.N. Mandisodza, A. Goren, and C.C. Hall. "Inferences of Competence from Faces Predict Election Outcomes." *Science* 308: (2005) 1623–1626.

· **5** ·

YOUR CONSCIENCE CAN BE WRONG

How your conscience, too, can become a means of running from feelings, and how you can reshape it.

Your conscience or superego is not a brain structure but a concept. It is an idea that helps make sense of distinct aspects of your mental life that relate to self control, pride, shame, and guilt. In particular, problems of the conscience are unique, and the process of repairing them differs from catharsis. Because it is so important in our daily lives, knowing about your conscience is extremely useful. Unfortunately, the study of psychotherapy for several decades has been very focused on early relationships and has largely neglected the conscience. When I began to realize how important and how distinct the conscience was, I went back to writings from the past. The development of the concept had been limited by the idea that the conscience forms around age five. While important parts of its formation do take place at this age, similar formative events happen over a much greater span of time from around age three through adulthood. Thinking of the conscience as more subject to change over time increases the usefulness of the concept. In this chapter I will describe how I came to see the conscience in a somewhat new way and how this understanding leads to clarity about how to change your conscience when it is wrong.

Emily

Emily, now eighteen months old, runs shrieking with delight into the kitchen where her mother is making dinner. Emily is confident that the world loves her and that all is well. She has already come to rely on her mother's cathartic ability to soothe her when she gets hurt.

Emily is about to do something her mother won't like. She feels a twinge of anxiety and hesitates. But the twinge isn't nearly strong enough to suppress her eagerness to explore. Emily opens the door to the lower kitchen cabinet and begins to pull out pots and pans. Her mother is cooking a complicated meal and trying to focus on timing; when she hears the clatter of the pots and pans, she snaps, "Emily! Didn't I tell you not to do that! How do you expect me to make dinner?"

Emily looks up for comfort but finds instead an angry face. Her world crumbles into tiny pieces and she begins to cry. The connection she relies on for emotional sustenance is shattered. Her tears turn to sobs.

Developing Internal Controls

Affect regulation is how we keep our feelings in a range with which we can cope. At eighteen months of age, Emily and her mother are already skilled at helping Emily feel better through catharsis—but now she has the physical ability to get into all kinds of excitement and trouble. This creates a new challenge for affect regulation. When she does things that upset her mother, the soothing face isn't there. Mother's scolding voice quickly takes Emily's affect out of the range Emily can manage. In a few moments they are both screaming.

Affect Regulation

How we keep feelings at a level that doesn't overwhelm us. One of the first forms of affect regulation we develop involves the use of empathic connection with the primary caregiver to soften the bumps and jolts of life through catharsis.

Up to this point, Emily and the family dog Fifi have had about the same level of self-control. Fifi has learned from experience that some things are okay and others not. She has to be reminded frequently, especially when her instincts are strong. What self-control they both have is based on the pleasure/pain system, the first layer of their motivational apparatus. They do their best to balance the pleasure of discovery against the pain of reprimand. Both Emily and Fifi lack the ability to generalize from a familiar experience to a new one or to understand that the same behavior can be acceptable in one situation and not in another.

What Emily needs now is a way to stay out of trouble in the first place. She needs to develop internal controls that will come into play before her mother becomes upset so she doesn't have to use her mother's reaction to guide her behavior, as Fifi does. Her motivational system needs a second layer to help her resist the considerable power of her impulses and curiosity. What she will need is a superego or conscience. That is the part of our motivational apparatus that is responsible for autonomous self-control so we don't have to be told each time what is okay and what isn't.

Superego (Conscience)

A part of the mind, independent of our wishes and impulses, that uses pride, shame, and guilt—along with the Black Box Motivator described in Chapter 2—to get us to follow its internalized standards even when we don't want to.

At eighteen months, according to Allan Schore, the right prefrontal cortex—the part of Emily's brain that will become the site of her conscience—is just developing the myelin insulation that will allow it to become a functional part of her brain. This physiological development will make it possible for Emily to show early signs that her conscience will soon be ready to come to the rescue.

Allan Schore (1943-)

Leading researcher in neuropsychology and author of *Affect Regulation and the Origin of the Self.*

The Two Elements of Self-Control

A functioning conscience requires two components. First, Emily will have to internalize templates of acceptable behavior. Second, she will need to develop an internal means of enforcement strong enough to override the powerful allure of the pots and pans.

The vague twinges of fear that guide Fifi the dog are also part of Emily's means of self-regulation (the pleasure/pain system), but they do not have sufficient power and flexibility to be of much help in her increasingly complex world. Yesterday Mom put a kitchen pot and lid in her playpen for Emily to play with; today, pots and pans are off limits.

What Emily has access to, which Fifi does not, is language. Take, for example, Emily's mother saying to her, "I don't want you to take things out of the cupboard unless I tell you it's okay." Without words, a rule like this would be far too complicated to learn. Trial and error and the old fear-based system would take too long to provide sufficiently subtle guidance about what is appropriate and inappropriate. Language is so important that it is not uncommon for children to repeat the rules out loud as if working to internalize them.

Understanding the rules is not enough. Society can pass laws, but we still need a police force to ensure that the rules are followed. For children at Emily's stage of development, the internal police force is shame, which is very powerful. According to Schore, the capacity to experience shame also develops at around eighteen months of age.

The combination of knowing the rules and self-administered shame forms the beginning of a self-control system that has enough strength, flexibility, and precision to align Emily's behavior with the expectations of her Mom. Of course, even with important elements in place by eighteen months, the system's ability to help with self control takes years to develop fully.

Four Types of Template Utilized by the Conscience

The conscience relies on four types of template. First and most obvious, *prohibitions*, like not getting out the pots and pans, guide our behavior. But the conscience also makes judgments according to internalized *values, ideals, and attitudes*. Together, these four elements have tremendous influence on our behavior and priorities. They become lasting and constant principles that form a part of our personalities and have a profound effect on our identities, choices, and lives. Note that while the superego or conscience includes all four elements, listing them each time is ungainly, so I will sometimes use the word *values* to represent all four. Together, they legislate what is valued or approved and what is not.

Shame, the enforcer, is a very painful feeling. We experience that feeling when we make a negative judgment of ourselves. The templates on which we base those judgments are just those values, ideals, attitudes and prohibitions that reside in our conscience. (Recall that shame is one of the secondary feelings that result from evaluating ourselves in the light of our superego templates, whereas primary emotions represent a direct reaction to some stimulus.)

Shame probably starts out, as does smiling, as an inborn reflex. When we are first rebuffed at an early age, shame and anger are very natural reactions. Soon the feeling of shame comes to be linked with taking the other person's point of view against our own. When we are shamed, we feel that the other person is right and we are wrong. Beginning as a natural reflex that has analogues in other mammals, our reflexive reaction to being disappointed or rejected develops into the two components that make up our conscience: values or templates and enforcement through positive and negative feelings.

In addition to shame, two other secondary feelings fill out the gamut of emotions utilized by our conscience to influence our behavior. If the self-judgment is favorable, then the corresponding feeling is pride, a source of positive reinforcement for good behavior. On the negative side, while shame represents a general feeling of inadequacy and embarrassment, people experience another secondary emotion, guilt. Developing a little later, guilt is a more specific feeling related to particular behaviors rather than to a person's entire self-worth. Guilt acts as a deterrent when people are tempted to go against a specific rule or principle. Guilt is more related to prohibitions, whereas shame accompanies failure in relation to values, attitudes, and ideals. Even more important than their role as punishers and reinforcers *after* we act, the anticipation of secondary feelings helps us exert control *before* we act. That is where they can help Emily to stay in harmony with her mother.

More on the Enforcers

We have already looked in general at our motivational system's power to shape all kinds of behavior. Recall the three layers: First, the pleasure/pain system that gives us pleasure when we behave in ways that are good for the species and pain when we behave in ways that are not; second, the conscience, as described here; then third, the Black Box Motivator described in Chapter 2, which reinforces the first two layers by sending out impulses and thoughts to further persuade us to do what our mind determines to be good for the species. Just as with the pleasure/pain System, the Black Box Motivator produces impulses and thoughts that are designed to "talk us into" behaving the way our conscience determines we should.

Going back to Emily, there is actually a degree of specialization between the pleasure/pain System, with its primary emotions, and the conscience, based on secondary emotions. Primary feelings of simple pleasure and pain generally tend to help us do what is best for the individual. Inevitably, though, there are pleasures we may seek as individuals that are not good for our relationships or for society. Eating as much as possible is a good way to protect ourselves against famine, but what about eating the other person's rations? Our conscience and its secondary feelings are most adapted to serve the requirements of social life. Pride, shame and guilt are more directed towards making us good partners and citizens who don't eat another's food.

Most of the time, we are not aware that our Black Box Motivator is involved in our moral life. Where it does play a role is particularly relevant to the subject of this book. Just as with the pleasure/pain system, it goes to work when our first level of self-control seems to be losing the battle for our free will. When our conscience says we are out of bounds and we persist anyway, that is the trigger for our Black Box Motivator to start sending thoughts and impulses aimed at getting us back to where we are "supposed to be." In many situations, such as John's, "supposed to be" is something established long ago that is now dysfunctional. Thus, the Black Box Motivator can be our most troublesome adversary when it comes to changing old dysfunctional patterns.

When the Superego Is Not on Our Side

Perhaps it comes as a surprise that our conscience can be wrong. We usually assume that, like the Disney character Jiminy Cricket, our conscience is incorruptible and always on the "right" side. Unfortunately, many of the most destructive patterns of dysfunction are due to our conscience having internalized defective templates. I first became aware of this when working with survivors of severe early life trauma. Like most trauma survivors, my patients had damaged self-esteem. The more I listened, the clearer it was that they had internalized the negative attitudes and values of just the people who had hurt them and this was the source of their damage. Attempts to change these attitudes and values soon showed that they were extraordinarily resistant. They had been incorporated into the conscience. This makes sense because we need our conscience to be resistant to our own selfish wishes. We need it to be incorruptible. This important characteristic of our conscience also makes it hard to change. What happens when we try to change a conscience?

First, of course, we are pummeled with shame and guilt. Next, should we persist, our Black Box Motivator goes to work trying to prevent change. Finally, internalized templates are very firmly lodged and inherently hard to change. All three factors conspire, for example, to keep trauma survivors from feeling good about themselves.

As I learned more about how the conscience operates, it became clear that many others beside trauma survivors also suffer from dysfunctional attitudes, values, ideals and prohibitions.

Emily grew and matured. By the time she was ten she naturally followed the rules. She was an excellent student and well liked by the teachers because she cheerfully did whatever she was asked. She was her family's model child. Emily's values were largely those of her parents. She believed in honesty and in helping those in need. She loved her elderly dog Fifi and never forgot to take care of her needs.

When Emily turned thirteen, her personal self-identity started to develop. She wanted to stay up late and spend hours on Facebook. Her family's rules began to seem limiting and silly. She questioned the importance of school.

Emily became a little overweight, and her mother expressed alarm about her eating habits. Home life was no longer free of conflict. As Emily prepared for the future, she put her energy into building relationships with peers rather than with her parents.

Emily started to make her own choices, moving from borrowed values to those she could call her own. As she gained more independence she wanted to choose her own food, and she wanted to text with her friends even when she had homework to do. With these temptations, her self-control was challenged and the consequences became more serious. In the summer after her fourteenth birthday Emily went to camp. While there, she decided that she wanted to be very thin. She ignored her hunger pangs and pushed herself to exercise for hours at a time. By the time she returned home from camp, she had lost the weight that concerned her mother.

Come fall, Emily went back to school and studied hard. Between Emily's weight loss and improved grades, her parents believed that Emily's self-control had returned and that their old Emily was back. Because Emily seemed to be doing well, they believed she was happy.

Unbeknownst to her parents, Emily was obsessed with counting calories. She exercised at least three hours a day. Although she grew thinner and thinner, she felt heavier and heavier, so she began to wear baggy clothing. Her weight continued to drop.

Eventually, Emily avoided eating in front of anyone, and she grew ever more obsessed with food and exercise. She rarely smiled. She isolated herself from her old friends. Emily was showing all the signs of anorexia nervosa.

Let's look at Emily's superego. When she wanted to lose weight, she worked to internalize a new value: *Thin is good.* Her motivational system was now divided. On the one hand, she was hungry. In response to her basic needs her brain said, "Eat!" On the other hand, in response to her new value, it said, "Don't eat!" Her conscience, with its new template, won out to an extreme extent.

Emily became dangerously thin. When hunger got the best of her and she ate, she felt deeply ashamed. When she looked in the mirror, she saw a failure. Her parents became alarmed, and, mostly against her will, Emily eventually agreed to begin treatment.

Emily continues to experience intense conflict between her species-preserving desire to eat enough food and her overdeveloped value of "Thin is good." Each time she follows the nutritionist's suggestions and eats a healthy meal, she feels shame and sees herself as ugly and self-indulgent. But when she disobeys therapeutic orders, she also feels shame. It will take her time and hard work to shift the balance towards the healthy values.

Not only did Emily's conscience steer her towards thinness at any cost, but also her Black Box Motivator fed her rationalizations to convince her she was doing the right thing along with impulses to skip meals and refuse food when it was offered.

Is Your Conscience on Your Side?

Once we accept the idea that the superego does not necessarily watch out for our best interests, there is an excellent way to evaluate our own superego. It is like a boss at work. An effective boss does not always agree and may criticize, but a good one does so in a way that is positive and supportive. A bad boss may give only criticism, or may do so in a demeaning way, or may ignore extenuating circumstances and effort. A truly healthy superego is one that helps us do our best in spite of our errant wishes. How would you rate yours?

Contradictory Values

There is one more characteristic of the conscience that can cause problems. Now that we see how templates of good behavior are internalized, it should no longer be a surprise that values can clash with one another. Nothing prevents one value from being contradictory to another. As long as they stay in our implicit mind, the conflict is not visible. Only when the superego attempts to enforce two opposing standards can the conflict become apparent.

In describing therapy to John, this concept was used to advantage. John held one value that doing one's duty is good and another that needing help is very bad. To make therapy more palatable, getting help was presented as a duty. One value was used to overcome the other.

On the other hand, conflicting values can create very painful situations in which no action satisfies our conscience. One patient felt so guilty that his superego told him he deserved nothing and should devote himself wholly to others. But, he also held the attitude that everyone deserves something. He could find no peace, because no matter what he did, he was in violation of one value or the other. Note that the logic behind these values was not that of conscious reasoning or mature thinking, but it came from the realm of early implicit thought where black-and-white absolutes had not been modulated by the realities of life. Once these thoughts became conscious, the work could begin to reshape them to a livable compromise.

Similarly, depressed people often cycle endlessly between blaming themselves and blaming someone else. As each of these judgments comes to consciousness, its wrongness becomes apparent. Blaming the self is unjust and blaming the other seems unfair. As each judgment fails to satisfy mature logic, the mind shifts to the opposite tack. The black or white quality of these internalized standards bears the stamp of the implicit world where anything bad must be someone's fault, either the self or the other person. In that world, there is no such thing as "just one of those things" where no one is to blame. Thus, the depressed mind is locked into two equally unsatisfactory positions with no escape.

Why Our Conscience Should Be Hard to Change

The conscience was originally designed to help us resist temptation. When our pleasure/pain system pushes us towards anything that feels good, we need an internal agency capable of saying no. Like the "untouchables," the FBI agents of the Al Capone era, we need a force that can't be corrupted by selfish desires. To fulfill this function the conscience has to be capable of resisting not only our impulses but also any efforts to bend our standards. As long as our values hold firm under pressure, the superego can do its job of fighting our own pleasure-seeking self. The superego can help us do our homework when there is a good TV show on, eat a healthy diet when the world is full of candy, and go to work when we would rather hang out.

Our conscience's resistance to change has another advantage. Our values help us maintain our individual identities in spite of external change. Even when our environment shifts dramatically, say because of a disaster or emigration, we know how to stay the same. Our built-in moral compass allows us to navigate and continue to find ourselves despite entirely new surroundings or circumstances. Is it any wonder, then, that our internalized values are hard to change?

How Values Are Internalized

As touched on earlier, it had become a regular privilege for me to help my trauma patients face their painful moments and experience the healing effect of catharsis. The dramatic results of this work felt good to them and to me as their therapist. However, this progress only underscored the existence of other consequences of abuse such as low self-esteem and even self-hatred. In contrast to the painful memories, these unhealthy values and attitudes failed to respond to empathic understanding and proved harder to reverse. Some patients even felt guilty towards the people who had abused them, as if the perpetrators were the righteous ones.

I tried the techniques that worked for catharsis. I listened, and together we explored the details of the negative attitudes. We were able to achieve understanding, but the attitudes didn't change. Catharsis simply didn't work. Seeking a different approach, I encouraged my patients to change their behavior. I suggested that they try treating themselves as if they were as valuable as anyone else. When they did, instead of seeing their attitudes and values change, they felt even stronger waves of shame and worthlessness.

Perhaps education would help. I tried to help my patients understand what had happened. I told them about the Stockholm syndrome, how people can identify with their abusers. When this didn't help, I became more active in urging my patients to adopt positive behaviors even when they felt resistance to doing so. I believed that we were going in the right direction, but the work was very hard and very slow.

Stockholm Syndrome

When people who are held hostage grow to sympathize with, like, and even identify with their captors. It is believed to occur in about a quarter of victims of hostage-taking.

It was not at first clear to me (as it is now) how these symptoms were different from those that could be cured by catharsis. Then one day I had a huge epiphany. It dawned on me in a flash that the healing of these negative attitudes must involve an entirely different change mechanism. Catharsis was rapid and its effects definitive, but changing the negative attitudes that were also consequences of early life trauma was slow and laborious. Furthermore, whereas catharsis was permanent, changes in attitudes towards the self were subject to relapse. All it took was a random negative event and my patient might feel unworthy all over again.

The idea of more than one basic healing mechanism was radical. In my years of training, psychic change was assumed to be and presented as a single process. Psychotherapy was supposed to make the unconscious conscious and then, as the patient gained insight, somehow improvement would happen. There would be "aha" moments when the insight would touch something deep, but exactly what was going on was a mystery. This was the formulation I took for granted. However, once I took the daring step of considering the existence of more than one healing mechanism, I began to wonder exactly how each might work and, more urgently, what exactly might help change the negative attitudes that catharsis could not resolve.

The Second Door

Soon, a second door opened. I realized that the mental attitudes and values my patients had acquired from their abusers were precisely the values, attitudes, ideals, and prohibitions that I had learned to recognize as contents of the superego. This too was a radical notion.

Standard teaching posited that the superego was formed around age five or six and remained essentially unchanged after that. If that was true, how could the superego acquire values and attitudes from undergoing traumatic abuse, particularly from abuse that occurred after age six? Could the experience of trauma in adulthood affect superego values as well? The answer was clearly yes.

Take Patty Hearst. From news reports (I have not met her and have no direct knowledge of her experience), it appeared that she internalized the values of the radical group who kidnapped and abused her in 1974. Some of my own patients also internalized negative attitudes and values from adult trauma. It seemed clear that values internalized in adulthood were as firmly lodged and no less difficult to change than those internalized in early life.

Then I made an intuitive leap; that is, I theorized that the mechanism for changing dysfunctional values would most logically be the same as the mechanism by which they were internalized in the first place. In this I followed the law of parsimony, otherwise known as Occam's razor, which states that one should prefer the simplest hypothesis unless the facts force adoption of a more complex one. Therefore, I hypothesized that the way to reverse the damage from toxic internalizations would be to help my patients internalize new, healthy values and attitudes "on top of" the old ones. The metaphor of layering is apt because it both represents how new values could supersede older unhealthy values and accounts for the fact that old, unhealthy values do not disappear but can still be reactivated by negative experiences. My quest now focused on learning how super-ego contents can be internalized.

What Did Freud Think?

Once again, I started with the collected works of Freud, who explained the origin of the superego as part of the process by which boys resolve the Oedipus complex—that is, the tension between their desire for their mother and their fear of their father's jealousy and retribution. Under pressure of this fear, boys were thought to internalize a prohibition against incestuous wishes. Sexual interests then disappear until adolescence, when they reappear in a new form, directed not towards the mother but towards other females. (Freud obviously did not consider homosexuality in this formulation.) The prohibition against sexual thoughts directed towards the parent of the opposite sex remains in place, a permanent part of the superego. Here was an example of a prohibition that has a clear social function.

Oedipus Complex

Named by Freud after the title character in the play *Oedipus Rex*, written by fifth-century B.C. Greek tragedian Sophocles. Oedipus unknowingly kills his father and marries his mother.

Another mechanism caught my attention as well. Freud spoke of "identification with the lost object," in which loss or separation could trigger internalization of characteristics of the person who was absent. Freud pointed out that "identification is the original form of emotional tie;" that is, the first bond to be formed. Identification with a lost object can, however, happen at any age. An example might be a widow or widower who takes on the profession of the deceased spouse.

Identification with the Lost Object

The phenomenon of taking into oneself, characteristics that formerly belonged to someone important to us whom we have lost.

More Examples of Value Internalization

A favorite professor of mine was a strong antiwar individualist. When he was younger, during the Vietnam War, he had been drafted. The thing he hated most in basic training was marching in unison, which he and his comrades were forced to practice for hours on end. In spite of himself, he became quite good at marching. At graduation, to his absolute horror, he realized that he felt pride in being able to march in unison. He had internalized a value with which he disagreed vehemently!

In a book entitled *Snapping: America's Epidemic of Sudden Personality Change* (1995), Flo Conway and Jim Siegelman focus on experiences through which adults suddenly and dramatically internalize new values. In some of the instances Conway and Siegelman describe, the change is voluntary, even strongly desired. In less benign situations, such as some examples of cult induction, the individual would be pulled into an emotionally charged atmosphere, often with sleep or food deprivation or other physical suffering. Whatever the circumstances, the authors describe the critical moment as follows:

> *The experience itself may give rise to a rush of physical sensation: a blinding light, a floating feeling, momentary paralysis, breathlessness, a flood of tears, a coursing of blood throughout the body, or a strong tingling that showers downward from the head with the surge of an electrical discharge... We were amazed to find that so many people were fully conscious of this exact moment when 'something snapped.'*

Many of my patients who were abuse survivors could also identify the specific moment when something changed forever.

> *When Margaret was six, her mother married Steve. One night Margaret's mother was working late, and Steve got drunk and made a sexual advance toward Margaret. Margaret ran from him, then locked herself into her room and waited for her mother to come and rescue her. When her mother arrived, Margaret realized in an instant that her mother was as helpless as she. Steve was out of control and her only option was to run out of the house, alone, into the night. When she entered therapy, all she remembered was headlights shining in her eyes. The feeling of powerlessness she struggled with as an adult had started at that moment.*

A final example of the internalization of values is toilet training. The value of keeping clean, developed in the first years of life, remains intact and able to generate shame in older adults who accidentally soil themselves, even when the event is completely involuntary and there is no longer a reason for feelings of shame.

But What Is the Mechanism?

These examples beg the question: what exactly is the mechanism of internalization? Some writers on trauma have identified powerlessness as a trigger, but there are times when an individual actively wants to internalize a new value. In the case of toilet training, acquiring and being able to act on the value of cleanliness is actually a matter of gaining rather than losing power.

My conclusion may surprise you. The factor that is common to all the above situations is the need for connection. People who join cults want to belong. Children who become toilet trained want to be better attuned to their caregivers. And, yes, even in cases of abuse, people need connection.

As mentioned in the discussion of catharsis, people in traumatic situations feel incredibly alone. Think of Margaret, in the earlier example, running out into the night. Trauma can lead to a degree of aloneness so painful that a connection to the abuser is better than no connection at all.

When people in traumatic situations have a comrade or supporter, they may be spared much damage, including internalized negative values. Prisoners of war often describe how maintaining some kind of relationship helped them to survive. In some cases, the relationship was with God. In others, prisoners managed somehow to communicate with other prisoners by notes on scraps of paper or tapped-out messages. These connections offer powerful protection. When no connection is possible, however, the stage is set for negative attitudes towards the self to be internalized.

I looked again at Freud's writing and realized that his examples involved the same common factor. Identification with the lost object is triggered by separation. The formation of the superego in the Oedipal situation also serves to keep the connection with both the mother and the father. Thus, I came to believe that a threat to connection is the triggering factor in the process of internalizing values and attitudes. To put it in a more succinct form, I'll call it "connection distress."

Connection Distress

Think back to the purpose of the superego self-control system. When a child's abilities grow to a level at which she could do serious damage to her mother's good will, the superego comes along to save the day—at least sometimes. Self-control in the face of instinctual needs and impulses, even if imperfect, is vital to the connections that ensure our survival as social beings.

When we feel most alone, the same system is activated to keep us connected to whomever might be available, even if the person is abusing us. Abuse survivors' low self-esteem is not simply an effect of being hurt but an internalization of attitudes implied or even expressed out loud by the perpetrator. And the drive to internalize comes from the need to cling closely to someone.

The evidence that these attitudes and values actually become part of the superego is this: When survivors try to go against those values or attitudes, they feel genuine shame and guilt. These are the hallmarks of the conscience in action. The superego has, in effect, been hijacked by the abuser. This is why my patients' negative attitudes were so hard to change. As far as the superego is concerned, any violation of internal values is wrong and should be punished. As a result, the victimization continues long after the abuse has ended.

In fact, the internalization of negative values is often the most damaging effect of abuse. Because the superego is naturally so resistant to change, it can be easier to heal memories of pain than it is to escape from self-condemnation, even when the values upon which self-criticism is based are wholly false.

Characteristics of the Superego

In summary, here is what I discovered about the superego and how values, attitudes, prohibitions, and ideals become part of the our templates of appropriate behavior:

- The superego is not built all at once but begins to develop at about eighteen months and keeps on being added to and shaped.

- Templates of good behavior that belong to our superego produce feelings of pride when met and shame or guilt when violated. These, in turn, influence our free will.

- Internalization is triggered by aloneness or, more exactly, connection distress.

- Internalization can happen suddenly or over time, perhaps as a series of small moments of change.

- The contents of what we internalize represent our version, at the time, of the values and attitudes of the person or people with whom we need to be connected, whether or not this is in our best interest.

- Contradictory values can and do exist in implicit form in the superego and can create situations where all possible actions violate one or the other value.

- Templates of good behavior become permanent parts of the superego but can be overridden by later templates.

The Superego in Perspective

Taking a very big-picture, perhaps existential view of the human condition, we are born and remain basically alone and vulnerable. The solution to the fundamental human problem of aloneness is relationship. Relationship is necessary for our physical and emotional survival. At the same time, relationship brings new problems because connections are fragile and can be broken. A tremendous amount of our personal and societal energy goes into reinforcing our connectedness. Shared values not only protect our relationships but also become an important part of our feeling of community. Reinforcing these values is the main function of the superego. In addition, much of the content of our rituals and even our casual conversation is aimed at reaffirming and maintaining the values, attitudes, ideals, and prohibitions we share. Just listen to gossip to confirm this observation.

Looking at the individual, it is clear that our values have a powerful role in shaping our identity. To a large extent, we make life choices based on these values. What we wear, the work we do, the people with whom we associate—to name just a few examples—are profoundly influenced by both the healthy and unhealthy templates carried in our superego.

Changing Unhealthy Superego Contents

Unbeknownst to me, years before my examination of the processes involved in internalization, Aaron Beck (inspired by Albert Ellis) developed cognitive therapy for depression based on the realization that depressed people hold negative "core beliefs." I perceive these as being the same as superego templates. In this way, cognitive-behavioral therapy complements our discussion of the superego, and as CBT has blossomed and expanded, it has remained focused on correcting irrational beliefs and attitudes. Over time, CBT has developed a repertoire of methods, honed by experience, to accomplish this challenging task. Whereas traditional therapists are trained to point out unhealthy values, cognitive therapists make changing such values a central focus with a sizable toolbox of research and methods.

Aaron Beck (1921-)

Beck is considered to be the father of cognitive therapy. He developed systematic treatment options for depression and anxiety as well as the Beck Depression Inventory.

Albert Ellis (1913-2007)

Ellis originated rational emotive behavior therapy (REBT), an early form of cognitive-behavioral therapy.

Whatever the theoretical orientation, changing values is hard work. First it is helpful, if not necessary, to clearly identify unhealthy or dysfunctional values. Otherwise we will continue to take it for granted that our values are right and that we should defend them to the end. We are proud of our values and feel attacked when they are questioned. We treat them as the social lifeline that they are meant to be, and once were. For this reason, it is critically important for therapists to approach issues involving values with care and respect.

As values are explored, they are brought out of the realm of the implicit and put explicitly into conscious words. Contradictions can now be identified as well as the unhealthiness of values that were internalized from deprivation or from people who have treated us badly. Through this process, we can begin to form a clear idea of the values we "really" accept and want to incorporate in our lives. This work needs to be done thoughtfully because our superego cannot be expected to let go without a fight.

The Role of the Therapist

Therapists try not to impose their values on patients. When they do, patients usually recognize that something is amiss. This is one reason therapists are reticent to say too much about their personal views. But, whether they like it or not, therapists do represent the value of health. When therapists point out that a patient's self-condemnation is not appropriate, they are expressing a value.

Making the situation even more delicate, we have already seen that connection distress is the trigger for internalization. Patients naturally feel a drive to get closer to their therapist. Therapist anonymity or aloofness, when present, is a source of connection distress. Given the combination of therapists representing healthy values and the therapeutic situation naturally creating a degree of connection distress, therapy can hardly avoid being conducive to the internalization of new values and the strengthening of older ones that are in line with the values represented by the therapist.

As a result, the therapeutic relationship has a great deal of power for good or the potential to do harm. This is an area where therapists bear a special responsibility (see Chapter 9, the Scarsdale Psychotherapy Self-Evaluation). It is also a place where an aware and educated patient is in a better position to make a thoughtful assessment of the values that he or she is thinking of embracing or rejecting.

Looking at the role of the therapist brings up a very important and interesting question. Is it best for therapists to be more warm and empathic, or more withholding? Most training for therapists prescribes a single, consistent stance. But this policy is based on the assumption that there is only one mechanism of change. We can see now that there are at least two and furthermore that the optimal stance of the therapist is different depending on which kind of change is required.

Therapists who work with people who have been traumatized know that warmth and unconditional acceptance are not only helpful but are often essential for gaining access to painful feelings and establishing the empathy that promotes catharsis. A stiff or excessively aloof therapist will have poor results in working with people who have been hurt. This is true in general when the goal is catharsis. What, then, is the optimal stance for internalization of healthy values?

If internalization is triggered by connection distress, then being too understanding and accepting could make internalization of new values more difficult to accomplish. Perhaps this will make more sense if we consider a problem that sometimes happens in therapy. When therapists are too accepting and passive, the result can be "enabling." Patient and therapist may collude to leave everything as it is. Completely unconditional acceptance can be misinterpreted as support for the status quo.

Consistent with this observation, the "neutrality" that is part of some traditional therapies—that is, the therapist who doesn't react—will necessarily generate a considerable amount of connection distress. This approach to the therapeutic relationship may be bad for catharsis but, depending on the degree of distress, can promote internalization of values. In a similar way, cognitive and behavioral therapists have a tradition of thinking of themselves as expert technicians who are there primarily to apply "protocols" to bring about change. When taken literally, this stance, too, will generate considerable connection distress. A side effect of such an emotionally distant stance would promote internalization of values. Is this the stance for a therapist to take when the goal is internalization of new values?

A concept that is helpful here is one I like to call "expectancy," an attitude on the part of the therapist that you are both there to accomplish change and that staying the same is not what you want. It matters to both of you that you are successful in your goal of change. But, if months and years go by with no change, the therapist bears a responsibility for failing to manage the process as it should be. Potentially, the patient bears some responsibility as well. To the extent that the patient contributes to blocking healing and growth, the patient has fallen short. Thus, in contrast to the usual dictum of "unconditional acceptance" on the part of the therapist, expectancy can be thought of as a slight degree of conditionality.

The word *slight* is very important here. Humans are extremely sensitive to their connections. The slightest distancing will be felt as very powerful. Thus, only the mildest degree of "conditional acceptance" or "expectancy" will have a profound impact on the relationship and the therapeutic work.

Having said that, I will suggest that, in practice, I believe most therapists actually do vary their stance depending on the work they are doing at the time. If they are working with painful feelings, where catharsis is the mechanism of change, then they will automatically show a little more warmth and acceptance. When they sense that the goal is to let go of old, unhealthy values and adopt new ones, they naturally show a tiny bit more expectancy. These may be very small variations around an established baseline. The baseline can vary a great deal. We become accustomed to our therapist's style but remain very sensitive to slight changes.

One way to express the variability is this formula: *"Maximum empathy + optimum expectancy."* Empathy—that is—accurate emotional understanding of the other person (or the self), is always good for therapy because it helps catharsis. Empathy does not carry judgment. It is neutral with regard to change. It is only an acknowledgment of what is. On the other hand, expectancy, the sense that the therapy has a direction and that making progress matters, is the part that often does, and I believe should, vary slightly depending on which change process is in focus. Within any therapeutic relationship, one degree of expectancy is, in my view, optimal for catharsis, and another is optimal for the internalization of new values.

Civil Disobedience

One of the main factors that keeps unhealthy values locked in place is that we consistently align our actions according to them. Acting like a second-class citizen makes one feel like a second-class citizen. The action reinforces the feeling and the value or attitude that underlies the behavior.

When we set out to change our values, after recognizing what needs to change, and talking back to our conscience, the next step is "civil disobedience;" that is, adopting behaviors that go against our unhealthy values. Let's look at how civil disobedience can help us heal and grow.

As we have learned, civil disobedience will predictably produce a storm of feelings of shame or guilt. Interestingly, like any other feelings, these too are subject to catharsis. As we share feelings of shame with someone who understands how strongly we feel them, but also how inappropriate those feelings are, we experience catharsis. The pain we experience is diminished, and it becomes easier to maintain behavior that goes according to our healthy values rather than the unhealthy ones. Think of the trauma survivor who practices taking good care of himself. As the shame subsides, he feels more worthy and positive. It becomes easier to continue acting and feeling like a worthy person in spite of the values internalized as a result of the trauma.

With ongoing self-talk that he is a worthy person and that the trauma was not his fault, the trauma survivor gradually absorbs a more positive attitude towards himself. The old, negative attitude is still there but it has been overridden by a positive one. Is this positive attitude a new one? Probably not. It was probably there to begin with and has been reactivated by internalizing the positive attitude of the therapist plus self-talk plus voluntary behavior change. Either way, starting fresh or building on early health, the same measures seem to be the ones that help restore health to a damaged superego.

Internalization: Slow and Fast

Earlier, we reviewed examples of "snapping," where internalization seemed to take place in an instant. There were also examples like toilet training, a process that extends over time. Until we can observe the exact synaptic connections where changes are taking place, it seems right to assume that the fast and slow versions of internalization make use of the same basic mechanism. Presumably, the process can be sudden and violent, or it can be broken up into very small increments. The end result is the same. The conscious desire to please and the automatic need to reinforce connectedness work together. In concert, they assure that values, attitudes, ideals and prohibitions become embedded in the superego so as to form a lasting and stable way of keeping our behavior consistent.

The rapid kind of internalization happens under conditions of massive connection distress. The absolute aloneness of humans subjected to trauma creates the greatest possible connection distress and produces the most violent internalization, which presumably makes it more likely and easier under terrible circumstances to internalize values that are the most toxic and contrary to our true selves. It also appears true that the more violent the circumstances of internalization, the stronger is our resistance to change. Values internalized under milder circumstances with less at stake are held more loosely and are easier to modify.

In therapy, we don't want to recreate conditions of trauma. Doing so risks generating feelings of powerlessness and reinforcing negative values towards the self. For that reason, psychotherapy (in contrast to cult-like activities) generally avoids the most dramatic kinds of internalization, favoring the more incremental ones.

There are interesting exceptions. The technique of planned intervention works by creating something of a crisis in the life of the addict. Even though it is presented with a great deal of love and support, the addicted person faces a hard choice. It comes down to a choice between the substance and family and friends. Addicted people usually put a high value on self-reliance, and recovery generally isn't successful until they give up that value and turn to others for help. Thus, hitting "rock bottom" can involve massive challenges to values and can put the newly recovering individual under a great deal of pressure. As wrenching as this is, the consequences of continuing the addiction are no less dire.

What happens next is very relevant to the discussion of internalization. Rehabilitation programs generate connection distress by physically removing the patient from familiar people and places. They then surround the addict with people who have a positive attitude towards health and ask the addict to act in a healthy way, especially by sharing feelings with others and turning to others for help. In this way the addict goes against his or her value of independence and self-reliance. The intensity is quite powerful and hopefully leads to a relatively massive internalization of values different from those that had been developing during the active phase of the addiction.

Similar approaches have been used in wilderness therapy for teens and treatment for younger children who suffer from attachment disorders. In these cases, the intensity of the situation is warranted by a high degree of resistance to change. Failure to use strong treatment can result in no change taking place and no therapeutic gain. On the other hand, controversy about these treatments and programs revolves around the issue of possible traumatization. Once again, the formula of maximum empathy and optimal expectancy may offer a guide to what is appropriate.

In psychotherapy, unlike rehab, the process of modifying attitudes, values, ideals, and prohibitions is usually slow and quiet work. Starting with clarity about the values we wish to embrace, we move to civil disobedience, acting in ways counter to the dictates of our unhealthy conscience. Working through waves of inappropriate shame and guilt, our resistance softens. Acting like a valuable person forces us towards accepting that we actually are valuable. The more our behavior becomes habitual, the easier it is to maintain. In the meantime, presumably a quiet process of internalization is taking place in response to both our desire to change and that minimal degree of expectancy built into the therapy.

These same principles have implications for child rearing as well. That subject is beyond the scope of this book, but I will suggest that much of what gives children lasting attitudes towards themselves, as well as what gives them a sense of how to be citizens of their community, follows the same principles of internalization.

Internal Electric Fences

We have looked at how healthy values are acquired in early life and how they help protect the connections to others that are vital to our survival. We have also seen how unhealthy values can be internalized in the context of desperate aloneness that often accompanies trauma. Now let's look at how the superego can help us avoid experiencing the same painful feeling over and over. That is exactly what happened to John in earlier chapters. Now we'll see how this type of Castle can become a Prison but how it can also be adaptive.

When Being Tough Is Good

Looking at internalized values from a fresh angle, we can understand that Mark Twain's Huck Finn, like John, coming from a background of deprivation, needs to be tough; he puts a high value on self-sufficiency and strength. How did he develop this value? Huck is the son of the town drunk. As a small child, if Huck asked his father for understanding or attention, he could expect to be hurt. At minimum, his father would refuse to meet Huck's needs; at worst, he would criticize or even beat Huck for having needs. For Huck, like all of us, being told "No!" can be very painful, and he is likely to have felt anger, shame, or both. Because of his dad's unpredictability as well as insensitivity, anger would not have gained Huck anything—and might have actually put him at risk—so feeling shame (that is, blaming himself instead of his father) would be the safer option.

Let's imagine ourselves in a situation like Huck's. There we are, in circumstances where asking for help gets us a harsh "No!" We don't feel safe enough for anger but we need connection, so we identify with the aggressor. We side with the source of harshness and feel shame when we are hurt. The person who says no embodies the value that we should not ask for help. Automatically, to stay connected, we identify with the negative attitude and feel unworthy or in some way defective for needing anything. After a few similar experiences, or perhaps a single, particularly bad one, we permanently internalize the value that we should never have needs or ask for help. Self-reliance becomes structuralized (part of our permanent makeup) in the form of a lasting internalized value.

This is the process that teaches Huck to value self-sufficiency and toughness. He moves from taking his father's point of view to internalizing his father's values as a permanent part of his own being.

Afterward, whenever Huck finds himself needing someone else, he experiences shame—even if he knows that the person will be quite willing to help out. Since wishes for support and nurturing are human and expectable, the fact that they are heavily suppressed in Huck tells us how powerfully our internalized values can override natural needs.

While Huck's toughness might look like pathology, it started out as a positive means of self-protection. Every time Huck was tempted to look for softness in his world, his superego made him feel shame and steered him toward being tough and self-sufficient. Thus, he successfully avoided repeated experiences of disappointment and pain. In this way, internalized values can form a kind of internal electric fence to keep us away from doing things that will predictably bring emotional pain. Fences like Huck's serve an important purpose: As long as our living conditions are harsh, expecting little and being tough are positive responses.

Internalized values can guard us from potentially painful experiences by deterring us from listening to our needs when we are likely to be hurt. Such protection can be helpful to individuals but also for groups and cultures. Where societies are harsh, toughness becomes part of cultural values. Because of constant warring during the Middle Ages, castles were advantageous for protection. In personal life, it is only when conditions improve that our Castles become Prisons. Otherwise, they remain truly useful. Internal electric fences—that is, value systems internalized for protection—continue to shape feelings and behavior whether or not conditions have changed. If Huck were to marry, he, like John, would have trouble accepting love and nurturing. Life requires a balance between toughness that protects us from hurt and softness that helps us be sensitive in relationships. In a surprising twist, it is often my good fortune to help people learn to adapt to softer, more nurturing conditions than what they had to cope with in early life.

Surprising but True

You might imagine that the young person who fights against his abuser would be able to resist internalizing that person's values. Unfortunately this is not so. Even a person who has a healthy sense of his own worth and feels anger when abused can still internalize an abuser's values. The film *Good Will Hunting* accurately portrays this phenomenon. Like Huck Finn, Will Hunting (played by Matt Damon) is the son of an abusive man. As a child, he had reacted angrily and fought back against his father. Nevertheless, he internalized a strong sense of being unworthy. As a result, he ends up as a janitor in a university where he could have been a professor. I have observed this phenomenon many times. The need to be in sync with the important people in our lives brings about the internalization of their values even when it is clear to us that they are wrong.

How Fences Hide What Lies Behind

Understanding internal electric fences helps us anticipate the reactions of those who possess them. First, knowing that internal electric fences are a part of the superego tells us that we can expect intense resistance to the very thought of change. Second, we can anticipate that letting go of these protective prohibitions, even when they are faulty, will likely take time and steady work.

Now an additional observation: Internal electric fences form such strong barriers that they insulate us from awareness of the original painful feelings that led to their formation. For example, Huck's (and John's) value of toughness is a barrier to feelings of hurt. Until this barrier begins to soften, Huck will not have any awareness of having felt hurt by his father, even if reminded. Therapists are often tempted to reach behind a barrier to show why the barrier is there. This simply won't work. It would sound to Huck like pure "psychobabble."

Therapists and even friends might want to bond with Huck by empathizing with the pain he must have experienced long ago. Instead of feeling understood, he would be offended at the suggestion that he might have felt hurt. Would-be helpers should keep in mind that they are up against an entrenched value and be prepared for rebuff.

The fenced-in person will need strong reasons to question his own value system. Remember John, who only entered treatment because he was facing the loss of his marriage. Anyone suggesting change will be suspect. Someone who questions our values will likely set off alarms making us ready to believe that they want to corrupt our conscience or make us into who we are not rather than help us.

Next Steps: How to Re-form Unhealthy Values

We treat our values as if they are the cornerstones of our existence, as in some ways they are. We are proud of them. It usually doesn't cross our minds that our values could be wrong, or that they might contradict one another. We generally don't consider the possibility that our values might be working against us.

If you experience shame and guilt when you shouldn't, then your life is being guided by unhealthy values. They need to be overridden by healthier ones. If you have realized this on your own, congratulate yourself on your unusually honest self-examination. If you realized it through someone else's input, congratulate yourself on being open to constructive input. And if you are beginning to realize it through reading this book, congratulate yourself on having the bravery to continue to read.

Helping Yourself

Change Your Behavior. The most important tool you have is voluntary behavior change. This means "civil disobedience," not living by your own unhealthy values, attitudes, ideals, or prohibitions. If your values say you don't deserve to stand straight, then you will need to make a point of standing more erect than is comfortable.

Dealing with Backlash. As you engage in a campaign of behavior change, your motivational system will send you guilt and shame. It may inundate you with anxiety, depression, restlessness, or feelings of being fraudulent. Your Black Box Motivator will go into high gear to discourage you. It will tell you that there is no point in trying to change or that it is just too hard, or even that you are wrong. It will try to convince you that every feeling and idea it sends you is the truth. It may succeed.

Your weapon here is knowing what to expect. Pay attention to your feelings and thoughts. Discuss them with your therapist and/or members of your support system. Ask yourself where your impulses are leading you. Unfortunately, your Black Box Motivator is excellent at disguising its messages and packaging your impulses in small, seemingly harmless steps. This is why an objective outside person can be so helpful.

Talk Back to Unhelpful Automatic Thoughts. In addition to changing your behavior, you can also change your thoughts. Talk back to your Black Box Motivator. You can thank it for trying to help, then explain that your life is different now, and you need new values to match your new (better) life. Changing your thoughts without behavior change may not be enough to change your values, but this is still an important ingredient.

Let Connection Distress Help You. As already discussed, the trigger to internalization is the longing to be connected: This is where the slightly aloof, "expectant" therapist can be particularly helpful. Your need to connect will trigger you to internalize healthy values. Just a small amount of connection distress can promote new internalization. For this task, a therapist who is too passive or too supportive may fail to help you feel the need to internalize new values.

Have Patience. Because your old values can't be erased, they will sometimes return, especially if you have an experience that mirrors the one that led to their internalization in the first place. The bad news is that you may need to do the work over and over. The good news is that it gets easier. And you are likely to be motivated to do more work after you experience the improvement in your life that comes with trying on new values. This work may well go on even after you have finished therapy.

References

Conway, Flo, and Jim Siegelman. *Snapping: America's Epidemic of Sudden Personality Change.* 2d ed. New York: Stillpoint Press, 1995: 13-46.

Schore A.N. *Affect Regulation and the Origin of the Self: The Neurobiology of Emotional Development.* Hillsdale, N.J.: Lawrence Erlbaum Associates, 1994: 348.

• 6 •

VOLUNTARY BEHAVIOR CHANGE

The role of behavior in avoiding feelings and finding them.

Key Concept:

Behavior change may be the holy grail of the twenty-first century as we succumb to the endless temptations in front of us. But the news is good: You *can* change your behavior—forever.

In this chapter we will focus on behavior patterns, one of the most important mechanisms that shield us from awareness of dreaded feelings. My own classical training had de-emphasized behavior. The focus had mostly been on distorted thoughts and how insight could give us access to what lay behind them.

In the 1980s my career path led me to work with people suffering from addictions. It didn't take long to realize that voluntary behavior change, especially choosing to abstain from the substance, was the *sine qua non* of treatment. Therapists who did not put behavior first were simply ineffective in working with addicted patients. My appreciation of the importance of changes in behavior soon extended beyond addictions to a wide range of problems in which behavior patterns were working against change.

Perhaps this evolution was in keeping with changing times. In the Victorian era, when Freud developed his ideas, the emphasis was on self-control. Good, middle-class Victorians might fantasize, but they were supposed to resist putting their desires into action. I grew up in the 1960s when the theme of the era was "sex, drugs, and rock & roll." The time had come to appreciate the power of behavior. Soon I learned how often behavior patterns are central to the Castles that were once erected to protect us from feelings.

The behavior patterns we will look at serve a common purpose, but they come in an exceedingly wide variety. The range is so great that to make sense of them we need to focus our examination on groups that are at least somewhat similar. The factor that is most important in determining the look and feel of these patterns is the age at which they presumably first developed. For this reason, I will divide them into five groups, roughly corresponding to five developmental eras.

Note that this dating is presumptive and based on observation rather than research. While I believe it will hold up to the test of time, it is not critical to understanding the patterns to be described and how facing feelings can bring about healing.

Five Developmental Periods, Five Groups of Patterns

Here are five broad groups of dysfunctional patterns—behaviors that are not random but repetitive in some recognizable way. They function to distance us from dreaded feelings and eventually block us from living healthier, more satisfying lives.

Age 0-3: Schemas. These are patterns of perception and behavior learned during early, preverbal years as trial and error guided us in avoiding pain and seeking out pleasure. Schemas are stored not in words but in implicit memory, and they form much of the knowledge of life that we take for granted without conscious thought. Fear of intimacy and issues with trust are typical. These patterns are a large part of the way we repeat in our adult relationships the assumptions and approaches that we learned from early interaction with caregivers.

Age 2-4: Inborn Strategies. This is my term to describe a group of patterns of reaction that are partly determined by genetics and chemistry and partly by experience. We have already discussed dissociation anxiety and depression as ways to avoid feelings. Obsessiveness works in similar way. All are symptoms that seem like problems in themselves, but they can equally be viewed as behavior patterns aimed at avoiding feelings. Looking at them in this way can open the door to change and help free us from their grip.

Age 3-4: Hidden Agendas. I have adopted this term to use as follows: By age three or four, children are aware of their lack of power to address their biggest problems and challenges. They know that the ones who can make things better are the adults. Hidden agendas are patterns of behavior originally aimed at trying to change important adults. When these patterns continue into adulthood, it is because the adults had not been listening or ready to change. As a result, these agendas involve nonverbal, indirect ways of attempting to influence others. Over time they become habit patterns whose targets and even purpose have long been forgotten. Clarifying the hidden messages behind the behaviors is the key to releasing feelings and seeking acceptance of what we once thought we had to change.

Age 4-6: Quests. A fourth group of patterns will be discussed separately in Chapter 6 because they are quite different from the others. When children reach age five, they gain the capacity to look ahead into their own long-term future. Being able to imagine a future in which they, themselves, can become different makes possible an entirely new way to solve the problems of childhood. "Someday I will be..." and then I will be able to overcome the difficulties and limitations that cause pain today. By changing myself at some time in the future, I will overcome the problems of today. This is how quests are born. The chapter will explore how quests, when they become hidden and secret, can also become Prisons.

Age 12+: Addictions. This fifth group of patterns will be discussed in this chapter alongside the other inborn strategies. By addictions I mean all kinds of compulsive behavior patterns when they do harm to our lives. Other than the fact that they develop later in life, they still have much in common with the other inborn strategies.

Patterns Have Inertia

While many behavior patterns or habits are effective and help us in life, most of us have at least some patterns that are dysfunctional—perhaps the ways we interact with others, the way we spend, how we manage time, the sort of people we choose or avoid. As long as these habits are not challenged, we don't think twice about them. They are the familiar Cave we live in, which makes it much easier to leave things just as they are. We have a strong tendency to accept, without too much question, habits in ourselves that actually rob us of life.

But when someone suggests that we could change, we feel discomfort. We begin to sense that something in us doesn't want to change. "I can't change that, I've always done it that way." Most likely we have years of rationalizations lined up to defend the status quo. "I never thought I'd live that long anyway." Until our comfort zone is challenged, we often don't realize just how protective we are of our habits. When we actually resolve to make a change, even one that is obviously in our own best interest, we are likely to experience real discomfort and inner resistance.

It is hard to realize that the comfort zone you are guarding is really not so comfortable and definitely less so than the one you have never experienced but will discover after you make changes and face your difficult feelings. As you encounter your own resistance, it is also important to realize there is no shortcut to defeating unhealthy patterns. There is no alternative to facing the feelings you have been avoiding. Reversing the order, I am saying two things: The only way to heal and grow is dare to cross the Bridge. Once you do, you will find a happier and more comfortable life awaiting you.

Schemas: What We "Just Know" about Life

We don't ask ourselves how to walk, we just know. There is a lot of background information about the world that we just know—that is, we have a lot of implicit knowledge—especially in terms of what is safe and what will bring pleasure or pain. If someone makes us feel uneasy, that feeling is probably based on implicit knowledge.

Implicit knowledge may feel instinctive, but it is actually built from experience and stored in many synapses throughout the brain. From the point of view of healing and growth, it is important to recognize that implicit knowledge can also be wrong—or, to put it more precisely, patterns based on the conditions of childhood may not be appropriate to the conditions of today. This is what makes the difference between healthy schemas that help us navigate the world and unhealthy, dysfunctional ones.

For example, if we are betrayed by caregivers early in life, we almost always have difficulty with trust. Is it any surprise that children who have never felt safe grow into wary teenagers and adults? As we maintain this vigilance, however, it severely limits our ability to experience intimacy and warmth, even when they are warranted. Vigilance also creates a self-fulfilling prophecy, because trustworthy people feel hurt by our lack of trust. They sense our guardedness and pull away (while genuinely dangerous people don't expect to be trusted anyway). We then misinterpret the trustworthy people's distance as lack of interest—or worse, we believe we were right to mistrust them in the first place. As a result, we unknowingly destroy opportunities for the very closeness that we so desperately want and actually need.

Schemas are learned through simple positive and negative rewards. We tend to repeat behaviors that bring pleasure and avoid ones that lead to uncomfortable feelings or pain. When children are faced, as they often are, with situations in which their behavior produces inconsistent or unpredictable reactions, they learn patterns to cope with helplessness and chaos.

How Can We Recognize a Schema?

How do we know that a schema is operating? In therapy, we might say something like, "Every time a new relationship gets to a certain point, I decide there's something terribly wrong with the person and

I somehow end it." With thoughtful exploration, we may find that associations lead us to the original situation, or we may be able to make educated guesses about things we learned long before there were words to describe them.

> *Laila had to start each session with small talk. Over time, we realized that whenever she had a conversation with her father, her first step was to check if he was drunk. As a result, she unknowingly needed to chat with me at the beginning of each session to make sure I was sober.*

> *Flo laughs affectionately at her husband Tony's foibles. Without realizing it, Tony is reminded of his mother laughing at him derisively when he had trouble with his toilet training. Tony's old schema of shutting down emotionally kicks in, which in turn sets off one of Flo's schemas from her early life. Without either having any conscious understanding of what is happening, they are soon well into their usual fight, the one they have had a million times.*

Many marital problems involve schemas that are based on concerns with safety and need fulfillment. These reactions developed when we, as small children, were instinctively fighting for our emotional and bodily survival. This gives them a life-and-death quality. What's more, they engage the more primitive survival-related parts of our nervous system. These primitive systems trigger responses so quickly that our conscious, thinking brain can't process what has happened. By the time we are consciously aware of what we have done, it is too late to take it back.

As we look at ourselves—especially at how we deal with intense interpersonal situations—with a moderate degree of self-observation and honesty, we can see where we have strengths and where we have difficulty. Matching this up with what we know about our early experience will very likely help us develop a working hypothesis about why we react the way we do. There may be early memories that resonate with here-and-now fears or reactions.

An example from my own experience is that when voices are raised in anger, I experience an impulse to cry and give in to the angry person. I have memories that resonate from times of chaos in my family during my first years of life. The best way to combat this schema has been first to heal the shame I used to have about it and accept that I still have the feelings. With openness and acceptance, they have lost much of their grip on my outward behavior. If I know I am heading into a tense situation where this schema is likely to be activated, with the knowledge I have I can prepare myself mentally to handle it appropriately.

In general, schemas are the most problematic in intimate relationships, where in early childhood the stakes were the highest. This is why intimacy, meaning the ability to tolerate and enjoy deep emotional sharing, is one of the most challenging achievements of adult life. But intimacy is not the only area that is affected by early relationships. The ability to be a good supervisor at work really challenges our schemas, as does being a parent. It takes an unusual individual to be able consistently to hold firm under pressure yet remain flexible and open to new ideas and influence. That's why really good bosses are so rare. In these areas genetics play a role in inborn temperament, but experience in a healthy early environment is also formative where ideally the degree of control and guidance from caregivers was gauged just right for the particular child to nurture self-reliance without over-or under control.

It is also interesting to note that great leaders often come from relatively deprived backgrounds where they had to develop unusual abilities to handle pressure. A difficult early life regularly produces unusual abilities as well as liabilities.

Schemas are at the center of the study of attachment; that is, our ability and style in forming interpersonal bonds. This area will be discussed in more depth in Chapter 8, when we look at emotional development in general as opposed to the individual behavior patterns that are the subject of this chapter.

Changing Schemas

Clearly, changing automatic nonverbal reactions is difficult. The first step is to recognize when we fall into an old, dysfunctional habit.

When these reactions take place in an intimate relationship, the person who still has some perspective may be the first to realize that some hidden force is at work. At first we may only recognize our schemas in retrospect; however, being able to put that recognition into words is an important step. Words give us a label, a handle with which to catch the schema instead of seeing it slip away in the stream of experience. In time we may actually be able to recognize our schematic reactions as they are happening. At that point, we are in a position to modify our behavior. As in the personal example above, letting go of shame is extremely helpful in our becoming open to change. Of course, the next frontier is to take hold of ourselves before we react.

The ultimate goal is to replace the old behavior with a healthier new one. Even if the dust has already settled, it is still a good idea to practice healthier responses. "Do-overs" are an excellent method. They give the person who has reacted a chance to practice a healthier pattern as well as expressing reassurance that the bad behavior is still forgivable.

As we try to change our behavior, our efforts can be expected to stir up some form of resistance. Our inner child is desperately trying to hold the line, fearing that pain will be repeated. With success in making changes we are likely to experience the strong feelings that the schema was originally designed to avoid. As you have come to expect, experiencing these feelings in a context of connection and safety is the formula for catharsis and healing.

Perhaps the new, healthy action is something as simple as expressing affection or asking for directions. If at one time that would have made us vulnerable to rejection, we are likely to find ourselves somehow resisting our own determination to carry out the act. When we succeed, the feeling is one of strangeness along with vulnerability on a child's giant scale. This is the feeling of crossing the Bridge described in Chapter 1. If everything goes well, we can still expect a backlash. Our Black Box Motivator will retaliate by telling us our success was a fluke. If the new initiative fails, it will tell us we never should have tried. Persistence is critical in the face of this kind of resistance. It will be made easier by expecting the resistance as well as asking for support from others who understand the daunting nature of the project we have undertaken.

Inborn Strategies

Whereas schemas are ways to regulate the impact of our environment, inborn strategies are ways to regulate the self. I am proposing the term to be as descriptive as possible, but you won't find it elsewhere. Inborn strategies start with natural reaction patterns that become incorporated into more elaborate and purposeful means of avoiding threatening feelings. Examples are anxiety, depression, dissociation, and obsessive-compulsive behaviors. Though they help us in early life to avoid painful feelings, later they become major sources of dysfunction and suffering.

Young children naturally rely on caregivers for help managing their emotions. When that doesn't work, they have little choice but to try to change themselves. It is not surprising that the means available at very young ages involve drastic distortions and sacrifices. As we will see, these inborn strategies, when they last into adult life, often constitute psychiatric disorders in themselves. I think of inborn strategies as having their origins around the ages of two to four years. Once again I will use the language of intentionality for something that I believe is often purposeful but not under conscious or willful control.

Inborn strategies are potentially available to all humans, but some individuals may lean more towards one than another. Genetics seem to have a lot to do with which inborn strategies we adopt. More often than not, a parent will have had the same or similar traits. Even so, when they become lifelong problems it is, in my view, in large part because they fulfill an emotional function. What they accomplish in different ways is to keep bad feelings out of our consciousness.

Inborn strategies are particularly important because, together, they represent the majority of emotional symptoms that lead people to seek professional help. How is it possible that anxiety and depression, unpleasant experiences in themselves, could serve to help us avoid feelings? Chapter 2 introduced the concept. Let's look further now.

Anxiety

This is not the healthy from of anxiety that signals real danger and triggers a fight-or-flight reaction designed to help us save ourselves. Instead, it is an irrational form of anxiety, in which we experience fear for no clear reason, or find ourselves afraid of something that is insignificant or unlikely to happen. This seemingly purposeless anxiety actually does accomplish one thing. It keeps us very far from the deep down fears that lie behind it. As we try to manage the anxiety, our preoccupation with fear becomes a diversion from real worries.

Actually the diversion has two layers. The real source of anxiety is obscured from the beginning. This is one layer. Then as we become more concerned with anxiety itself, our preoccupation with avoiding anxiety becomes a new focus and takes us even farther from the original feeling. Think of Andrew from Chapter 2, who invented worries where none existed. First his focus moved away from the original fear onto something implausible, then he put his energy into controlling his anxiety, further distancing the feelings themselves.

Yes, here we are again. As children we adopt and adapt approaches to keep as far as possible from feelings that are beyond our limited coping ability. Once established, they can stay with us, even when they are no longer of use or are actually destructive. Once again, our Castles turn into Prisons. The answer to anxiety, like the other inborn strategies, is to face the original feelings. Therapy aims to help us see clearly how it is better to face our anxieties and befriend them than to avoid them. As we do so, feelings are unmasked and become accessible to healing and growth.

By age three, perhaps the prime age for inborn strategies, most of us have accomplished certain important developmental milestones. We have a firm sense of our physical body. We are clear that we exist as a separate being from others, and we have a very modest ability to cope with being alone. We know that we do not rule our world but that we have a right to existence and dignity.

However, the problems of three-year-olds can be major. At this age, we are still weak and dependent compared with older siblings and parents. The superego with its self-control is still quite weak. We follow our best schemas to get attention or have our needs met. When this doesn't work, when the adults don't respond as we need, the level of desperation escalates. Seeing that our attempts to get the attention of caregivers are not working, we turn to the self.

Perhaps the core fear comes from hearing the parents arguing in the next room. The child feels a twinge of helplessness that he or she can't put into words. The first step is to substitute a more identifiable fear for the real one. Perhaps it is a fear of monsters coming into the bedroom at night. Then the focus is placed on measures to control that fear such as leaving the light on. Over time, children usually cope with these worries and they seem to pass. But later in life, adult circumstances may reawaken the original fear, which was never really allayed in childhood.

Panic Attacks

In adulthood, panic attacks such as John's are perhaps the simplest of inborn strategies. These come for no apparent reason, with a feeling we can't get enough air, rapid heartbeat, dizziness, and a sense of something terrible happening. All this scary feeling is simply the mind being reminded of far distant worries and telling the body that something is dangerously out of kilter.

For John, panic came from nowhere but was really related to a scary promotion. The parts of his brain that are specialized in spotting danger had picked up the similarity between his promotion and the thing he most dreaded in early childhood. Back then, since his parents weren't there when he had minor needs, his child logic was that if the situation was really bad they would certainly not step in to help. Therefore, his worst fear was that he would have to be the grownup in some situation that was critical, and, being a child, he would fail to handle it and all would perish. For years this terrible worry stayed in the back of his mind. He honed his survival skills, but because the old fear remained buried, his adult abilities never fully allayed the old fear.

On the surface, John's job promotion felt good, but he worried that he wouldn't be up to the challenge. Deep down there was turmoil. Not being sure of having the strength or resources to succeed was a very close match to his deepest dread from childhood. And this implicit thinking part of the brain doesn't possess the subtlety to know that the situations are not really the same. It would take words to get to that level of precision.

On the other hand, John's defenses don't want to admit fear or weakness. Sure he can do the job. He even has adult experience to convince him he can do the job. For a while, adult knowledge holds back the rising waters of doubt. But finally, fear of a catastrophic failure gets the upper hand and breaks into consciousness. It first emerges as a pure physical reaction with a large dose of adrenalin to cause shaking, pounding heart, and a feeling of impending doom. John attaches this to the idea that he is surely having a heart attack and will die.

Unlike the version presented in Chapter 2, let's say this time John doesn't get therapy. The emergency room staff give him Valium, which calms him and send him home with a recommendation to go to the hospital's psychiatric clinic. He declines but begins to worry about when panic will hit again. He stops going to the gym for fear that his heart may not really be that strong. He worries that his anxiety is visible to everyone at work. The boss is surely going to see how weak he is and take him off his new assignment. He becomes so distraught that his boss suggests a few days off.

If he follows the thoughts and impulses coming from his Black Box Motivator, he will do everything possible to lessen his anxiety. That will mean doing less and less, finally becoming emotionally disabled and invalid. Let's hope this doesn't happen. As we saw in Chapter 2, what helped was the opposite of his natural instinct.

It was to re-experience his fear in a safe setting knowing that it could not cause him harm. As you will recall this is the formula for catharsis, which could be accomplished in at least two ways: behaviorally by giving him tools to master the fear so he could allow himself to experience it in life, or by helping him imagine his adult worst-case scenario and exploring it in depth back to the original version from his early years.

Obsessions and Compulsions

Even without having the full-blown diagnosable syndrome of obsessive–compulsive disorder (OCD), many people suffer from useless obsessing over thoughts that lead nowhere or actions that accomplish nothing. The thoughts often come in a setting where we are dealing with a problem we can't solve. Compulsive actions often seem like they will make us feel more comfortable or less anxious. For some time now it has been observed that medications that enhance the neurotransmitter serotonin (such as serotonin re-uptake inhibitors like Prozac) can lessen these symptoms. My favorite example is a woman who had to clean the grout around her kitchen sink till it was spotless. She would work until 3 a.m. to get the job done. With medication, the clock struck 1 a.m., and she said to herself, "That's enough, I'm going to bed." Even without complete relief, she felt much better.

What is even more remarkable is that simply stopping the compulsive behaviors can produce the same changes in the brain chemistry that are produced by medication (Linden, 2006). This is one clear instance in which therapy can be shown not only to be beneficial but also to produce measurable changes in brain chemistry.

The problem, of course, is that for people who suffer from obsessive–compulsive disorder, it's very difficult to change behaviors. Not performing usual rituals causes powerful anxiety. Even just thinking of skipping a ritual produces uncomfortable feelings. Similarly, stopping obsessive thoughts requires serious work helped by tools of cognitive-behavioral therapy. As a result, sufferers must be strongly motivated and have plenty of support to push their way through. When they do, however, the rewards are great.

How do obsessive thoughts and compulsive rituals serve to avoid feelings? We have seen how helplessness is one of the most painful, even toxic feelings humans can experience. Children are especially prone to helplessness, having few strengths and limited outside resources. For those who are genetically prone to develop obsessions and compulsions, thoughts and actions that give us the illusion of control over our environment, provide solace, and allow us to deny the helplessness we would otherwise have to face.

Many obsessions relate to self-control, such as hurting someone or forgetting to lock the door. Some naturally lead to behavior patterns aimed at calming the worry. We can put all the knives out of reach or go back multiple times to check the door. Unfortunately, these measures only emphasize that there is no sure way to gain control. The more we seek to control our worries, the more insistent the worries become. Most of us can see that this is leading nowhere, but for some, it seems unstoppable.

These patterns of thought and behavior probably start as strategies to deal with young, wordless fears that remain lodged in our implicit memory. Later they become translated into specific adult concerns: "If I check once more, I won't feel so worried that I have forgotten to lock." A compulsive behavior becomes a way to allay the surface version of a deep and hidden fear. Even when there is no behavior to give the illusion of control, the act of worrying "binds," or provides a concrete focus for anxiety, which seems to feel less out of control than free-floating uneasiness.

As with anxiety, there is usually some symbolic connection between the thing we are ostensibly worried about and a deeper, more frightening concern that we are afraid to face. What is remarkable here is the mind's capacity to substitute something that seems more controllable for something we deeply dread. This ability to substitute something more adult and acceptable for something deeper and unacceptable is one of the mind's basic techniques. Unfortunately, the connection is not usually available to our conscious awareness.

The best example I know of one thing standing for another is in anorexia nervosa. Individuals with this disorder focus a tremendous
amount of energy on controlling their food intake. Working with
them makes it very clear that the thing they most want to control
and can't is their own human neediness, so they control food. As
John was troubled by his needs and tried to suppress them, sufferers
from anorexia (at least those I have known) are most deeply concerned about suppressing their need (appetite) for a very young kind
of parental love. Deep underneath layers of avoidance, they have a
voracious appetite for the all-encompassing kind of love that is basic
for the smallest children. This appetite becomes all the more intense
due to efforts to suppress it.

What happens next is that food becomes a substitute for love. The
individual can't get enough of it, which even further intensifies the
fear of losing control and becoming fat. A war breaks out between
impulses to eat and measures to control eating. Food becomes an ob-
session, and control of eating becomes a compulsive and very dangerous behavior pattern.

As described earlier with the Black Box Motivator, we can't see into
the place where the connection is made between the appetite for
early love and the appetite for food. We are left to make an educated
guess based on the inputs and outputs. In a similar way, a person
who is experiencing rageful feelings but has no awareness of them
might also be experiencing obsessions about having an irresistible
impulse to pick up a sharp knife.

Thus, obsessions and compulsive behaviors can function to cover up
real concerns, often with roots going back many years. And—to reit-
erate—the real way to control these concerns is to face the dreaded
original fears. How can we do this? First by voluntary behavior
change; that is, by refraining from the behavior patterns and learning to stop the obsessive thoughts.

Relinquishing the behaviors that distance from feelings, the emotions that have been suppressed begin to enter consciousness. Not
checking that the door is locked leads to intense anxiety about what
might happen if the door were accidentally left unlocked. Following

the trail of anxiety leads to catharsis, and then to deeper layers of anxiety and new levels of healing. While voluntary behavior change is the key to non-medication treatment, I believe it accomplishes cathartic healing of the underlying painful feelings, now brought to the surface.

The Remarkable Power of Feelings

An indication of the power of feelings is how deeply we resist encountering them. Our resistance is not only strong but also subtle, even uncanny. With the best of intentions to change unhealthy behavior patterns, our own Black Box Motivator can often conjure up ways to look like we are making real changes when we are not. A relatively simple and common example is to do something covertly unhealthy to counterbalance a step in the direction of health. In doing so, we may change superficially without actually challenging our emotions.

Another indication of how strongly we resist feeling is that when we are successful in pushing ourselves towards healthier behavior and coming closer to dreaded feelings, our stress level can increase to the point of bringing on medical conditions such as autoimmune illness.

> *Alex worked hard in therapy and let go of his obsessive and compulsive inborn strategies. As he did so, he found reasons to be excessively critical of his wife. Even though he was aware of using flimsy excuses, he justified his verbally abusive behavior towards her. This allowed him to ward off yearnings for her to pay attention to him. She wisely refused to engage with him. She remained warm towards him while refusing to accept his abuse. Soon, he developed not one but two autoimmune illnesses. When these conditions gradually resolved through medical treatment, Alex had no "choice" but to traverse his feelings. Once he finally did so, catharsis could work and he was able to begin making real changes.*

Dissociation and Depression

As described in Chapter 2, dissociation and depression can also function as inborn strategies for avoiding feelings. As with the other inborn strategies, the feelings we once avoided were more than we could handle. Depression is a natural, biologically based reaction to the threat of helplessness and hopelessness. As described in Chapter 2, it can also be a strategy for salvaging a small ray of hope from utter blackness. It is a way of turning passive into active, from something done to us to something we do. In addition, depression can serve to channel rage towards the self, where it feels less dangerous.

Dissociation is a skill with biological roots, one for which some people are naturally more gifted than others. Under conditions of severe stress, dissociation allows us to distance from overwhelming affect so as to preserve our ability to do what we must for survival. This costly strategy can save lives but is also the source of the symptoms of PTSD, in which buried feelings can wreak destruction for years if not brought out and healed.

Hidden Agendas

As described in the introduction to this chapter, I use the term hidden agenda to describe behavior patterns originally aimed at influencing the adults in a child's life. I think of these patterns as dating from age three or four, but I wouldn't want to be strict about the age range. At these ages, children know they are relatively powerless to solve problems on their own. Especially when it comes to basic needs, their only hope is to look to the adults in their lives. Hidden agendas would not exist if the child were simply able to ask for what she or he needed. The problem is either that the child is inhibited from expressing needs or, more likely, the adults are in some way not responsive. The end result is that the child must either face helplessness or devise some indirect way to try to get the adults to change.

Children simply won't and don't accept hopelessness. So the child focuses on finding an alternative way to influence the adults. Since words were not effective, the message must be delivered without them. The thought might be, "If only they understood, then they would see the light and change." The result is covert communication, what I call "smoke signals"—that is, nonverbal or indirect ways to communicate a message. When these patterns last into adulthood, they drain energy and life and are even less successful than in childhood. The recipient of the communication may feel the silent pressure, but since demands are not made directly, the impact is not one the recipient can easily respond to. Even if the recipient identifies what is going on, the person with the agenda will probably possess long-established ways of denying any such thing.

The most damaging aspect of hidden agendas is when the message is to show the adult how wrong they were in their parenting. The main way to demonstrate this nonverbally is a prominent display of some kind of failure or damage. How can a child communicate that the parent is doing a bad job? By showing the results. That means unconsciously exhibiting some kind of failure by doing harm to the self. A possible tip-off can be that the person seems overly accepting of their own failure.

At age three or four, big problems might involve loss of love and attention when a sibling is born, having a depressed parent who rarely gets out of bed, being unfairly punished, or being afraid that we might have to shoulder responsibilities beyond our resources and ability. These are genuinely stressful and difficult problems where hopelessness looms right around the corner.

David suffered throughout childhood from his parents' apparent disinterest in helping him navigate a world that seemed much too harsh. The problem had been continuous from an early age. Even when he went to college they put him on a train, wished him well, and turned their backs till it was time for him to graduate.

He sought therapy in his forties for feelings of hopelessness and depression. He described how he had lost a good job over a decade before. He had ventured out on his own as a freelance consultant and had done all right until a bad economy led to a slowdown in his industry. Now he and his wife were struggling financially, and he didn't know where he would get his next assignment. He felt overwhelmed, discouraged, and very depressed.

As I listened to David's story, it became more apparent that he had been dragging his feet in marketing his own business. He had contacted a volunteer business consulting organization and had received excellent counseling, but he had been slow to contact them in the first place and was slow to implement their suggestions. His wife was upset with him and, instead of supporting his efforts, criticized him for being irresponsible. He felt he was doing the best he could and felt hurt by her disapproval.

At first, my efforts to point out that he might do more were met with denial. He felt strongly that he was at his limit. On the other hand, focusing on specific steps seemed to help him. He made progress but could not see that he was capable of more.

What David couldn't see was that his tiredness and procrastination were more a communication than a reflection of reality. It was his unconscious way of saying, "It's too hard, I need more help." In spite of himself he made progress in his business, but the agenda stayed active. He was also overweight. The situation came to a head when he joined a weight-loss program but found that he couldn't get himself to follow it. This, too, was a communication. He was sending the same message: "It's too hard, I need more help."

Imagine if he actually followed suggestions and was successful. Then the childlike communication that he needed support would fail. The message would be, "I'm okay, thanks"; that is, he would be relinquishing his claim that the others in his life should do more for him.

This will make more sense if we picture the childhood situation. David couldn't criticize his parents for neglecting his needs. They wouldn't have accepted that at all, and he might have lost the love he did get. So his only way to influence them was to demonstrate that he was struggling and needed more help. If he stopped struggling or had no need to struggle, his parents would have concluded that they were doing a great job and didn't need to change. So not only did David continue finding ways to dramatize his struggle, but he also developed a habit of rationalizing that he was really doing his best. In his own mind he was quite heroic, so anyone who might suggest differently was seen as hurtful and unsupportive. He was truly stuck.

Without any conscious awareness, he was waiting for his business consultant, the weight loss program staff, his wife, and even his

therapist to try harder. Meanwhile his adult-life helpers were waiting for him to follow their counsel. Just this kind of impasse, in both
real-life settings and in therapy, is typical of people who are following a childhood agenda.

> *Slowly we began to break up the logjam. In spite of himself, David took small*
> *steps to improve his business and work with the weight-loss counselors. He*
> *began to recognize that he had experienced a great deal of deprivation in his*
> *young life. With this awareness, he began feeling a hurt in his chest, especially*
> *on the way to his therapy sessions. Finally he began to connect the feeling*
> *with the years of unspoken pain at having to find his own way in the world.*
> *At last he could do the work of facing his feelings of loss and anger. He began*
> *to follow the weight-loss program much more actively and accelerated his*
> *work with the business consultant.*

Agendas focus on a variety of needs. Some are focused more on issues of justice or blame. Frankly self-destructive behavior can be a
smoke signal to say, "Look what you did to me." Exaggerated and
unjust self-blame can carry a message such as, "Don't you see, it is
really your fault." Self-defeating or self-destructive behavior can express a hidden agenda of revenge, too, a way to hurt those who have
not done their job. Living with someone who seems to insist on self-
harm is not just painful, but it also creates feelings of helplessness
and frustration for significant others when efforts to address needs
of the one with the agenda are not allowed to succeed.

Like David, people with hidden agendas are not only unaware of the
messages they send, but they also place high value (meaning the
conscience is involved) on being "good people." They themselves
are especially intolerant of anything suggesting willfulness. As a
result, any attempt to point out how their behavior is painful to
others will be met with powerful defensiveness. Not only is the
individual reluctant to admit to ulterior motives, but someone's
pointing out that she is doing it "purposefully" will elicit the most
intense reaction. Remember that the agenda was formed in the
first place to deal with grownups who refused to take responsibility
for their behavior. In many cases they will actually have blamed
the child for their own failures. So it is no wonder the child, now

grown up, reacts defensively to being told (once again) that she is responsible for her self-destructive behavior. It feels wrong because at one time it *was* wrong.

It is not easy to let go of hurt and resentment, especially when they are multiplied by years of pain. Change for the better feels like defeat. It feels like letting the real perpetrators "off the hook." In addition, giving up this sort of hidden agenda leads right to the original feeling of helplessness—helplessness from childhood needs that were legitimate and real but that could not be met. All the years of hoping that the grownups would get the message have left the original feeling of loss or deprivation untouched and as big as when it was buried. Only a force as strong as catharsis can bring about healing.

Failed Rites of Passage

Another important form of agenda revolves around what I call "failed rites of passage," in which the older child or adolescent puts his or her development on hold, waiting for a parent or parent substitute to provide the sponsorship needed in order to move to the next step of maturity. I once heard an interview with the actor Burt Reynolds. His words were memorable: "You're not a man until your pappy says you are... and mine never did."

In some cases, the patient sees the therapist as the one who can provide the sponsorship and eventually interprets that the therapist is refusing to give it. The hidden agenda then focuses on changing the therapist, once again by hints and smoke signals. To make matters worse, neither patient nor therapist at first understands what the signals mean. Here is another example of transference. It can begin to be worked out when the patient becomes aware of his agenda. Only then can the two come to understand what the patient was hoping for and how those needs might realistically be addressed.

Agendas are often even more costly than these examples might suggest. Gerald Jampolsky, M.D., known for the Attitudinal Healing Center he founded, says it succinctly: "Peace of mind comes from not wanting to change others." Agendas do just the opposite, they focus on trying to solve problems by changing others, and the result is inevitably loss of peace of mind. To make matters worse, their destructive energy is usually unconscious, where it is inaccessible to change.

Who Is the Bad One?

Whereas most of the hidden agendas described so far represent attempts to change someone else, some agendas aim is to identify who is the "bad" one. Here, the sufferer inexplicably repeats destructive and often genuinely bad deeds in an attempt to reenact some situation from the distant past in which it was unclear who was to blame. Was it the child or the perpetrator? The confusion is understandable since there are so many situations where parents or others do wrong but don't take responsibility. Inevitably the child's mind splits, with one part believing he or she is "right" and the other siding with the adult.

James's father was violently abusive towards his mother. His son was a helpless witness to beatings and verbal attacks.

In later years the son, who prided himself on his fairness and decency, found himself repeatedly mistreating women. He felt guilty, but he could not stop.

As we explored the dynamics, it was clear that the constant question deep in James's mind was whether he was to blame for his father's attacks. So repeatedly the son, through his actions, would argue both sides of the question. He would prove that he really was a bad person and simultaneously that he was a caring, decent person.

Of course, the question could never be answered through action. The evidence mounted up on both sides, but there was no clear answer. There could not be an answer because humans are neither "good" nor "bad." These are childhood concepts based on our emotional brain's binary, black/white nature. In fact, humans are all, as one wise physician put it, "flawed children of God."

The only permanent way to untangle James's agenda was to bring it into the explicit realm of consciousness and explore what was really going on. Only after revealing his agenda could he work on ending the destructive, abusive behavior pattern.

Acceptance and Forgiveness

One final aspect of hidden agendas is how they can block acceptance and forgiveness. There are many things that happen in life that we need to get past either by accepting reality and moving on or by coming to forgive someone who has harmed us. What if there were a secret agenda of changing reality or getting the person who did wrong to take responsibility? As long as the agenda is secret, then the owner will keep waiting for reality to change or for the other person to change. Either way, the end result is that the person will not be able to accept or forgive.

As pointed out in Chapter 4, the secret idea that we may not have to accept or forgive can block acceptance or forgiveness. This hope can became an agenda. Whenever something seems to be holding up the natural process of grieving over what went wrong and moving on, we do well to look for a hidden agenda that was originally devised to keep hope alive but is now preventing closure.

Let's look at an example of acceptance. The most common reason we cannot find the serenity to accept something we are not happy about is that, without realizing it, we still have some hope that the problem will be fixed or resolved so that we won't have to face the pain of loss.

John could not accept the inadequacy of the parenting he had received. Without consciously realizing it, he still hoped, as he had in childhood, that if he was responsible enough and asked for little enough, someone would take notice and reward him with the nurturing he had missed. Of course when he married Jen, he had no awareness that this was an agenda from childhood. No wonder he was disappointed when she gave up on helping him.

What John needs is to move into true adulthood and ask for support in open, healthy ways. Unfortunately, a child within is still stuck hoping to get what he needs by earning support but not asking for it. That didn't work in the first place, and it won't work now. For him to change course, he will first have to admit to having needs, then he can begin sorting out which needs can be met in adult life and which childhood shortfalls will never be made up. As is quite common, there are two layers of cover-up. First, John's conscience won't allow him to need anything. Next, there is the secret agenda of getting someone to repair his childhood so he won't have to face the loss. Only as he works his way through those two layers will he be in a position to face the longing and disappointment associated with needs that will never be met. When he does, he will experience true grief over losses that can't be made up for. Once again, the healing mechanism is catharsis, but it will first require that the hidden agenda be brought to light and relinquished. As the emotional healing is accomplished, John will then be ready to get on with his life in a healthy way.

Addictions

Addictions were discussed in Chapter 2 because they are the result of the motivational system being hijacked in the service of "getting high." There is good evidence that genes have a lot to do with who develops an addiction and who doesn't, which makes addictions somewhat like inborn strategies. On the other hand, addictions are different in that they generally develop much later, during the preteen or teen years, or even later.

Other compulsive behaviors, also act more or less like chemical addictions. Compulsive overeating, compulsive gambling, and compulsive sexual behavior are examples. What makes them like chemical addictions is that sufferers are genuinely unable to control the behaviors even when they are doing real damage. The motivational system is most likely compromised in a way at least similar to the way chemical addictions do it.

What makes these patterns relevant here is that they too effectively cover up feelings. In fact, the longer the addiction goes on, the more it becomes a universal coping mechanism for every stress. When emotional pain is a major contributor to the original development of the addiction, it will probably be necessary for the person to face the feelings at some point in recovery. In addition, the Black Box Motivator develops a whole system of rationalizations and denial. Facing these honestly is also a large part of recovery. Thus, like all the behavior patterns in this chapter, the essence of recovery is to face reality honestly along with the feelings that have been covered up and avoided. At the end of this chapter there is a special "next steps" section devoted to addictions.

Approaches to Behavior Change

Even when we are clear that behavior change is a necessary part of healing and growth, it is not so easily accomplished. Resistance is high, and each of the three layers of our motivational system is set against us. The pleasure/pain system sees uncomfortable feelings ahead. Our conscience very likely has values that stand in the way of change, and finally our Black Box Motivator is there to talk us out of what we really want and need. How, then, can we prevail?

Traditional talk therapy has, from the beginning, been weak on behavior change. Therapists in these traditions are generally taught to "interpret acting-out defenses." This means pointing out to the patient that a behavior is standing in the way of understanding and feeling. Then the patient is supposed to realize that changing the behavior would be a good idea. In the 21st century this method seems, and often is, far too weak. In this area behavioral and cognitive-behavioral therapists have shown a greater recognition of the importance and challenges of voluntary behavior change.

James O. Prochaska and Carlo C. DiClemente studied behavior change in one of the areas in which it is hardest to achieve, alcoholism. They developed their transtheoretical model of behavior change, recognizing that there are five stages of change and that matching the approach to the stage is far better than a cookie-cutter approach. More recently, John Norcross introduced the notion of "Changeology" in a popular book (2012) incorporating 30 years of research on behavior change. Other important ideas about voluntary behavior change come from cognitive-behavioral therapy (CBT) specialized in counteracting the rationalizations and other automatic thoughts produced by our Black Box Motivator to discourage us from trying to change.

James O. Prochaska (1943-) and Carlo C. DiClemente (1942-)

Prochaska and DiClemente developed the transtheoretical model of behavior change, a method by which a therapist can assess whether a person is ready to change and then guide the person through adopting and maintaining a new, healthier behavior.

John Norcross (1957-)

Distinguished researcher, teacher, and clinician who has focused on behavior change and psychotherapy. Collaborated with Prochaska and DiClemente. He has championed research demonstrating the crucial importance of the therapeutic relationship in psychotherapy success as well as what works to make lasting changes in behavior.

If voluntary behavior change is a challenge for you, I recommend Norcross's *Changeology*. In the next sections I discuss some of my own perspectives on the difficulties you may encounter when you try to change entrenched behavior patterns. Then, based on experiences and observations throughout my career, I share some methods of dealing with those difficulties.

Behavior Change Math

Unhealthy behavior forms an amazingly effective barrier against feeling. You can think of action as the opposite of feeling. Here are of some of the ways this can work:

- Constant activity distracts us from inner feelings. People who are constantly active may sometimes be running away from a painful feeling.

- Acting out our feelings distances us from consciously experiencing the affect. Hurting others can keep anger at bay. Hurting oneself can distance feelings of low worth. Eating to fill an emotional void can briefly take away feelings of emptiness.

- When we try to control other people, we focus on them and distance from feelings about ourselves.

- Doing less than our best can keep us away from anxiety or discomfort associated with success and failure.

These mechanisms are extremely powerful. I have altered Einstein's famous equation to show just how powerful behavior can be:

$$E = BC^2$$

In this equation, C still equals the speed of light—186,000 miles per second—but E is *emotional* energy, and B stands for behavior. Because C^2 is such a gigantic number, even a small change in behavior (B) results in a huge change in emotional energy (E). In simpler words, even a small behavior change unleashes a huge amount of emotional energy. With such a large amount of emotional energy at stake, the process of behavior change is highly charged and can even be dangerous. The better we understand the process, the more surely and safely we can navigate.

The Grow Graph

The grow graph below shows what happens when we push to make positive changes, and it also shows how problems can surprise us when things seem to be going well. I originally developed the graph to describe recovery from addictions, but it applies to any situation in which we strive for healthier living against internal resistance.

The graph shows that there is a level of behavior where our stress is at its lowest—our comfort zone. Pushing toward healthier living (i.e., to the right on the graph) raises our stress level. Pushing too hard can bring stress into a danger zone where people with addictions are likely to relapse, and others may self-sabotage or show severe signs of stress.

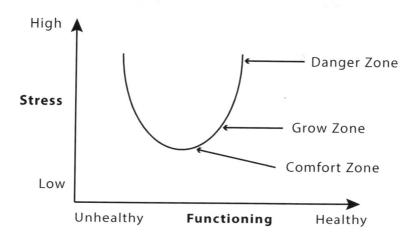

Level of Functioning Related to Stress

When people become angry, irritable, agitated, and judgmental, the first thing I think of is that they are on the "backside of the curve." They have fallen back into old, unhealthy behaviors. Even though it may seem the easy way, the result of backsliding is greater stress, as shown on the graph. It is as if we know we are doing the wrong thing but don't want to admit it or give up the behavior. The result is that we become unhappy with everything and everyone.

The positive goal is to make frequent excursions into the growth zone but to go back from time to time to the comfort zone to refuel. As we practice being in our growth zone, it becomes easier, even exciting, especially when our growth zone is correlated with less stress.

As the next graph shows, the effect of long-term growth is to shift curve down and to the right. The comfort zone becomes even more comfortable as we become healthier, and what used to be stressful is less so. This can be shown by drawing a new curve further down and a little to the right. The interesting part is that there is still plenty of challenge, because there is always room for more growth.

When we understand this behavior change math we may be more motivated to move ahead in spite of our uncomfortable feelings. We may also be better able to identify those feelings, even when they show up in disguise. Most importantly, we can then anticipate problems before they ambush us. When we are trying hard to change we may experience simple anxiety or depression. More insidiously, our

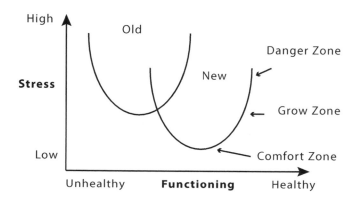

Healthier Functioning *and* Lower Stress

Black Box Motivator can trick us with feelings of restlessness and impulses to do things that seem positive but are unconsciously designed to thwart growth. For example, a common pattern among people with more severe problems is to decide prematurely that it is time to seek employment. Predictably the result is a failure that discourages further growth. The Black Box Motivator is using a very sneaky kind of reverse psychology to protect the status quo.

The preceding graphs reveal that we actually have control over the speed and intensity of the change process. I like to tell people that they control their own gas pedal. They can go faster or slower, and how hard they press determines the amount of stress they will experience. The feeling of driving at eighty or ninety miles an hour is a good analogy to how it feels when change is going too fast.

Finally, the graphs illustrate that we can't spend all of our time outside our comfort zones. Constant change is not possible or desirable. We do our best when periods of growth are mixed with time to rest and refuel.

Next Steps: How to Practice Voluntary Behavior Change

So, how do we change our behaviors? Especially, how do we change schemas, those automatic behaviors we cannot initially control and that can be so very distressing? Say you are feeling close to someone you are dating, and then suddenly, with no warning, words pop out of your mouth that push the other person away. You have no warning, so you have no ability to prevent these behaviors. But even though you cannot prevent them, and even though you have no control right now, there is much you can do.

Use Words as Handles. At first you may only be able to identify a behavior after it is too late. As you observe yourself in action, however, you will start to recognize not only the pattern but also its triggers. Schemas exist in the implicit part of the mind. Moving them to the explicit area will help a lot. Here are some steps to take:

- Identify a behavior you want to change. Give it a name.
- Describe the behavior and its patterns and triggers.
- Define the new behavior you want to put in its place.
- Mentally practice the new, healthier response to the triggers you identified. Mental practice is almost as useful as the real thing—ask any ski racer.

Reach Out to a Loved One. Our problematic behaviors often show up in the middle of emotional interactions with people who are important to us. Typically at these times we have no perspective at all. Your partner may be better able to spot a pattern before it escalates.

If you both feel comfortable with this idea, consider enlisting your partner to warn you when one of your behavior patterns pops up. Since words can easily trigger emotions, I recommend that you and your partner agree on a nonverbal sign. For example, your partner might hold his or her hands in the T sign for "time out."

When your partner does this, you may feel anger or shame. Take a deep breath—or take an actual time out in another room. Over time you will be able to gain perspective and take control.

Be aware that in asking for help from your partner you may be off-loading your own responsibility for your actions. If your partner refuses, it is probably not a lack of willingness to help but perhaps because it feels (and likely is) a trap in which you will take less and less responsibility as your partner takes more.

Use the Undo Feature. If the involuntary behavior is one you can take back, make a practice of doing so as soon as you realize what has happened. For example, if your pattern is to say something hurtful, be sure to apologize and then to say the non-hurtful thing you really want to say. Practicing the right thing will help to cement the new behavior as well as soothe the person you might have hurt. See if your partner will be comfortable with a "do-over." His or her acceptance will further reinforce your healthy behavior.

Unfortunately, with some compulsive behavior patterns—especially those involving anger and violence—apologies and explanations may not be enough, or may even make it "all about you." In those cases, only a very serious investment in change will work.

Recognize Growth. There is a human tendency to discount what we've achieved and focus on what we haven't (the Black Box Motivator in action). But every little step is important, as is recognizing and giving yourself credit for your accomplishments. Try to find a somewhat formal way to congratulate yourself. Keep a journal in which you list what you've done well. Put a gold star on your calendar.

Outflank the Behavior. A trick that can help you deal with emotion-avoiding patterns is an outflanking maneuver or "end run." The steps are simple (though not necessarily easy!):

- Determine what feeling the behavior is meant to avoid.

- Address that feeling in a healthy way so as to starve your old pattern of its reason for existing.

Outflanking a behavior means deliberately bringing an emotion to the surface despite the behavior pattern in place to avoid it. This is a mainstay of talk therapy. For example, if your depression is based on suppressing anger at someone important in your life, bringing the anger out in therapy will help it to heal and will take away much of the power behind the depression.

If your repertoire of behavior includes passive-aggressive patterns in which you express anger indirectly, the solution is again an end run. By acknowledging the anger you can bring the feeling out in the open where it may be possible to process and heal it. Then, the need to act passive-aggressively hurtful will be reduced. (A therapist can be particularly helpful here by pointing out the passive-aggressive pattern if you are unaware of it.)

To summarize, outflanking maneuvers—taking care of the emotion behind a behavior pattern so as to remove its reason for being—won't eliminate habitual behaviors, but it will lessen the drive behind them, making it easier for you to succeed in bringing about change.

Stay Safe. It is important that voluntary behavior change be truly voluntary (stopping drug or alcohol abuse is an exception; see below). Pushing yourself into something that doesn't feel right may fail or worse, backfire. If you have doubts about the safety of a new behavior, honor those doubts and take time to carefully examine the pros and cons of change:

- Are you really ready to try something new?
- Do you believe that the benefits will outweigh the dangers?
- What might you gain from the new behavior?
- What might you lose?
- Is this a good time in your life to be making this change?
- Are you feeling pressured into a change, against doubts?

Taking seriously any concerns you may have will help reduce the stress of voluntary behavior change. If you don't, you may be storing up resentments that can cause trouble later. Hopefully, as you carry out your analysis of the situation, you will discover that your reluctance relates more to your distant past and less to the present.

The right to consent—or not consent—also applies if the change is just too hard or you're just not ready. Even if your partner or therapist is convinced that the change is a good idea, you are the one who has to do the hard work and feel the uncomfortable emotions. Attempting to change works best—and is least stressful—when you control the timetable and can lift your foot from the gas if you find yourself going too fast.

Override Your Inborn Strategy. Although the patterns I have called inborn strategies are involuntary, they don't have to stay that way. Today you may have no control over dysfunctional patterns, but as you work at it, the day may come—and I have seen this many times—when you begin to have some say as to whether you become depressed or afraid. Imagine getting bad news and realizing that you don't have to assume that God or Nature is systematically against you. This skill grows with practice, and it will get easier as you focus on understanding, feeling, and trying out new patterns.

Talk Back to Automatic Thoughts. Your Black Box Motivator thinks that the status quo is much safer and sends you thoughts to steer you away from change. If you recognize them for what they are, it will help you keep moving anyway. Asking someone you trust is the most reliable check on whether the thought is a healthy one or not, but another good test is to ask where the thought is leading you. Does it lead towards positive results, or will it take you a step closer to a goal that is dear to your brain but that you don't want?

Nancy was trying to break out of her isolation. When she was at the grocery, she bumped into a friend. They chatted for a while, then Nancy went back to shopping. She didn't realize how much time she and her friend had spent together, and when she got outside there was a parking ticket on her car. She felt anger start to boil within her, and old messages started flashing in her head: "Just my luck" and "I'm such an idiot."

Nancy said to herself, "Black Box Motivator, I hear you telling me I'm bad. You are wrong. Actually it was a good conversation. It was worth the ticket." Then

> she got into her car, plugged in her earbuds, and started playing one of her
> favorite songs. She could immediately feel her self-esteem coming back. She
> even felt proud of herself for identifying her real source of distress and taking
> action to escape it.

Her automatic thought betrayed its source by its end result. Focusing on making her feel even worse and blaming herself would certainly push Nancy back to isolating. This dead-end thought would only make her feel worse and foster less healthy behavior, not more.

This skill can be tricky to learn. You may feel silly saying nice things to yourself, even though you have plenty of practice saying mean things to yourself! What can you do to learn this skill?

- Tell your old messages, "Thank you, but you're old. I'm moving on."

- Replace the negative thought with one that is more in tune with your true values.

- Keep practicing talking back, even if it feels silly.

Find Cheerleaders. Voluntary behavior change is hard and the tendency to lose sight of original good intentions is strong. Having a rooting section can keep you motivated. Once you share your desire to change with friends and family, many will volunteer for the role of cheerleader. They will want to know how you are doing, and they will cheer you when you do well. Your internal chorus of negativity may not be impressed by your efforts, but words of encouragement from your friends may get through. *Note:* Family members and others sometimes have their own fear of change. If you are getting mixed messages, don't wait for others to change, find people who are wholeheartedly with you.

Parent Your Inner Child. Remember that your fear of change started out a long time ago. Thinking of your inner resistance as a child begging you to stay out of danger will put it in a more accurate perspective. When children are needlessly afraid they need reassurance, and when they can't accept your words, they may need you to apply gentle firmness: "It's okay, come with me and you'll see I am right." On the other hand, if the child is too terrified, you might do better to go slowly. Approaching your inner child with kindness and understanding but clarity that you are the one in charge will put you in the right frame of mind.

Plan for Relapse. Slipping back is part of the game. It is rare not to have an occasional setback. John Norcross rightly suggests having a plan to deal with the inevitable slip.

Hang in for Ninety Days. This is another tip from John Norcross. Research shows that people who can hold to a new behavior for at least ninety days have a much greater chance of keeping it. So don't let your Black Box Motivator tell you it's too much trouble, or that three months is an eternity.

Stay Hopeful. Losing hope is a serious problem. When backlash is making you feel worse rather than better, reach out for help and support. Talk to your role models and cheerleaders and therapist. Focus on the concrete ways your life has improved. Expect some backsliding and leftover consequences of old bad decisions. Don't let your Black Box Motivator tell you your life will never get better. Persistence is very powerful.

Cognitive-behavioral therapists often use charts and written plans to track progress. If this suits your style, it can be a good way to shore up your resolve. And if your gains are modest, consider pushing yourself a little more so that you can see results, even if the work is stressful. When change is too slow, you may get tired before you reach your goal. Once you can actually feel that you are doing better, the whole process becomes easier.

Dealing with Addictions

Unhealthy behavior patterns, such as chemical addiction and compulsive behaviors, take on a life of their own, co-opting our biological survival instincts. Food, sex, and drugs, in addition to their effectiveness in covering up feelings, give a reinforcing shot of dopamine to the pleasure centers in parts of the brain that are intimately involved in our basic survival systems. As mentioned before, the brain undergoes a switch and begins to treat our unhealthy appetites as necessary for the species. When the two forces, biology and emotional needs, team up to hijack our motivational systems, the result is extremely powerful. For this reason, addictions are even more potent than behavior patterns whose original purpose was solely to avoid uncomfortable feelings. Change will require the most powerful tools available.

Behavior Change Comes First. When dealing with addictions, whatever will work to get behavior change started is good. This is where it doesn't matter at first if motivation comes from inside or outside. When you are too close to your last binge of addictive behavior, your brain is just not much help. You don't have to "want to change" to benefit from a planned intervention. In your raw state, going into an inpatient treatment program may be the only effective way to get started. Be willing to do whatever works, and don't kid yourself with halfway measures and substitutes. Moving to another state or starting a program of healthy eating and exercise won't cut it. Substituting another addictive drug or behavior won't work either unless it is a chemical blocker.

Develop a Support System. Since your own free will has been compromised, having an outside support system will help rebalance the forces for change. Twelve step programs remove the excuse of not being able to afford a support system. Even more importantly, other recovering people understand addiction and know a lot about recovery, whereas most lay people simply don't understand how you can "choose" to do the wrong thing.

Make a Plan. You will need a plan for recovery. Every successful recovery program has some kind of organized plan. The reason is that you will need to have a clear definition of the behavior you want to achieve. Without clarity, your Black Box Motivator will find a way to slide past your good intentions. A simple resolution to "cut down" is almost never strong enough to resist the power of addiction.

For drug and alcohol addictions, what works best is to stop the behavior altogether. Black and white are clear, but once you accept gray, your brain will begin playing with "what shade of gray?" until you are back where you started. As people in Alcoholics Anonymous sometimes say, the best approach is the simplest: "Don't drink. Go to meetings." This advice combines behavior change with a simple-looking but really sophisticated approach: substituting healthy human connections for chemical anesthesia.

Since it is impossible to totally stop eating, the Overeaters Anonymous approach is to define "abstinence" as following your personal, clearly defined, food plan.

Embrace Slogans. Slogans boil a lot of other people's experience into a few words. They may seem corny, but when your brain is working overtime to return you to unhealthy behavior, simplicity is power.

> *One day at a time. Fake it till you make it. Don't judge your insides by other people's outsides. The worst day sober is better than the best day high. No day is so bad a drink can't make it worse. Easy does it. First things first.*

Each of these slogans is based on the distilled wisdom of people who have been there.

Beware of Your Bright Ideas. We've discussed the need to beware of the seemingly good ideas your Black Box Motivator may concoct to lead you astray. But how can you tell a healthy idea from an unhealthy one when your brain labels both of them as healthy? Remember, other recovering people and your sponsor don't have your blind spots. If they seem shocked or roll their eyes, your bright idea is probably not one you want to follow. For example, "This experience was so terrible, I'm sure I'll never be tempted again" may feel ironclad to the newly abstinent person, but others will recognize it as the first step towards complacency.

Find Sober/Abstinent Role Models and Friends. Role models and sponsors serve two important purposes. First, they prove that success is possible. There may be times when you will need to be reminded of this fact. Second, when you are deep into an addiction, you probably can't imagine what life sober would be like. You might imagine a yawning abyss of boredom or an endless obstacle course of pain. If, however, you have sober/abstinent role models, you can see that their lives are far from boring, that they often experience joy and happiness, and most importantly, that they continue to grow and heal.

The most powerful tool for recovery from addictive behaviors is human connection. Our need for fellowship has almost as much evolutionary weight behind it as the need for physical sustenance. Joining others in recovery is a way to harness this deep, biological source of motivational power to bolster your commitment to work against addiction. To get an idea of the power of fellowship, consider soldiers charging forward in the face of gunfire. Do they do so out of patriotism? No. They do it to support the other members of their platoon. Fellowship is that important, which is why it is one of the few things that can outweigh your compulsion.

References

Linden, D.E.J. "How Psychotherapy Changes the Brain—the Contribution of Functional Neuroimaging." *Molecular Psychiatry* 11 (2006): 528–38.

Norcross, John C. *Changeology: 5 Steps to Realizing Your Goals and Resolutions. New York:* Simon and Schuster, 2012.

· **7** ·

DREAMS AND QUESTS

How dreams, quests, and ambitions can
cover up feelings, too.

Dreams are what fuel our greatest accomplishments. Even when they are improbable, they spur us to reach for the sky and surprise ourselves with what we can do. When they are crushed, we mourn deeply because these are often the things that mean the most to us in all the world. We do well to nurture them in others and to listen to them in ourselves. However, dreams can also go awry. This chapter is about dreams that doom us to fighting ourselves.

The behavior patterns described in the last chapter were the best solutions we could come up with when we invented them. They helped avoid and cover up pain and gave us the hope of getting our grownups to rescue us. Unfortunately, those approaches were costly. Keeping feelings out of our own awareness means loosening our grip on reality. Trying to change others who don't want to change is one of the least rewarding of all human activities. Approaches born of desperation often have desperate consequences.

When we are around five years old, however, cognitive development opens the door to a completely new technique for dealing with insurmountable challenges. Utilizing our newly developed capacity to imagine a distant future, we can picture a scenario so wonderful that our pain will vanish. Even if we don't have the strength or power to solve our problems in the present, we can create hope by imagining a future where we will gain all the strength and power we might need. Imagination doesn't compromise reality, for anything is possible. We can tell ourselves, "Yes, it is bad today, but someday I'll be older, more beautiful, stronger, more powerful, and then my dreams will surely come true!"

Someday

Around age five children begin to take an interest in fairy tales that start with "Once upon a time" and end with "happily ever after"—that is, stories about a rich future, such as poor mistreated Cinderella marrying the prince and becoming a queen. Rather suddenly, the dimension of time gives a fullness to imagination beyond anything that was possible before. Soon we imagine our own "somedays." And if we believe that we will become a princess, a soldier, a rock star, or president, no one can say with certainty that it won't really happen.

Younger children, before age five, are fully capable of imagination. But their fantasies consist of images lacking the dimension of time. In the here and now, they picture something great that gives momentary satisfaction at the expense of reality. Imagining you are a superhero feels good to younger children, but soon it gets hard not to realize that you are just a kid. With a growing grip on reality, the truth of being small and having limited power becomes all the more painful. Finally at about five and a half, the ability to see oneself in the distant future becomes possible. Add the dimension of time to a wish-fulfilling fantasy and you have an entirely new creation. As Piaget says, "Grasping time is tantamount to freeing oneself from the present."

Jean Piaget (1896-1980)

Piaget was a developmental psychologist and philosopher who pioneered understanding of children's cognitive development.

Soon the image of future achievement acquires intention. And intention turns to determination: "I will be…" As in fairy tales, there are steps along the way. Fantasy begins to acquire the attributes of a plan, a series of willful actions leading to the end result. What is a journey leading to a goal? A *quest*. Under good conditions, five-year-olds', someday plans or quests are often beginnings that lead to real adult accomplishments and even careers.

Naturally the plans of five-year-olds need adjusting. For example, the plan to become a princess might evolve into an interest in high fashion and a career as a clothing designer. The plan to become a pro baseball player might evolve into a lifetime of athletic activity. Some plans don't need to be adjusted at all; many doctors, teachers, writers, and others will tell you that they have always known what they were destined to be. And, of course, a few people actually do become princesses and professional athletes. The variations are endless because the ambitions that suit the needs of children are endless.

When Plans Are Buried

It sounds as though five-year-olds have found the solution to life's problems, with an eternal source of hope. There is a lot of truth to this, especially when the plan takes its place in the conscious mind. Most of us have such plans. There are even some plans that don't make it into consciousness but stay quietly in the background, energizing our teen and adult efforts without our knowing quite what we are looking for. These, too, can be a magical source of energy and creativity. But this is not always the case. Sometimes, quests become hidden or buried because of shame or guilt. When that happens, following the principle that "what isn't conscious doesn't change," healing and growth are blocked. When they are actively hidden from consciousness, quests become frozen in time, retaining the imprint of a child's mind.

The problem is that some of the most highly valued five-year-old plans are also the least acceptable. What if a quest is shameful or prohibited from within? Such plans can be pushed out of consciousness or "repressed." The freezer effect then takes hold, keeping the childhood quest unmodified by reality. Do such plans stay entirely dormant? No. Without our knowledge, they have access to the our motivational system. The mind waits, scanning for opportunities at last to put the plan into action. First steps are tentative and partial. For this reason, it will not be apparent where they are leading. The mind is expert in the art of "one thing leads to another." One small, disguised step leads to the next, and only after many steps have been taken, can we begin to guess where they were heading.

If this sounds like the work of the Black Box Motivator, it is. After all, that is the part of the mind that is in charge of producing thoughts and impulses leading in directions perceived as essential for life. In this way, covert and forbidden plans continue to influence our feelings and behavior while failing to keep up with adult realities.

Even as a child, Valerie had known that her parents were too young and immature to handle the job of parenting. Their lives were all about parties and socializing, and they spent little time focusing on Valerie's needs. So Valerie made a plan: someday she would find a prince who would give her the guidance and discipline that was missing in her life. He would love her endlessly and would need nothing but her limitless love. He was the essence of a father and a prince charming rolled into one.

This fantasy remained with Valerie into adulthood as an unconscious plan, leaving her with a significant problem: No real man could ever satisfy her. She was looking for a man who would be both the parent she didn't have and the mate she dreamed of. Unaware that her feelings were, literally, childish, she was disappointed with every man she dated. When she finally did marry, her husband was unable to fulfill her unrealistic dream, and the marriage ended in divorce. Valerie went back to searching in vain for the perfect man.

Hiding the Plan

Sometimes as five-year-olds we hide our plans because we fear they are shameful or "bad"—that is, we suspect that our parents would not cooperate or might even find them unacceptable. As discussed in Chapter 5, as children we can set up value systems as internal electric fences to counter our own desires and help us to resist temptation. When we cross or even go near those fences, shame and/or guilt set in, keeping us from acting on wishes—or plans—that we think we shouldn't have.

But we can't fully relinquish the plans we make as five-year-olds. After all, these quests are the ultimate solutions to our problems, providing the happiness and security we most want and need. They are central to our emotional survival. Somehow we manage to keep them alive. Even against our conscience and strong values, we continue to harbor secret desires to carry out our plans.

The end result of any attempt to relinquish our cherished plans is banishment from consciousness, not elimination. Even though they may be hidden, buried, and lost from awareness, they are far from abandoned. Despite an uneasy sense of guilt or shame, our minds remain secretly on the lookout for opportunities to execute all or parts of our plans which can go on indefinitely.

Can such a quest still influence us, even in our fifties or later? Absolutely, and this is one of the things that convinces me that the dimension of time is an integral part of our buried quests. Not infrequently, the only apparent reason for a plan coming to the surface is that an older adult senses, on some level, that time is running out. Suddenly out of nowhere, late in life, decisions are contemplated that seem driven only by the sense that we must act now or forever lose our chance. Thus at age fifty a man who had always been faithful suddenly initiates an affair with a woman he has admired since his twenties.

Reenacting Unfinished Business

How can we tell that such a plan is smoldering somewhere under the surface? The hallmark is that our most cherished goals repeatedly slip through our fingers. Perhaps something always goes wrong with our intimate relationships. Or perhaps we can't quite reach our career goals. Maybe we convince ourselves that we have bad luck—or maybe we suspect the truth, that we are actually sabotaging ourselves. Whatever the specifics, there is a strong chance that we are unknowingly trying to solve problems we couldn't solve when we were five by reenacting unfinished business from the past. The reenactment includes both the unfinished plan to find happiness and in addition the guilt-driven need to make sure the plan is never executed.

Just as our plans haven't evolved, neither have the value systems set up to block their execution—and our Black Box Motivator is representing both sides. The mind is set on fulfilling our quest, and at the same time it is making sure that our prohibition is respected. The result? Just as we are about to achieve a desired outcome, we make some fatal miscalculation. We choose the wrong person or make a wrong move. Our Black Box Motivator is protecting us from the painful feelings of guilt or shame, just as it is supposed to do.

Guilt and shame are only part of the reason for repeated failures. Cliffhangers in movies and books are only satisfying when the hero or heroine is genuinely trapped—for example, the innocent girl is tied to the tracks in the middle of nowhere, just when a train is coming. Similarly, our reenactments, to be fully satisfying, must resemble precisely the childhood problems that long ago couldn't be solved. Take, for example, a girl who wanted to win the love of a father who couldn't connect. As an adult she will very likely seek out a man who also has trouble making connections. Her plan is to win his love, but she has chosen just the person with whom emotional intimacy is impossible. Created to overcome the disappointments of youth, our quests are crafted to prove that what seemed impossible then might actually be attainable. Triumph can only come if our reenactments are every bit as dire and unworkable as the original situation. Predictably, the result is not triumph but yet another failure.

Snatching Defeat from the Jaws of Victory

The happy ending we secretly hoped for doesn't happen. Is that the end? Do we stop setting up reenactments? Of course not. To give up would mean facing the feeling of hopelessness that we couldn't deal with in childhood. Instead, our plans go underground again while we continue to scan for new opportunities. As the cycle repeats, once again we end up snatching defeat from the jaws of victory. Here is an in-depth look at how this works:

As a child, Lawrence suffered because his parents were self-centered and unavailable to him. They also had loud, angry fights, and Lawrence's father would storm out of the house. Each time this happened, Lawrence feared that his father would never come back.

At around four years of age, Lawrence developed a wish to find comfort in physical contact with his mother. He saw his parents in bed together each morning, getting along well, and he came to associate their bed with a comforting and satisfying place. He was also curious about his mother's body and wanted to explore. By five he understood that these wishes would not be well received. His father might go into one of his rages. His mother would very likely say, "What do you think you are doing?"

Did Lawrence give up on his wishes? Certainly not. He built them into a quest. Someday he would be rich and strong and he would woo his mother away from his father, who was usually angry with her anyway. He would charm his mother in all the ways his father couldn't. She would be so pleased and impressed that she would allow him to explore as much as he wished. (If this sounds to you like Oedipus, you are right, but the details are unique.)

Lawrence kept his plan secret but he added more details. Along with being rich, he would be famous—he knew that would impress his mother. And when he was grown up and strong, his mother would not be dismissive of his interest in her, as he knew she would be of his five-year-old's desire to explore.

Soon, Lawrence's plan became buried in his unconscious. At the same time, his superego internalized a prohibition against sexual exploration. He went through his grade-school years with little interest in bodies, though he did have a lot of curiosity about other things. As he came into puberty he was not attracted to his mother, but he still felt uneasy about his sexuality. He believed that there is nothing wrong with sex or with wanting sex, but he still harbored an uncomfortable feeling that there was something inappropriate about his particular desires.

Without realizing it, Lawrence was attracted to girls who reminded him of his mother. He wanted to touch them, but the guilt he internalized remained, leaving him somewhat shy and inhibited. He felt that the girls he found attractive wouldn't be attracted to him. He imagined they would say, "What do you think you are doing?" Again he fantasized about becoming rich and successful so that he would be able to attract a woman who would love him the way he wasn't loved long ago.

Lawrence married and built a good career, but he now feels that he can't satisfy his wife because he's not successful enough. He continues to worry that his sexual wishes are somehow bad, and he feels like a fraud at work even though others clearly don't see him that way.

This case is a little different from those described in earlier chapters. Like a hidden agenda, the quest is ultimately aimed at changing the adults. But this time it is by earning or winning the adult's willingness. Furthermore, the surface manifestations are not so obvious and the reasons are not so apparent. On the surface, Lawrence seems quite intact. He is professionally successful, though not as much as he might wish. His marriage appears as good as any. But he remains subtly unhappy. The traditional word for problems like this is *neurosis*, referring to emotional problems that are less severe and, more precisely, built around unresolvable conflict between a person's ambitious quest and his internal prohibition.

What we see on the surface is a pattern of wishes or ambitions that are never quite fulfilled. When we examine closely the thoughts and feelings around these, we can begin to discern a childlike quality. Lawrence worried about being "bad." Asked what that meant, he couldn't come up with a rational adult idea. This is similar to the earlier example of Valerie. When asked to describe her ideal of a husband, she became uncomfortable to hear herself describe qualities far beyond those of any normal adult.

Neurosis

Usually neurosis refers to milder emotional problems that can still ruin lives. In this book it refers to dysfunctional patterns in which we somehow defeat ourselves when trying to achieve our cherished quest.

Slipping and Sliding Away

To paraphrase a famous Paul Simon lyric, the closer you get to your goal, the more you find yourself slipping away. The exact thing the individual wants most in life is what he or she is somehow never going to achieve. This is the telltale sign of a buried quest.

J. Paul Getty, who was thought to be the richest man of his time, said, "I hate to be a failure. I hate and regret the failure of my marriages. I would gladly give all my millions for just one lasting marital success." Could it be that his quest was really for forbidden love?

The Patient–Therapist Relationship

From its beginning over a century ago, traditional psychoanalysis has focused especially on the subtle emotional symptoms that grow out of our inner five-year-old's plans. Psychoanalytic therapists have sought to understand the relatively complex and hidden ideas, conflicts, fantasies, and wishes that underlie these symptoms. Over time, traditional talk therapy and psychoanalysis have developed techniques especially adapted to deal with resistance to discovering our buried quests.

Free Association

Our minds work to produce an almost constant stream of spontaneous thoughts. Cognitive-behavioral therapists see these thoughts as sources of error that need to be corrected. Freud, among the first to take a serious interest in what he called free associations, saw these as a window into the unconscious world. In the terms of this book, these same thoughts are the outputs of our Black Box Motivator, dutifully steering us towards the goals it considers vital to our lives. These conscious products are probably the closest we will come to actually knowing the quests and prohibitions that presumably occupy the inaccessible reaches of the mind.

As discussed, when we try to get healthier our Black Box Motivator fights harder to maintain the status quo. Since therapy inevitably moves towards change, our stream of spontaneous thoughts soon gathers intensity. The more we try to change, the more our Black Box Motivator senses an impending clash and sends us thoughts, impulses, and rationalizations to dissuade us. Since our buried quests are prohibited, spontaneous thoughts from both sides—that is, desire and conscience—become more insistent. For those in therapy, it is fortunate that these same thoughts constitute the best clues we have for understanding how our deepest ambitions and strongest values might be at war with each other.

The Relationship

Even more powerful than free association is Freud's next tool: the patient–therapist relationship. Freud found that this relationship is fertile ground for reenactment of unfinished business from childhood, providing a glimpse into what early life really felt like. As we have seen in the earlier discussion of transference, this reenactment provides not only a window on the past but also an opportunity to resolve what could never be resolved before.

The therapeutic relationship is a place where hope of wish fulfillment brings desire out into the open. With increasing intensity, wishes as well as guilt and shame become clear and explicit. This makes the therapeutic relationship an ideal stage on which to bring out the subtleties and complexities of someday quests and the values or prohibitions that oppose them. The dramas that unfold in the consulting room are most often about relationships. Here, the therapist can play any and all roles. Since five-year-old quests were buried because they were not acceptable, they necessarily involve conflict, and the conflict soon engulfs the therapeutic relationship. How does this look and feel?

Recall that emotional problems start with needs whose fulfillment is somehow impossible in childhood. Five-year-olds gain the ability to translate their needs into a vision of an improved self and more willing others. But when the vision is clouded by shame or guilt, and goes underground, the force of the conscience remains locked in opposition to fulfillment of the quest.

In the human mind (as in families), roles are relatively freely exchanged. In therapy, the therapist can be cast in the role of the source of fulfillment or, just as easily, in the role of the killjoy conscience. With a good deal of fluidity, these positions can change from moment to moment. In practice this fluidity is not as confusing as it might seem; a small number of configurations will soon become familiar, allowing patient and therapist to gain familiarity and understanding.

Wish Meets Disapproval

As five-year-olds we buried our plans because we believed our wishes would be met with disapproval. At first, presumably, there was the actual experience or expectation of disapproval, anger, even danger. As described in Chapter 5, an internal electric fence was soon constructed with an internalized prohibition saying that our wish is "bad" and should never be granted. From here on, attempts to seek fulfillment are met with firm resistance from the conscience, enforced by feelings of shame and guilt. Does this stop the desire? No, nor does it stop secret efforts to find a compromise or some alternate way to succeed. Under such superego pressure, no such intentions will be expressed openly or gain consciousness.

Faced with such disapproval, shame, and guilt, what would you expect a five-year-old to do? Naturally the child resorts to guerrilla warfare. She goes underground and watches for an opening. The therapy situation presents itself as just such an opening. Here is a grownup who is amazingly interested. Maybe he will be open to influence. To avoid experiencing shame or guilt, she starts with very subtle hints, so subtle that neither she nor the therapist can guess what they mean. As the hints are ignored, instead of giving up, she redoubles her efforts. The intensity level rises. She realizes that carrying out the plan will require a bolder approach.

At this point, we, our therapist, and our inner child have incompatible goals. Therapists want to understand us and to help us let our feelings come to the surface where they can be resolved by catharsis. Our adult self agrees with the therapist. We crave understanding in order to make sense of how our lives work—and don't work. Our inner child, however, wants desperately to avoid shame and guilt, and yet succeed in winning over the therapist to her cause. So she keeps her plans to herself and works to thwart any attempt by the therapist and our adult self to gain understanding. If the therapist knew, he would surely disapprove. With no idea that any resolution other than successfully carrying out the plan is possible, our inner child continues to try covertly to get the therapist, the grownup in our drama, to see the child's point of view and grant fulfillment of the quest. Fortunately, therapists are facilitators, not solutions!

The Black Box Motivator Enters

The increasing tension engages our Black Box Motivator to produce an array of thoughts, dreams, and impulses that reflect the concerns of all of our different parts, albeit in disguised forms. These products of the mind point ever more clearly at what is really going on inside us. Hopefully an alert therapist helps our adult realize that something is taking place under the surface. As we listen to the "chatter" coming from the Black Box, our understanding can advance, even while our inner children grow more frustrated.

The Therapist—Inner Child Relationship

Let's take a closer look at the interaction between the inner child and the therapist. From the child's point of view, the therapist is giving mixed signals, on one hand being encouraging and trying to understand the inner child, but on the other hand taking no action to support fulfillment of the quest. The child becomes more and more frustrated and eventually concludes that, like the child's parent, the therapist doesn't *want* to say yes. This is a perfect recreation of the original problem, and the inner child redoubles her efforts to overcome the therapist's unwillingness to move from no to yes.

This may sound clear and straightforward but that's not how it feels. Our inner child's thoughts and feelings are rationalized as they filter into consciousness. What can't be said directly in its original form is translated into a form that seems more reasonable. Sooner or later we manage to find a "real" issue with the therapist. The issue may be trivial, but we respond with an intensity of feeling more in sync with the childhood need. The conflict that results feels very real. A good example is the patient who quit therapy after several years because her analyst refused to adjust the thermostat.

You and Your Inner Child May Disagree

Under any circumstances, moving the discussion from the therapist's "bad" behavior to the patient's childhood plan is a delicate operation when feelings are strong. One patient was furious with her therapist for taking vacation at Christmas time. How could he, a supposedly sensitive person, take vacation at such a difficult time for his patient? At the time she would not have been at all ready to hear that her anger had more to do with past neglect than with her therapist's judgment. Fortunately, before it comes to this kind of confrontation, there are usually hints of what is coming. That is the time to lay the groundwork for identifying and dealing with the inner child's feelings of anger and disappointment before they are so intense that they threaten the therapy. Hopefully, with a positive history between patient and therapist and some advance warning, when the disappointment surfaces it can be healed by catharsis rather than a breakup of the relationship.

In real life the drama plays out in steps such as these:

- The patient expresses disappointment with the therapist.
- The therapist replies with answers that satisfy only the (adult) patient.
- The inner child is not satisfied, taking the therapist's response as a refusal to understand or change.
- The inner child vows to persist and becomes even more secretive.

- The inner child finds an issue (something like the temperature in the office) that the adult also sees as important and brings it up with the therapist.

- The therapist is kind and open to discussing the issue, but the inner child becomes more and more convinced that the therapist is covering up another self-centered, unhelpful refusal, just as the patient's parents did so many years earlier.

These interactions between the therapist and the adult patient are intense, because the inner child believes that his or her needs and survival are at stake, as they were years ago. It takes a lot of open talk and catharsis before patient and therapist can honestly and accurately sort out what happened. That is what I mean by working things out.

When you do work things out, the plan and the feelings that go with it will be clear and accessible to catharsis. It will be possible for the patient to reshape expectations and look for fulfillment of needs that are more appropriate to adult life.

Therapists Are Human

The interaction is intense and emotionally engaging. In spite of their training and self-awareness, therapists can unwittingly become caught up in the action. This is why boundaries are so important within the relationship. As long as impulses and wishes do not result in action, then harm is much less likely. A therapist who is able to acknowledge his or her personal reaction will help the patient gain clarity about his or hers. Clarifying the situation may take genuine openness and self-examination on the part of the therapist. This process will be worthwhile for both the therapist and the patient, because clarity is necessary to understand the patient's inner child and secret plan.

The Scale of Young Wishes

The inner child expresses very young wishes, and the ones that first become visible are only trial balloons. Filtered by consciousness, they seem modest and plausible. "Would you mind if I sat in the other chair this time?" This minor request might be a test of the therapist's willingness to change and of whether the wish itself is a "bad" thing. What the inner child really wants to know is this: Will the therapist take over where the parent failed? Of course the answer is no.

This seems simple enough. Therapists are there to help us find fulfillment of our needs, not to be the ones who fulfill them. But the problem is actually much bigger than that. Childhood wishes, just like childhood feelings, are very big. Similarly, the younger the wish, the larger its scale. The inner child, being a child, has boundless wishes. They are on the scale of what children *perceive* that parents can do for them, which may be beyond what parents can really do and very far from what adults do for one another. Valerie wanted not only the perfect husband but also an ideal parent, one who would nurture her growth and development and protect her from pain and adversity while making no demands.

As therapy brings wishes to the surface and as they become more intense, their true scope becomes more apparent. The intensity and the breadth of the child's wishes keep expanding until the therapist's "no" recapitulates the original failure, completing the reenactment.

Adult Solutions to Childhood Plans

What is the solution to this seemingly impossible dilemma? The problems of our inner child, the ones that cause emotional ramifications far into adult life, persist because what we once needed was so vital to growth and development that acceptance of defeat was not a consideration. That's why our inner child is still trying to get grownups to fix our problems: we want to fulfill our potential the only way we know how. The inner child simply can't imagine another solution.

In order to resolve the problem, the inner child must realize that the solution is for the *self* to change, not the therapist. This is totally revolutionary. Having spent a lifetime trying to influence others, your inner five-year-old finds that the therapist, the only "other" who seemed even slightly open to seeing the light, is definitively not going to change. The only answer is for the child somehow to do the work. This realization is naturally met with a great deal of anger and disappointment, all the more because it echoes the parents' original "unwillingness." But what is "the work"?

To the inner child, "doing the work" means having to supply one's own love, support, encouragement, discipline, etc. These are things children can't do for themselves, so the child is right to be disappointed. But in therapy, the work means something very different. As an adult, having somehow grown up in spite of whatever was missing, the work means grieving for what we didn't have, grieving for the parts of the quest that will never be fulfilled, and, finally, accepting that we must make the best of what we have.

Solving Your Inner Child's Pain

Even if therapists can't be the solution as originally envisioned, through catharsis they can help resolve our inner child's pain by understanding it and being a witness to the real anguish of failing to gain something we cherished and believed was an absolute need. The therapist can help us understand that there are other options, and that we can make many of our wishes/dreams come true, though likely in different ways than we may have imagined.

Lawrence, the man who thinks he has to be rich and famous to impress women, tells his analyst about going to an important event filled with famous people. Without realizing it, he is trying to impress her as the first step in carrying out his inner child's plan.

Lawrence's unconscious inner conversation goes like this: "Did she notice? She doesn't seem impressed. Maybe she senses that I want something from her that I shouldn't even wish for." Lawrence's plan goes back underground. Will his inner child give up? No, but his next attempt will be more careful.

Lawrence tells his analyst about his dream of a brightly colored bird hopping on one foot. The analyst asks for his associations, and Lawrence admits that the bird is himself and that he is showing off. He tells her that he feels shame. The feeling dissipates (catharsis working here).

> *Lawrence and the therapist discuss his reasons for showing off. This leads to*
> *the next cycle of feelings and wishes coming to the surface and being clarified.*

What if both Lawrence and his analyst failed to pick up on Lawrence's clues? Lawrence's attempts to impress the analyst would have become more intense and desperate. His dreams and thoughts would have become more vivid (to get her attention) but less obvious (to avoid feeling shame). His level of anxiety would continue to rise, and his inner child's plan for changing the therapist would continue to intrude on both his and the therapist's ability to elucidate his needs. If neither person figured out what was going on, disappointment would likely lead to anger and then perhaps depression, and ultimately to giving up on therapy. Sadly, this sort of impasse is one of the most common reasons for the failure of psychotherapy.

On the other hand, when an analyst and patient do catch one of these potential moments of healing and turn it into insight, the patient is presented with a new chance for growth. Here's how it worked out for Lawrence:

> *Reluctantly at first, Lawrence began to be able to share his need for attention*
> *from the analyst and feel the pain of not receiving the total attention he*
> *wished for. He began to grieve for both the attention he craved and the love he*
> *hadn't received as a child. He began to accept that his idea of how to get love*
> *was actually misguided (not surprising for a five-year-old's idea).*

> *Lawrence reevaluated his ambition of being super-successful as he learned*
> *that, in his adult world, love was not as hard to win as he thought. He came to*
> *accept that he didn't really need the analyst's love or even her approval. Over*
> *a long period he was able, step by step, to go through the feelings of loss for*
> *what he could never have and to reevaluate his quest.*

> *Lawrence began to do the slow work of changing his unhealthy superego*
> *prohibitions against sex and success, knowing that they were created in a*
> *context that was no longer applicable. He became able to use the skills he had*
> *honed in his search for unlimited success and apply them to more appropriate*
> *adult ambitions.*

Chances to Grow

Deciphering and outgrowing the buried someday plans five-year-old is challenging and sometimes painful, but we gain endless chances to grow and seek out all that life has to offer.

Next Steps: You and Your Plans

Do You Have to Be in Therapy? More than any of the types of problems discussed in this book, someday plans are subtle, hidden, and hard to uncover. For this reason, in-depth therapy is the ideal place to resolve them. However, there is much you can do to open yourself to know your inner wishes and plans. Consider this a prelude to therapy, because going all the way to resolution is usually not something you can do on your own. It is simply too easy to get lost in your own mind's blindness.

Slipping Away. How can you identify the someday plans of your inner five-year-old? Do you find that your most cherished goals are, time and time again, slipping from your grasp?

What do you want more than anything? Because repeated failure to achieve what you want most is the best clue to a hidden quest, write an Autobiography of Near-Misses. Look for patterns. Do you sabotage yourself? Do you wonder if you will ever get there? Do you keep telling yourself, "someday"?

The true meaning of your inner child's plans is likely to be buried in shame and guilt, so you may not find clear answers. Don't dig too deep: that will engage your intellect when it is your inner child who needs to become ready to talk. The goal is not to analyze but to encourage your inner child to reveal his or her secrets. What awaits is a trade-off, but one in which you are the winner. Trade in fantasy wishes that can never be fulfilled for dreams that are real.

Following Your Inner Plan. Think of yourself as working to liberate your own inner plan. It is true in general that one of the best ways to succeed in life is to follow the path that reflects what is dearest to your heart. Your inner plan is the one with all the energy and passion, so following it will ultimately contribute to the success you have been looking for. Doing the things in life that hold the most meaning for you can release a level of drive that would not be available otherwise.

This is a well-known truth, which is why self-help books frequently address finding and following your own personal path. And it's not just the self-help books: I once heard a minister explain that the way to know God's will is to identify the things that are most deeply meaningful to you.

What Is Your Real Purpose In Life? As suggested by personal development blogger Steve Pavlina (www.stevepavlina.com), write a list of everything you might want to do, not just careers. Include fantasies and far-fetched ideas—at this stage, the goal is to listen to your deepest wishes, not to edit them. Which touch you the most? When you come to the one that makes you cry, that's the one.

Put yourself in the mind of the five-year-old you. Do your most private ambitions bear signs of a much younger you than you might wish? Are they unrealistically grand? If so, what would those ambitions have brought to you as a child? What are the needs that have been neglected? Are those needs really so impossible? Are you afraid to go for what you really want? Is it really bad? Is it really shameful to have ambitions?

This exercise is aimed at opening doors. It's best if you look at this dialog with your inner self as getting practice being the adult who tells you "Yes!"

Reference

Jean-Blaise, J. Piaget, F. Orsini, et al. *The Child's Conception of Time.* Translated by A.J. Pomerans. New York: Basic Books, 1969.

· 8 ·

ARRESTED DEVELOPMENT

*About emotional development, how its arrest can cover
feelings, and a look at three critical periods*

Whether we are 15 or 50 or 105, we can still grow and develop. It's
not fun facing our flaws and immaturity, but all it takes is some
bravery and determination.

We all have an area, or areas, where we wish we had greater maturity or, to borrow Daniel Goleman's phrase, "emotional intelligence."
We might hate talking on the phone or feel uncomfortable when
not in control. We might cry too easily or have trouble making firm
decisions. We laugh when Jerry Seinfeld jokes about his characters'
immaturity, but we are ashamed of our own. We may try to ignore
our shortcomings, telling ourselves, "That's just the way I am." In the
end, though, we will do better to face our immaturity and go forward. This chapter is about emotional development and how facing
feelings is once again the key to healing and growth.

Daniel Goleman (1946-)

Goleman, a psychologist and journalist, authored the highly influential
1995 book *Emotional Intelligence*, arguing that success in life depends on
skill with emotions and relationships as much as cognitive ability.

About Emotional Development

When we think of psychological development, we traditionally think in terms of stages. Stage-based models provide useful guidelines, but they shouldn't be applied too rigidly. What's more, we can be at different stages at the same time. For example, a top executive or even CEO might be better than most at handling decisions under pressure and yet have great difficulty coping when he or she is not in control. Part of our psyche can be stuck in a childhood stage while the rest has moved on.

Another way to think of development is that each of us has a portfolio of developmental acquisitions. The way we come by these acquisitions does tend to be sequential, with each development building on previous ones. But developmental arrest is more likely to affect only certain areas, leaving others to keep moving forward. A definition of emotional development might be this: *the semi-ordered acquisition of emotional skills that tend to build on one another.*

It's also important to remember that we experience physical, hormonal, and brain development along with psychological development and that each of these can influence the others. Adolescent hormonal changes regularly upset teens' psychological balance, and create new challenges for the young person and the parents.

Development and Our Motivational Apparatus

Not surprisingly, our entire motivational apparatus seems to regard growth and development as highly important for the survival of the species, especially where it concerns our social milieu. The first level of motivation, the pleasure/pain system, provides intense pleasure when we find new power and freedom. Our conscience, based on valuing maturation as a social asset, further rewards us with feelings of pride when we see ourselves capable of new skills. Both of these pleasurable feelings influence our free will to try more. Of course, the contrary is also possible. When attempts to grow meet failure or when newly acquired abilities are discouraged or criticized, we may lose our motivation to grow.

It is hard to overemphasize the role of the conscience. Our superego measures us according to internalized standards and gives out feelings of shame or pride according to our values. We naturally have very strong values favoring growth and development and as a result, we experience feelings of pride when we advance, and powerful shame when we fail. As we will see very soon, shame related to our immaturity can be one of the greatest barriers to growth.

The third level of our motivational apparatus, the Black Box Motivator, is right there playing both sides. It is ready to provide us with thoughts and impulses aimed at driving us forward in development, but it is just as alert to protect us from possible failure and pain. In the latter case, it will shower us with good reasons *not* to try anything new or unfamiliar. This, of course, can lead to our avoiding new experiences, which in turn results in areas of arrested development.

Can We Really Grow at Any Age?

Can development really take place at any age? Yes. One strong piece of evidence is that older people succeed in adapting to huge changes. We almost take it for granted that seniors can handle gigantic changes like moving from a lifelong home or dealing with widowhood or facing a terminal illness. These are among the largest emotional challenges that any human can be expected to meet, yet the majority of older people adapt and do so with grace. Yes, old dogs certainly can and do learn new tricks.

Restarting Development

All that is required to restart is to try new behaviors and experience the feelings that once were—but are no longer—beyond our capability. In doing so, once again we use catharsis to make the feelings manageable. We don't have to unlearn or let go of anything but our fear of new experience. Growth, even when delayed, is still accompanied by the excitement and pleasure of new experiences. We naturally value "growing up," so our conscience even rewards our efforts with feelings of pride.

The Biggest Obstacle: Shame

With all these positive factors favoring emotional growth, why do we still hold onto old, immature ways? Paradoxically, the first barrier to growing is our pride. In childhood our superego internalizes such a strong value on being "grown up" that admitting to be less than fully mature makes us feel ashamed and inadequate. The main barrier to emotional growth is accepting that we are not fully mature.

Do you remember how proud you felt when your grandfather exclaimed how big you had grown? Do you remember trying hard not to cry when you skinned your knee? When we are young, we internalize values around the importance of growing, maturing, and gaining self-control. Even as adults, when we become aware of acting immature, our conscience mounts a chorus of shame.

What our superegos don't know is that problems with development and maturity are very fixable. Ironically, it is the superego itself that gets in the way of repair. Shame makes us reluctant to admit and face our developmental shortcomings. Denial blocks us from growing. Once we get past the shame, we can grow and change using the same tools discussed in Chapter 6: practicing new behaviors and going through the feelings that result.

Perhaps the key to growth is to discover kindness towards the less mature parts of ourselves. Think of how you might approach a three-year-old beaming with pride for having dressed himself, but with his pants on backwards? This is not a time for shaming, but for understanding and warmth. The same goes for our own immaturity.

Emotional growth and development is a lifetime project. Each new experience or challenge adds something to the person we have become. We seek new experiences for the same reasons as always: growing is exciting, interesting, and pleasurable. Once we are past the barrier of shame, resuming neglected growth has the same positive qualities that accompany any new discovery.

Development Compared to Dysfunctional Behavior Patterns

How we acquire emotional skills is in many ways similar to voluntary behavior change as discussed in Chapter 6. The difference is that the discussion of dysfunctional behavior patterns focused on individual adaptation to specific problems, whereas development focuses on general solutions to problems that we all face.

Furthermore, the patterns of Chapter 6 were dysfunctional habit structures, aimed at avoidance of painful and uncomfortable feelings. In contrast, developmental skills are positive patterns that continue to be effective in minimizing discomfort and maximizing pleasure and satisfaction in life. Failure to develop, or arrested development, represents the absence of such positive behavior patterns.

In Chapter 6, voluntary behavior change was presented as a way of unmasking feelings that were once beyond our coping ability and then using adult assets to face them and heal. What was challenging about change was our natural resistance to encountering feelings. Development also requires facing uncomfortable feelings. This time, however, discomfort is a natural accompaniment of the unfamiliar, counterbalanced by the pleasure and excitement of doing something new.

Not infrequently, excitement is replaced by dread. In addition to our natural fear of the unknown, we may have had unfortunate experiences making us believe that what is new is not safe. Greater inborn sensitivity to discouragement may take the shine off discovery. Similarly, when success is blocked by circumstances or personal limitations we can become discouraged and prone to protecting ourselves by not trying. These are times when parts of development may be sacrificed in the interest of safety and comfort.

Growing should be fun. Feelings of pleasure are a large part of what motivates us to grow and develop as young people. As we overcome the shame that makes us reluctant to admit our immaturity, we can begin to enjoy the positive feelings built into our motivational system to assure our psychological development. If the feeling of risk and dread is too strong, then we need to seek out safe people and places so that trying new behaviors does become the thrilling adventure it was meant to be.

An Outline of Emotional Development

Innocent Obliviousness (0-6 mo.)

During the first months of life, babies are highly sophisticated at catching the attention of caregivers and getting their needs met. Starting with inborn reflexes, they busily develop schemas based on the pleasure/pain system of their motivational apparatus to maximize pleasurable activities and minimize pain. Very early there is evidence that they react differently to the primary caregiver, but they don't generally exhibit fear of strangers or of aloneness. Those come at the end of the period and signal the next phase.

This phase does not include words or symbolic meaning, but associations are being laid down. The "obliviousness" of this period gives the baby some insulation from unhealthy relationship dynamics that may be going on in the family. The main dangers are gross neglect or abuse.

Separation and Individuation (6mo. - 3 years)

This is Margaret Mahler's term for the critical period during which the child in some way grasps his or her separateness and vulnerability and learns to navigate the perils of depending on someone we can't control. The first indication of this new phase is the child's showing distress at being left alone or put in the arms of a stranger. These reactions indicate some kind of awareness of vulnerability. In some way the innocent obliviousness of the baby is broken forever. The solution is for the baby to begin to depend on the process of communicating distress to the caregiver and being heard—that is, catharsis.

During this period, the child shows sharp distress at being left alone. Attachment researchers have shown four different responses to reunion after a brief separation. Most children quickly get over their distress and re-bond with mother. "Ambivalently attached" children fuss and cling for a while. "Avoidantly attached" children show that they don't need anyone anyway, and children with a "disorganized" pattern don't seem to have any reliable formula to deal with the situation. Which pattern the child develops depends largely on the way the child and mother interact and tend to follow the mother's style of attachment. Patterns developed at this time have considerable influence on the long term development of personality.

This is when children discover that their will and Mom's don't' always coincide. When there is a disagreement, this creates a new and very serious challenge: learning to lose battles gracefully, to be discussed in the next section.

By the end of this period, children begin to have some capacity to tolerate separation from the caregiver. As discussed in chapter 3, Margaret Mahler called this "object constancy," where "object" means the other person and "constancy" means that the child has internalized a representation of some kind so as not to feel completely alone and disconnected even if the mother is not physically present. As discussed, this internal representation is vulnerable to stress and can be unavailable when the child most needs it. I have called this internalized presence the "internal rechargeable battery pack of connection."

My hypothesis for how this internalization takes place is that, as it is for internalization of values, connection distress is likely the trigger for development of the internalized battery pack of connection. My sense is that it is the act of saying good-bye that little by little cements an internal presence for the child.

Difficulties with any of the "subphases" or components of this period are frequent sources of major troubles lasting into adult life. Issues such as "borderline," narcissistic, and antisocial personality characteristics tend to derive from this period. Even more common, problems with the ability to self-sooth derive from this period. Along similar lines, behavioral and addictive problems involving cutting, eating disorders, promiscuity or drug use seem to involve trying to find substitutes for a very young kind of love.

In my view, emotional intelligence and resilience are adult qualities based largely on the availability of a strong internalized rechargeable battery pack of connection or, to use Mahler's term, object constancy.

Learning to Lose Battles Gracefully (age 2)

This critical subphase of the separation-individuation period is what is commonly referred to as the "terrible twos." At this time, children begin to engage in power struggles with the primary caregiver. They have strong wills, but, as pointed out earlier, also depend on their emotional connection with Mom for their stability. Temper tantrums happen when the child is caught between rage at mother's refusal to do what the child wants and fear of losing her. At this age, the stakes are life and death, which is why tantrums are so violent.

As indicated earlier, a successful outcome is that mother holds her ground at least much of the time, but helps the child to manage the rage so that no damage is done. A bear hug until tears start is an example. Punishment tells the child that it isn't OK to have wishes different from Mom's, which is not a good outcome. Giving in sends the message that the child is on his or her own, which is even more frightening. Going cold or giving a time-out, in this situation is the same as a punishment, since the child is already in severe connection distress.

Learning that we can disagree with Mom and still be lovable, even when we do not have our way, gives the child the freedom to develop as a separate, distinct individual. Failure in this area can lead to borderline personality in which positive experiences with Mom are kept separate from negative ones. This has been described as having two file drawers. When the good one is open, then the bad one is completely inaccessible. When the bad one suddenly opens, then the good one is closed.

Failure to traverse this developmental challenge can also produce malignant narcissism, in which the individual cannot tolerate losing a battle or being wrong. This will be discussed in detail later in this chapter.

Even without a full blown personality disorder, many of us have some degree of trouble dealing with conflict with those who are important to us. Solutions such as "people pleasing," a pattern of always giving in to the other's wishes, do address the problem of disagreeing, but probably develop later as a hidden agenda aimed at showing the other person how wrong they are to impose their will.

Internalization of Values (3-)

While, as mentioned in Chapter 5, superego precursors begin at age 18 months, internalized templates of good values and behavior don't begin to have major importance until about age three. At this point, children do have ideals and a sense of fairness. They can understand the value of treating others as they would like to be treated. From here on, internalized values, attitudes, ideals, and prohibitions form a bulwark against self-centered pleasures that threaten to disrupt our important social relationships.

As mentioned in Chapter 5, in my view, the trigger for internalizing values is connection distress. Unfortunately, abuse and other toxic situations can produce severe aloneness and connection distress, and as a result, can trigger internalization of unhealthy and self-destructive values.

This is the period when children can learn to cope with disagreement with caregivers by turning against the self and building "internal electric fences" that inhibit them from activities that are healthy and positive.

Learning the Rules (3-)

From three on, the child's intellect develops rapidly along with use of language and ideas. This is where I believe hidden agendas originate. Where open communication has failed, nonverbal behavior patterns seem to follow a logic aimed at teaching lessons and righting wrongs. As long as they remain nonverbal and unconscious, these patterns distort and disrupt relationships but continue, as they first did, to fail to accomplish their childlike goals.

Imagining Someday (5-7)

As described in detail in the last chapter, the acquisition of the dimension of time future allows the child to enlist imagination in solving problems "someday," without trampling on reality. Only when quests are driven out of consciousness by conflict with the conscience do they cause long-term trouble.

Becoming a Competent Child (7-12)

From age eight-on I think of children as increasingly competent at being children. They know the rules and, much of the time, have the self control and skills to do what is expected. They respond well to clear guidelines and dutifully adopt the values of their family. In the absence of major stresses or chaotic, unpredictable surroundings children tend to do well in this period.

This is the age when children will argue interminably about whether a peer has played by the rules. When children do face personal challenges, they often try to apply "the rules" out of a need to control a difficult and unruly world. The logic is, "If I follow the rules, then why don't you?" This rarely works, but can be carried into adulthood.

Adolescence: Accepting the Passing of the Baton (12-?)

Adolescence brings huge new challenges. Life is no longer a game with arbitrary and logical rules. The world is an unruly place where people often must feel motivated before they will do what one wants them or needs them to. Motivating others is an exceedingly complex and uncertain interpersonal task. Compromises need to be negotiated in which each person comes out richer in the exchange.

If one is to be ready to sacrifice for principle or values, then values "borrowed" from parents will no longer do. Adolescents must decide what they really believe and "own" those values.

Competing and striving to meet challenges gives the young person, for the first time, a gauge of the self. "How do I measure up compared with peers?" "Am I beautiful, smart, strong, etc." "Am I special?"

Perhaps most important, parents are trying to "sell" their adolescents on taking responsibility for themselves. Adolescents, accurately recognize that this "gift" may be more of a burden than a privilege, and are not so sure they want to buy. Over a few years, a dance ensues, where both adolescents and parents struggle with ambivalence. They both yearn for the order and carefree feeling of childhood, but they also want the freedom that goes with becoming adult. Adolescents want to be free of parental control and parents want to let go of being responsible for their children. On the other hand, adolescents are afraid of responsibility and parents may be afraid to let go.

Successful adolescence gives the young person self-mastery, a sense of his or her limits and identity, owned values and ideals, an ability to navigate complex relationships, and a sense of ultimate responsibility for his or her own life.

Obviously, this is an ideal and it is easy to enter adulthood with less than full achievement in any one of these areas. When is adolescence done? Perhaps the best measure is when the young person no longer has to pick fights with parents and authorities, but can treat them as peers.

Adult Development

Development doesn't stop with the end of adolescence. In underdeveloped areas we can continue to grow. New skills can be added and our perspective on life inevitably grows with experience. What makes adulthood quite different is that development is more individual and variable. Rather than following common pathways and predictable challenges, adults tend to develop their own unique portfolio of experiences and strengths.

Developmental Problems

Now let's take a closer look at how arrested development can be a tool for avoiding feelings, and how facing feelings can lead to further growth, regardless of age. Going through new experiences is how we grow and mature. Avoiding experience effectively stops growth. When we avoid experiences in order to keep painful feelings at bay, the result is arrested development. Like each of the mechanisms discussed in previous chapters, developmental arrest carries a heavy price to be paid later in life. Passing up developmental challenges leaves us not with new dysfunctional structures but with an empty place. Immaturity is neither Castle nor Prison, but an abandonment of territory that should be ours. This fact makes arrested development one of the most hopeful issues we can face—hopeful because it is never too late to restart.

Focusing In on Three Critical Areas

In a sense, developmental problems have been woven throughout this book. Each of the ways of avoiding feelings has been described as coming out of a developmental period with its challenges. In this section we will examine three particularly critical periods where failure to progress emotionally—that is, developmental arrest—has frequent and seriously damaging results.

First, the period described above as "separation and individuation" is critical in the development of healthy schemas for navigating important relationships. The passionate intensity of marital conflict is a regular reminder of the fact that important relationships continue throughout life to bear the life-and-death stamp of this early period.

Second, the subphase in which we learn to "lose battles gracefully" is absolutely critical to our ability to deal with conflict. Once again, a look at the headlines of the newspaper will show how important conflict and its resolution are to adult life. Developmental arrest in this crucial period produces severe distortions of personality that are the primary source of most of the world's trouble.

Third, adolescence is a period where almost everyone has trouble. Getting through adolescence is inherently a troublesome process and there is hardly a graceful way to do it. Arrest in any component of adolescence is highly likely to lead to adult dysfunction. Given the universal messiness of going from childhood to adulthood, this developmental phase warrants special attention.

Separation and Individuation

Small babies don't know that they are alone in the world. They are oblivious to how large the world is and how small and vulnerable they are. They recognize their mothers' voices but they are happy to be held by anyone. They are unaware of the existential problem of aloneness and isolation that has troubled philosophers, but soon they will discover not only the problem but its solution as well.

At around six months of age, babies begin to show distress when the mother (or the primary caregiver) leaves the room. They begin to react to aloneness. At this age, they may still accept comforting from a substitute person. However, at around eight months of age, as mentioned in the summary above, an abrupt and interesting change takes place. Babies begin to react differently to strangers. It is as if they suddenly become aware of their vulnerability and aloneness. They cling to their mothers while they peek out to inspect new faces. If a stranger attempts to hold them, they are likely to show strong resistance and crying.

No one knows exactly what is in a baby's mind, but clearly there is a change in the relationship to the world at around eight months. The world is now a place where danger lurks, and only familiar people can be fully trusted. The infant's solution to the problem of aloneness is the same as that of the philosopher Camus: relationship. The baby clings to the mother. Being connected is the antidote to aloneness, the solution to the existential dilemma of our ultimate isolation.

Albert Camus (1913-1960)

Camus won the Nobel Prize for Literature in 1957. His most famous works are *The Stranger* and *The Plague*. He was also an existentialist philosopher and a journalist.

Relationships: Vital but Fragile

If only it were that simple. Relationships are indeed the solution, but they are fragile and fraught with problems as well. Over the next two or three years, the child will become aware of how easily relationships can be disrupted. The people we depend on can leave us. They can stop loving us. They can require things of us that we can't provide. They can force us to give up what we most desire. They can die.

Children must confront these perils without the equipment to handle them. At first they don't even have the mobility to follow their mother as she moves through the house. They lack the ability to distinguish between a temporary absence and a permanent one. Even when these problems are on the way to resolution, children still lack the ability to tackle larger problems like death or more subtle ones like a relationship with impossible conditions.

Perhaps there is a reason for this cruel circumstance: It motivates children to learn the complexities of relationships. With a biology that is already dedicated to social existence, the human child is highly driven to learn how to adapt to and to motivate others—especially the mother—to assure ongoing connection.

Developing Relationship Tools

At first the baby has only a few tools: smiling, crying, cooing, and imitating. These start as reflexes, but by the time the eight-month awakening occurs, they are used purposefully to influence others. Caretakers, especially mothers, are biologically and psychologically programmed to respond. But what happens when the mother is in the midst of a postpartum depression? She may not respond, or she may do so without enthusiasm. Or perhaps the mother has an addiction and is sometimes responsive and sometimes not.

Babies with nonresponsive or inconsistently responsive caregivers try all the tricks they know. When these don't work, the babies are threatened with the toxic feeling of helplessness. To survive they have little choice but to form schemas of avoidance, which will be liabilities in their later lives.

Even under ideal conditions, by our first birthday the task of entwining our mothers into a safe and secure relationship becomes complex. As one-year-olds, we are already adept at the communication of feelings back and forth, and we are in intimate contact with our mother's inner states, with all their complexity. At the same time, our mother is teaching us about feelings and sensations by putting them into words: "Oh you want to get changed, yes, it must feel terrible to be all wet."

Ideally, our mothers accurately understand our feelings and needs. They help us when we need help and let us learn for ourselves when we are ready. They articulate concepts for us that we don't understand and make us feel loved and valuable. Of course, perfect attunement all the time is impossible. Sometimes our mothers don't understand us and sometimes they are preoccupied with their own needs. As long as these occasions don't occur too often, they are actually valuable; they help us learn the important developmental skill of self-soothing.

Attachment Theory

Perhaps it is surprising that the Victorian era not only frowned on the overt expression of sexuality but also tended to look down on the warmth and nurturing that we now accept as vital to raising healthy babies. Even through World War II, the best orphanages, as well as educated parents, followed scientific principles of hygiene and made sure that the children would not become unduly attached to or emotionally dependent on their caregivers.

A few workers disagreed and in 1951 the World Health Organization commissioned John Bowlby to write a report entitled *Maternal Care and Mental Health,* which was widely disseminated. He argued that rates of death and disease among the many orphaned children left by the war would be drastically reduced if the children and the individuals responsible for their care were not only allowed but encouraged to form affective bonds.

John Bowlby (1907-1990)

Bowlby, a British psychiatrist and psychoanalyst, championed the then-novel idea that children need emotional bonding with caregivers in order to thrive.

The ideas developed by Bowlby and others have turned out to be extremely important for two reasons. The first is that patterns learned in early life tend to remain and color the way people handle relationships throughout childhood and beyond. This in turn has powerful effects on those around them, which reverberates back to the individual. Imagine a child who learns not to trust. Soon teachers and other children are keeping their distance, because that child doesn't allow easy interaction; this reinforces the mistrust. The effect becomes self-perpetuating.

The second reason for the importance of attachment is the light it sheds on marriage. Marriage (or any other very important relationship, such as therapy) brings out very powerful feelings because we experience our primary connection as a matter of life and death. It may be our young mammal brain that sees the connection this way; when things get intense between spouses, that is the part of the brain that is running the show. Thus our most important intimate relationships are lived in the shadow of early experiences with our primary caregiver and, without our awareness, take on characteristics from so very long ago.

Bowlby and Mary Ainsworth built a body of research and a theoretical tradition around the four typical reactions children showed when temporarily separated from their primary caregiver. The *securely attached* one and two-year-olds were upset when their mother was out of the room but easily allowed themselves to be soothed when she returned. Another group, described as *avoidantly attached* would act as if the mother's return didn't matter to them. A third pattern, *ambivalent attachment*, was where children were the most distressed with the separation. They might cling or could push the mother away and not allow themselves to be soothed by her on her return. Later, a fourth pattern was identified and called

disorganized, in which children showed no consistent way of dealing with separation, as if they had not found any schema that consistently brought comfort.

For more about attachment theory, see Robert Karen's lovely book,
*Becoming Attached: First Relationships and How They Shape Our Capacity
to Love*, Oxford University Press, 1998.

Karen, Robert

Psychologist in New York and author of books on attachment and
forgiveness.

Meanwhile, I would like to share with you an unusual, almost-first-
hand account of the specific issues involved in becoming attached.

Three Principles of Attachment

*Vivian was a librarian with a professional demeanor. However, when she
started therapy, she complained of not feeling "real." Over the next decade,
adult Vivian went through the attachment steps that one usually goes
through as a very young child.*

In doing so, she taught me much of what I know first hand about
attachment and very early development. She had come to me with
a unique intersection of characteristics. Her self was divided into
isolated parts (dissociative identity disorder or multiple personality). Some were adult and functioning on a high level, and others
were protectively stuck in childhood. What was unique about working with her was that adult parts of her could describe and explain
things about the children that a child would not be able to articulate.
In this way she was able to give both of us a rare window into many
of the universal challenges of early development.

*Unlike many "multiples," she had not been subjected to severe physical or
sexual abuse. Her parents did not take pleasure in making her feel powerless
and, in fact, they loved her. But they had problems in the way they formed
attachments. Her mother cared but approached child rearing as a duty. At*

times she would be more focused on her graduate studies and career. At other times she would suddenly become frustrated and utter rejecting words to her child. Only late in life was she able to relax enough to show the love she had for her daughter. Vivian's father seemed more warmly connected to his daughter, but it all had to be on his terms. He would control the smallest details of her life to teach her the strange principles and practices he believed were necessary for her well-being

For Vivian, adapting to her parents' requirements, getting her needs met, and maintaining some sense of self were simply incompatible. The only way for her to survive emotionally was to split into separate selves separated by dissociative barriers. One was adapted to banter with her father, another to comply with his requirements. Some remained lost, as if abandoned in some very early age, and yet another set off in a perpetual search of a mother. In the meantime, parts of her went to school and appeared to function as a normal, though anxious, child.

Vivian's adult selves were able to articulate a number of basic insights about attachment, which I describe here as principles. These are not unknown to developmentalists, but Vivian's observations are unusual in that they are nearly first hand.

The First Principle: To Know You Exist You Must Be Seen

When Vivian first explained this principle to me, I was a bit surprised. I took existence for granted. Vivian, or at least some parts of her, did not. As mentioned, Vivian often complained that she didn't feel real. When she came across concrete evidence of her existence, such as a photo or a letter, she would feel elated because it showed that her experience, her existence, was authentic, "real."

When Vivian was about one year old (according to both her mother and her aunt), she was in her room with the door closed, crying with an unusual tone of distress. Her mother wanted to go in and comfort her, but her father, who lived by bizarre intellectual principles, blocked her mother. With the idea of training his child not to cry, he physically held the door shut and did not allow Vivian's moither to enter. He prevailed and Vivian was left with not even a word of comfort.

Vivian's adult problems make perfect sense as reactions to this and other instances of emotional abuse. In addition to learning to dissociate from her feelings so as not to cry, she learned not to rely on the grownups in her life. With no worldly relationships that she dared to count on or take for granted, she continued to feel that she was not real.

The earliest splits in Vivian's mind caused some very young parts of her to be isolated from the rest of her life. These parts remained immature; Vivian called them "babies." They were nonverbal, uttering only strange sounds, and their greatest need was to gaze into the eyes of another person and see themselves reflected and acknowledged. In this way, they could begin to grasp their own existence. In therapy, Vivian's babies and I shared long exchanges of eye contact over many sessions. Because they had experienced being seen, they could begin again to grow. Soon they disappeared, having merged with other parts of Vivian. Simultaneously, the adult feelings of being unreal began to abate.

The Second Principle: Feelings Are too Big and Too Frightening to Cope with Alone

We already know that catharsis makes use of empathic understanding to bring intense emotions to a level where they can be processed. For Vivian, even ordinary emotions were often too much to deal with in the absence of a safe outside relationship. Her solution was to invent her own, imaginary, but reliable connection, which she called the "Atmosphere." She based the Atmosphere on an encounter at age six. A graduate student in her mother's class asked to use Vivian as a subject to practice intelligence testing. This was one of the rare times that Vivian encountered an adult who expressed genuine interest in what she personally felt.

She then amplified this experience into an imaginary presence made up of kindly beings, some of whom had human counterparts. She imagined them diffused into molecules that were omnipresent and mingled with her own so there could be no break in their continuous connection to her. This is why she called it the "Atmosphere." In this way she was in constant contact with a warm and caring presence. It had the following traits:

- The Atmosphere was omnipresent.
- The Atmosphere was static and constant.
- The Atmosphere was completely and exclusively attentive to Vivian as an individual.
- The Atmosphere had no needs of its own.
- The Atmosphere had no feelings of its own, but was fully empathic with Vivian's.

This extraordinary presence was so effective that it created a new problem. Those parts of Vivian that depended on the Atmosphere did not learn how to experience feelings, since the feelings were immediately shared with, and their intensity absorbed by the Atmosphere. It was as if catharsis happened so rapidly and completely that Vivian didn't get a chance to feel. The end result was that parts of her were entirely unable to handle feeling. Only very gradually did she go through the very basic developmental process of learning to hold onto feelings and to make use of an outside witness for catharsis. As indicated in Chapter 3, these are skills that are usually learned in the first and second years of life.

Most of Vivian's therapy was about the gradual loss of the Atmosphere. In the beginning, parts of her imagined that I, her therapist, was part of the Atmosphere and therefore merged with her. In a series of painful awakenings, she came to understand that I did not exist in the Atmosphere but was a purely terrestrial being. Once she encountered a detour on the way to the office and called for directions. When I told her which landmarks to watch for, it caught some parts of her by surprise. Those parts had not realized that I had knowledge of any place other than the office I inhabited. She was shocked and upset for days. Beyond that, I was missing many of the traits of the Atmosphere. I could only be in one place at a time. I sometimes didn't understand her. I had needs of my own and was occasionally distracted.

As I slipped (from Vivian's point of view) out of the Atmosphere, she had to experience emotions on her own. Her experience must have been something like that of a newborn baby accustomed to the insulated womb and suddenly exposed to the outside. The bright light, cold air, and loud sounds must be overwhelming. It is no wonder that a baby's first act is to cry.

For Vivian, real emotions were overwhelming. She couldn't handle them alone, so most of the time she would slip into a personality who had no feelings at all. Dissociation wouldn't let her have the feeling experiences she most needed to have in order to grow. A few times, however, she was able to share feelings with me while she was having them. These were very important moments of catharsis between two separate beings.

Gradually, one experience at a time, those parts of Vivian that had been insulated by the Atmosphere began to be able to tolerate, and even appreciate, emotions. She learned to hold them till our next session and then feel better by sharing what she felt.

The Third Principle: An Internalized Sense of the Presence of Mother Allows Us to Cope with Aloneness

This is the same rechargeable battery pack of connection discussed in Chapter 3, the internal presence that makes aloneness tolerable. Vivian had elaborate ways of shielding parts of herself from the knowledge that, between therapy sessions, she was actually on her own. At the end of each session she would say, "Please don't forget me." She feared that if she slipped from *my* mind she would be completely alone. I pictured her mother involved with her career and showing no lingering interest in her child. Vivian was so afraid of the time between sessions that for years she avoided any reference to "next time," to maintain her denial of the span of time between sessions.

Denial allowed her to avoid going through the pangs of loss with each separation, but gradually those parts of herself that had been shielded from reality came to recognize that we really were separated. As this happened, she felt a sense of loss and began to link it with the anticipation of reunion. Over the course of many partings and returns, she began to develop a broad confidence that our connection did not depend on continuous physical presence. She was internalizing a sense of being connected.

Vivian's story gives us a glimpse into the world of nonverbal schemas where adverse experience can teach us how to avoid what is painful or unsatisfactory. Her extreme defenses show how too much shielding from distress can block the internalization of the sense of connection that will allow coping with the inevitable breaks in attunement.

Now let's look at the second developmental area chosen for special attention.

Learning to Lose Battles Gracefully

No sooner do we acquire the skills of closeness and harmony then we are confronted with the problem of conflict. Eighteen-month-old Emily, the child from Chapter 5, was happily playing with her Mom's pots and pans when an angry voice interrupted her joy. Her harmonious world came apart in a second, and her attempts to seek comfort from Mom failed because the mom with whom she tried to make comforting eye contact was not the soothing, loving mom, but a frightening, angry mom.

Learning that you can be weak or make a mistake and still be lovable, learning to lose a power struggle and still be lovable, learning that you can disagree and still be lovable, these are the lessons of the "terrible twos." Without satisfactorily traversing this difficult period and learning the important lessons, we are left with developmental deficits so critical that they can form the psychological basis of the three most serious personality disorders: borderline personality, narcissistic personality, and antisocial personality. Let's look in more depth at one of these problems. The reason I have focused on pathological narcissism is that relationships with individuals with those characteristics have had profound effects on so many of my patients, as spouses or children or even employees.

Narcissistic Personality Disorder

A severe personality disorder in which an individual cultivates and believes in a persona of superiority unrelated to his or her actual level of success. Behind this front is a life-and-death struggle to ward off humiliation that undermines empathy and any regard for the feelings of others.

Narcissism and the One-Way Relationship

Have you ever experienced a one-way relationship? That is, one in which the other person feels entitled to do all the taking while expecting you to do all the giving?

> *Susan was angry because her husband Chris felt perfectly justified having his every wish fulfilled, while he did almost nothing for her or their children. Every time she tried to point out the unfairness of their situation, Chris turned the discussion into a criticism of her.*
>
> *Chris walked away from their discussions 100% sure he was right. Susan, in contrast, spent hours wondering if she might really be the terrible person Chris said she was.*

Chris had no idea that there was any other way to live. He thought he was fine, even better than fine, but in reality he suffered from pathological narcissism. Categorized as a personality disorder, narcissism starts with failures of development, which can happen when small children miss out on experiences that might teach them that being wrong or vulnerable or powerless is not the end of the world.

Narcissism can lead to high position or villainy, or both. To bolster their flawed self-esteem, malignant narcissists often seek out power. Not infrequently, political and business leaders have narcissistic personalities. The sense of entitlement that is part of their pathology convinces them that they don't have to follow rules. When their lies and crimes are discovered, the pubic is shocked by the outrageousness of their behavior, while the narcissists are shocked by what they perceive as the pettiness of their accusers.

Humiliation Is Worse Than Death

This section focuses on the full-blown syndrome of narcissism; however, many people manifest lesser versions. Also, the terms *malignant* or *pathological* are used because a healthy personality includes a good deal of self-esteem, even self-love. It is when self-aggrandizement becomes desperate that it enters the zone of pathology.

The key to understanding narcissists is comprehending their hatred and fear of humiliation. To narcissists, humiliation is worse than death and must be fended off at any cost whatsoever, especially if they can make sure that the cost is borne by someone else. This is where they have not succeeded in learning that conflict with the important people in one's life can be resolved without anyone being crushed, that one can lose a battle without losing love.

How do children become narcissists? One prevailing theory is that constant rejection and humiliation make self-esteem a matter of life or death. But in some cases there has not been harsh treatment. An alternative theory is that overindulgence and excessively high expectations can create the same feeling that anything less than perfection would be unforgivable. Extreme rejection and extreme indulgence are both damaging to the ability to develop healthy self-esteem. It is likely that genetics play a role as well.

The first, and perhaps worst, casualty of narcissism is empathy. To feel empathy towards others one must first be able to empathize with oneself, which grows out of the ability to acknowledge and accept, with warmth and understanding, one's own weaknesses and limitations. Narcissists, however, experience vulnerability and weakness as unacceptable and humiliating personal failures. Having no tolerance for human limitations in themselves, they are unable to tolerate them in others.

Lacking empathy puts severe limits on narcissists' ability to understand other people, often at a high cost. For example, narcissists testifying in their own defense will lie and make excuses even when an expression of remorse would result in a shorter sentence. Being incapable of forgiving themselves, they expect a jury to have the same harsh attitude that they have. For them, there is no choice left but to lie. One would think that blindness to empathic understanding of others would make narcissists inept at dealing with others. Often they are, but they can also be masters of manipulation. They know just what to do, not through empathy but by careful observation. They are like sharks who make up for poor vision by overdevelopment of other senses.

With no ability to forgive failures, narcissists' superegos make judgments that are harsh and cold—including self-judgments. This is so painful that they learn to dodge their own self-condemnation. They blame others, make excuses, and rationalize to avoid acknowledging failure or imperfection.

Narcissists need to be appreciated, even adulated. Like a leaky tire, they require constant pumping from those around them to keep their egos inflated. They want to be seen as the epitome of whatever ideals they espouse. To obtain this adulation, they may work hard and accomplish extraordinary things. Even then, however, they tend to cultivate an image greater than their actual achievement warrants.

Narcissists' intolerance of humiliation is so powerful that they will change reality rather than face the pain. People in relationships with narcissists find this hard to understand or even believe, and they are baffled when they hear their partner tell lies to win an argument and clearly believe the lies. But to narcissists, reality is whatever will support the conclusions they need rather than an independent set of facts and truths. Obviously, arguing with a narcissist is an exercise in futility.

An Image to Live Up To

Narcissists are driven to convince the world that their self-images are reality. These false selves are completely free of defects and weaknesses. (Very early cognitive development has no place for gray, only black and white.) Those close to the narcissist are criticized and bludgeoned into supporting the pretense. For example, a narcissist would humiliate, without mercy, a spouse who dressed "terribly" for an office party. On the other hand, outsiders are treated with the greatest care, lest they see what is behind the curtain.

Narcissists cannot trust. Trust is based on empathy; we *feel* the sincerity of another person and know that what she says is honest and real. Narcissists must rely on learned patterns and guesses about the inner workings of other people. Having no way to compare themselves with others, they assume that others are no different from themselves. Everyone has an image to sustain and everyone is as ruthless as they are. The result is paranoia, seeing the world as a dog-eat-dog place full of self-serving predators.

The last casualty of narcissism is kindness. Without empathy, narcissists don't feel the pain of others, and they have no appreciation of the hurt they inflict. They may be particularly unkind to people who have the same weaknesses that they work so hard to deny in themselves. They often project their weaknesses onto people who don't actually share those traits. This ability to transfer or project one's weaknesses and imperfections onto others is the basis of one of the narcissist's most common behaviors: putting others down. A pattern I have seen many times in marriages is that the narcissist, who has put down his or her spouse for years, eventually believes that the spouse is a person of little value and initiates a divorce.

Life As a Zero Sum Game

Schadenfreude, feeling good about the failures and misfortunes of others, is a distinguishing characteristic of narcissists. People capable of empathy may occasionally experience envy or pleasure at others' misfortunes, but they also feel sympathetic about other people's pain and happy for their success. Narcissists don't. For them, life is a "zero sum game." Your loss is my gain and vice versa.

Can Narcissists Change?

I have said that development can be picked up at any age, and I still stand by that view. On the other hand, to change these patterns, the narcissist would need to acknowledge and accept personal defects, which is precisely what he or she dreads the most. They need to face feelings that long ago were beyond their capacity. As we have seen throughout this book, that is standard procedure for healing and growth. Unfortunately, the narcissist's readiness to distort reality makes it hard even in adulthood for him or her to be aware of or admit to any defects. The mainstay of change for others is trusting an outside person. For the narcissist, this is one of the greatest threats to self-esteem. Being understood feels like humiliation rather than comfort.

For treatment to work and change to occur, the narcissist must value something or someone so highly that she will suffer humiliation rather than lose the relationship. Sometimes failures in business or in relationships can bring the individual to this level of desperation. Interestingly, this is exactly what makes two-year-olds ready to accept the discomfort that goes with growth. The reason they are willing to learn to lose battles is because their need for connection with the caregiver is so desperate. Being accepted by their primary caregiver is so crucial that they are ready to give up being Emperor of the World.

Successful therapy requires that the narcissistic person come to depend on a therapist to a highly uncomfortable degree. Otto Kernberg, a key theoretician and expert on narcissism, pointed out that success in the world is a bad sign for therapy. With worldly success, narcissistic people are more likely to abandon their therapist and cling to their admirers so as not to have to acknowledge their imperfections. Only when their world is caving in are they likely to accept the humiliation of dependence on another.

Otto Kernberg (1928-):

Kernberg developed important theories about people with borderline personality organization and narcissistic pathology. He is a psychoanalyst and professor of psychiatry at Weill Cornell Medical College in New York.

When a narcissistic person does let another person witness his weakness, a huge developmental step is being made. Accepting the empathy of another is rare, but when it does happen, there is re-lief. Eventually this can even lead to the development of empathy for others.

Unfortunately, most narcissists will wiggle past empathy. They might say something like, "Okay, I have my weak points, but I'm stronger than so-and-so." The "but" nullifies the admission. This is just one of many ways a person can go through the motions of acknowledgment without feeling it.

Being in a Relationship with a Narcissist

Malignant narcissists don't seem to have any difficulty finding fol-lowers and devoted mates. This is no surprise, because they are very good at creating the appearance of an amazingly desirable individ-ual. Especially susceptible are those who started out life in a fam-ily dominated by a narcissist, where the children learn not to notice the shortcomings of the parent. The narcissistic person gives clear signals to the children that she is not to be questioned and that if something is not right, it must be the other person's fault.

Susan underwent a kind of brainwashing. She tried to please Chris by aligning herself with his thinking. Maybe it was her fault. She should try harder. Over time she became more and more convinced that she was seriously flawed. Chris, on the other hand, experienced so much success in business that he became a strong supporter of his favorite charity. Outsiders thought he was the most generous and charming person they had ever met.

This convinced Susan even more that she was barely if at all worthy of her husband. It hurt her deeply when he criticized her, and she wished she could do better. At times, though, she felt angry and hurt. When she tried to point out an occasional instance when she was clearly right, he would simply change the facts: "I never said that." He was so sure, yet she trusted her memory. Or could she be losing her mind? She didn't dare talk to her friends for fear of being disloyal to her husband.

When he announced his decision to divorce because of her inadequacy, she was shocked and devastated. She sought out therapy and gradually began to see that he was severely impaired in ways very similar to her father. She began to learn that she was actually the healthier of the two, except for internalized attitudes and values that she was unworthy. She had acquired these in childhood, but they had been further reinforced by the trauma of living with Chris.

In the Next Steps section at the end of this chapter, I describe how to survive or end a relationship with a narcissistic person.

The next critical period to be discussed is adolescence. Here, again, failures in making the transition from childhood to adulthood are as common as they are costly in adult life.

Adolescent Development: Owning Your Self

The feelings being avoided may not be as much a matter of life and death as in the earliest years, but facing a harsh and competitive world is still very difficult. Family turmoil, ADHD (attention deficit hyperactivity disorder), or any other handicap makes the task of becoming adult all the more frightening. For many if not most young people, falling back on parents' beliefs and accomplishments is no longer reassuring. Having questioned parents' views and feeling the need to establish an independent basis for being valued, young people must rely on themselves. Yet they don't have a large portfolio of skills or accomplishments. They don't even have a clear idea of who that self is or what principles they stand for. Faced with high expectations and not sure of being able to measure up, it is all too easy for young people to step away from trying.

Unfortunately, failing to engage in challenges and explore the limits of one's capabilities means failing to develop and take ownership of critical attributes. Among these are impulse control, self-definition, adult values, and the ability to work closely with others.

David's story is all too common. It has many parallels to that of Justin whom we met in Chapter 2. This time, we'll focus on adolescent psychological development. David was a good student in elementary school, though not as diligent as his older brother Luke. His intelligence and ease at class participation allowed him to get good grades without much effort. He was charming and had many friends. When he started high school, his parents had great expectations for him.

David's mother was overprotective and worried that he would injure himself on his skateboard. His father was a lawyer from a strict religious family. While the father demanded that the children attend church every Sunday, in subtle ways, like the enthusiasm with which he told stories about the "bad" kids from his own school days, he encouraged his son to act out his own unconscious resentment of authority.

Setting his sights on his brother's high grades, his parents' expectations, and the challenges of high-school work, David began his freshman year working very hard. However, he soon felt overwhelmed and started spending more time with his skateboarding friends and less time on homework. He decided that he would rather develop a more "laid-back" lifestyle than his father's daily grind. Maybe he would become a professional surfer.

At the first parent-teacher conference, David's mother discovered that David hadn't been handing in his assignments. She became alarmed and started asking him every day if he had homework to do. He would answer, "No, not today" or "I did it in homeroom." At first his sincerity made her believe him, but she soon realized he was lying. She tried, unsuccessfully, to get him to talk about what was going on.

As the year passed, David started responding angrily to his mother's questions, slamming doors and throwing things in his room. His mother didn't want to trigger his rage but was very worried. When David received a C-minus on his report card, his father had a "heart-to-heart" talk with him. David's father then told his wife that he and David had "connected" and that things would get better. He added that David needed to make his own mistakes and learn from them.

David's grades got even worse. His mother worried more and more and his father withdrew; when they did talk about David, they fought.

Though he would never admit it, David was in incredible pain. Unconsciously, he felt the pressure of his parents' and his own expectations. He wondered if he was as smart as Luke. He was secretly terrified that he might be a failure.

When David's concerns about his future came to consciousness, he tried talking to his friends, but they weren't comfortable hearing his doubts. Instead they would change the subject to surfing, how they hated school, and the future they imagined on the beaches of California.

> *When David smoked marijuana with his friends, his uneasy tension lifted. The drug made his parents' anger and disappointment feel insignificant.*

David was experiencing developmental arrest. Development happens when we do things that challenge us and go through the resultant feelings. With support from his friends and from marijuana, David decided to take it easy in his comfort zone. Emotional development was not progressing. Instead he was honing new skills of avoidance.

Staying in the Comfort Zone

We might think of David's pattern of avoidance as a choice, but it really wasn't. He slid gradually into a habit of avoiding whatever was uncomfortable and using his excellent social skills to avoid being confronted. By the time he was fourteen, he was already able to lie with the most sincere and endearing look. It was so automatic for him to turn away from effort and stress that he wasn't even aware he was making a decision.

> *In contrast, well before high school, David's older brother Luke had learned to make himself sit down and finish boring assignments. As he gained a reputation as a good student, he began to enjoy being a success. David, on the other hand, was able to get by without being so diligent. By not forcing himself to do the hard, dull work, David skirted the experience of self-mastery. Even when he wanted to learn to play the guitar, he lacked the self-discipline to practice. The only thing he stuck with was the skateboard. He missed out on the positive cycle of fulfilling expectations of teachers and*

receiving praise. With each repetition of this pattern, David fell further behind in his development. By high school, with help from his friends and covert encouragement from his father, he rationalized his avoidance and suppressed most of his feelings of shame and distress.

By the end of his freshman year in high school, despite increasing pressure from his mother and teachers, David didn't even bother to try to succeed. Instead, he became more and more skilled at manipulating everyone and everything in his environment to avoid discomfort and most of all to avoid having to give up the drug that kept him from having to think about making a change.

Success in life requires a balance between manipulating one's environment to make things easier and adapting oneself to life's demands. Like most teenagers with behavior problems, David became an expert at shaping his environment for his comfort. On the other hand, any ability he had gained in adapting to life "on life's terms" was fast slipping away due to disuse. Many if not most of the experiences that develop character are the ones that come from grappling with circumstances that are beyond our control. David was systematically avoiding these experiences.

Impulse Control and Other Acquisitions

High school is where we develop impulse control. We learn to do things we don't want to do—and to value the relatively mild rewards that result. By leaving our comfort zones to meet challenges, we learn the measure of our true capabilities and begin to develop a realistic sense of who we are.

In adolescence, we can no longer simply borrow our parent's values. We must come to own our personal standards and ideals; this is accomplished when we face real dilemmas and make hard choices.

Key Concept

We gain our sense of our identity by making hard choices in life.

Gaining self-mastery, learning about ourselves, and building personal values are among the most important developmental tasks of the teen years. David's unwillingness to leave his comfort zone denied him these new acquisitions.

Another important developmental milestone is the ability to form deep relationships. David and his friends had an active social life but systematically avoided the subtle experiences of personal vulnerability and honesty that lead to deep relationships, finding them much too intimidating.

> *David did not date much in his teens. He told himself that he preferred to hang out with his friends, but the reality was that attempting to be close with another person was way outside of his comfort zone. It was easier to get stoned with his buddies.*
>
> *David dropped out of college in his freshman year. He knew on some level that he couldn't meet the challenge, so he rationalized that college was stupid. In his twenties, he tried therapy, but he always quit when the going got rough.*
>
> *At twenty-six, tired and depressed, David decided to try to get clean and sober. He didn't really want to change, but he had run out of options. He took a minimum-wage job and lived in a dilapidated halfway house for recovering drug addicts. He hated the place. Without making a conscious choice, he had begun to face life on life's terms. Going through the real pain of stopping his drug use, David began, to his surprise, to feel proud of himself. He actually liked going to work and doing his job. This gave him the strength to pull away from his old friends, one of whom told him, "I liked you a lot better stoned."*
>
> *When he had been clean for six months, David made use of his formidable manipulative skills. Since he was very young he had been the charmer in the family. Further honed to support his addiction, his ability to motivate others was a strength. So he talked to the dean and was soon readmitted to the college. As he struggled to complete his courses, he did a lot of catching up on his self-mastery, honesty, and values development. When he graduated he took a position in sales. As he faced the challenges of his job, he grew more confident and discovered that his charm and chattiness were real assets. When he won a small sales award, he was very happy and proud.*

David's story demonstrates the continuum between the universal developmental issues and the acquisition of individual skills and assets. His drive to avoid challenges led him to develop interpersonal skills, which turned out to be very useful later. Even when parts of development are lacking, other areas can and often do become strengths. As a teen, David lagged behind his brother in the development of self-mastery and personal identity, but he was ahead of him in the ability to charm and influence others. Adversity is regularly a source of positive attributes as well as of pain and dysfunction.

Humans Are Individuals

From a practical standpoint, it is helpful to have a framework and even a timetable for "normal" development. At the same time, this framework should not be thought of too rigidly. Nor do we all need to have the same developmental assets. It has been essential to the flourishing of civilization that individuals have different personality types and characteristics, allowing us to specialize in different roles.

Biology and genetics, too, are factors in determining how we function and what directions we take. For example, David showed some characteristics of attention deficit disorder (ADD). His difficulty concentrating in school contributed to his difficulty with self-mastery and his preference for risk taking and high levels of stimulation. However, ADD has a positive side. His need for stimulation pushed him into a range of experiences that another person might never have tried. With experience comes skill and breadth of capability. Furthermore, part of the ADD syndrome is the ability to "hyperfocus," meaning a laser-like attentiveness to the exclusion of all else when the subject is of passionate interest. Whereas biology plays a role in the great variability in our native strengths and weaknesses, the developmental process shapes the end result.

Developmental Arrest Is a Good Problem to Have

Development is a major theme in this book partly because it is essential in understanding the variety of ways that early life avoidance of difficult feelings can lead to problems later. It is also a theme because it is underemphasized as a source of hope. It is too easy to think about dysfunction as illness without seeing how often change is simply a matter of doing now the emotional work that was missed years ago. Unfortunately, our healthcare system emphasizes diagnoses, illnesses, and disorders and tends to ignore development.

Even with a biologically based handicap, there is room to develop compensatory strengths. Opting for the developmental point of view helps us focus on creating new experiences that will lead to life-enhancing growth.

All developmental problems—both those seen in David's story and those that relate to early development—can have a profound impact on adult life. Developmental arrest coming from earlier years may have even more life-limiting effects, since it tends to revolve around such fundamental issues as trust, safety, and the ability to accept limitations in power and control.

As we grow into adulthood we learn to cover and deny our developmental deficits. Our shame makes us explain away immature behavior as a personal preference or to blame outside forces. Too often, the pattern of not questioning our own habits and quirks keeps us from thinking about their cost. Because development is about experiences we have never had, it is also hard to imagine the benefits that might come from change. The end result is that too often, limitations due to arrested development remain in place without being questioned or addressed.

About Stress

Throughout this book I have advocated getting out of your comfort zone, but isn't this adding stress to our lives, and isn't stress a bad thing? It is true that medical research has shown that stress causes illness and undermines our physical ability to combat disease. The answer is that there are different kinds of stress. Doing something difficult, when you know you are likely to succeed and have emotional support, is actually a positive experience.

The toxic kind of stress comes from feeling that you *must*, in some life-and-death way, do something that you *can't* do. It may be as simple as a boss's demanding that you do more than you can possibly accomplish in a day, under threat of termination. Or it might be having to choose between two paths: one violates your deepest values and the other that may cost your life. Lurking behind the toxic kind of stress can you see helplessness, the feeling that is most harmful to humans and other species?

At times, emotional problems—especially those derived from early years that have a life-and-death quality—may put us in a position of toxic stress. It is important for us first to seek emotional clarity that the stakes are not as high as they seem. Then, voluntary behavior change can be seen as a more benign exercise in going outside one's comfort zone.

Life Is about Growing

On our planet, life has always involved struggle. All animals struggle to survive and prosper. They compete with each other, fight to keep from being destroyed by forces of nature, and struggle not to be devoured by some larger creature. Humans are no different. Deprived of struggle, we tend to stagnate and lose our abilities. To fulfill our potential we need challenge—not the toxic kind, but the kind that leaves us feeling stronger than before.

In general, getting out of our comfort zone on a regular basis is among the best things humans can do. Whether it is to make up for lost time and to gain developmental skills that others already have or to push into new areas and gain personal strengths we might never have thought of, the cycle of venturing beyond our usual limits and then refueling in safety and comfort is what makes us thrive.

Next Steps: Restarting Arrested Development

I marvel at our capacity as humans to protect ourselves from damage by putting our development on hold. I am equally amazed to see how we can pick up the trail of development regardless of age. When we restart our arrested development, we opt to go through uncomfortable feelings we have avoided for years. Bravely we step onto our rickety Bridges and cross over our personal chasms.

In practical terms, the job involves three tasks. To some extent they are the culmination of this book.

Task 1: Explore Your Worst Fears. Before embarking on voluntary behavior change, it is important to feel that you will be safe. You need to know that your personal Bridge, while scary, is strong enough to hold you. Of course you can't be absolutely sure, but exploring your fears, ideally with a therapist, will teach you about yourself and your limits and will help you figure out what you want to change.

There is another benefit to exploring the exact nature of your fears in therapy. Each time you get close to one of those feelings in a context of connection, catharsis will occur and you will become less afraid. As you continue to explore and understand yourself, your giant childhood fears will steadily shrink down to adult scale and then grow even smaller.

Task 2: Practice Voluntary Behavior Change. Although you may meet powerful internal resistance, you can nevertheless change your behavior and experience all the benefits that come with that change. Think of the resistant part of yourself as a small child who is afraid. Comfort the child with your adult confidence and empathy. This is a major first step.

I often think of voluntary behavior change—and other forms of growth—as "making bricks," because each person's growth tends to be made up of many repetitions of the same steps. Once you have made the first one, it is easy to see that you can make a second one and a third. If you can make three, then you can build anything. In the same way, once you have successfully traversed your own personal moment of change, each repetition is like making another brick, not that hard to do and almost sure to be successful. With the experience of making a single brick or a few of them, you are assured that you will be able to go as far as you wish.

Task 3: Overcome Your Backlash. When you have successfully changed, even a tiny bit, your Black Box Motivator will try to convince you that you made a big mistake. It will tell you that change is bad, that failure is inevitable, and/or that your new behavior will cause the gods to be angry. In other words, your Black Box Motivator will lie to you. Be aware of this phenomenon so that you can persist in your growth. A trusted supporter and/or therapist can help you figure out which internal messages you can rely on and which are not in your own best interests.

A particularly sneaky form of backlash is seeming to move forward while actually setting yourself up for failure—for example, "biting off more than you can chew." Again, a trusted person can help you see if you are about to make a mistake or, if you do make the mistake, can help you process it in a way that encourages further growth.

As you move ahead, you will go through your uncomfortable feelings and they will be healed by catharsis. Unhealthy values will give way to more positive ones. Eventually what was uncomfortable will no longer be so. Your moments of healing may be tumultuous or frightening, but they will ultimately give you new abilities with which to create and enjoy a happier and healthier life.

More Next Steps: How to Handle a Relationship with a Narcissist

Why have I spent so much time looking at narcissism? As it turns out, this kind of relationship is one of the main causes of the suffering my patients have experienced. A surprising number of people in my practice have been damaged from growing up with a narcissistic parent or from being in a current one-way relationship, or both.

I have known people who were able to turn the relationship into a tolerable one, others who have chosen to leave, and still others who have been rejected by the narcissistic person. The pros and cons are very individual. The one generalization is that people don't change easily, and narcissism is one of the hardest things to change.

The Narcissistic Parent. People who grow up in the household of a narcissist even as children learn that their job in life is to support the narcissist's ego at their own expense. They may even feel guilty about taking care of their own needs. They learn to ignore how unhealthy this is, and their blindness leaves them vulnerable to selecting narcissists as partners and starting the cycle all over again. In later relationships, when transference sets in, it will mean that even a healthy partner's ordinary needs will be interpreted as absolute requirements.

The Narcissist Partner. If you think you are in a relationship with a narcissist, I strongly suggest that you speak with a professional. Dealing with a narcissist is extremely difficult because your natural instincts will lead you to react in ways that only make the situation worse. For example, you will want to explain and get the narcissist to understand, and this will be experienced by that person as an attempt to humiliate. Remember that trying to change the other person gives away your power and makes you vulnerable to being hurt.

Three Rules. If you remain in a relationship with a narcissist by choice or necessity, there are a few rules that may help you find your way. Human beings are infinitely complex and full of surprises, but pathology tends to make us more rigid and predictable. Narcissists have no choice but to focus most of their energy on the single task of avoiding humiliation, hence making it possible to formulate some universal rules.

Rule 1: Communication Doesn't Work. Communication is effective in healthy relationships because of the power of empathy; narcissists not only lack empathy, but they are actually threatened by other people's empathy. Giving emotional support (as opposed to vindication) will actually backfire. Therefore, in contrast to most relationships, it is usually best to keep things unsaid. The exception is that there may be times when it is helpful to state how you will react to a particular situation. "If you do this again, you can expect me to..."

Rule 2: Protect Yourself. Narcissists resort to bullying in order to feel big and strong themselves, but don't allow yourself to be put down. The more the narcissist devalues you, the more he will see you as inferior and of less and less use. In the end you will be likely to be discarded. This might be your liberation, but better *you* should decide when to leave.

The way to escape from the grip of devaluation is to *disengage*. When the narcissist is being abusive, step away physically or emotionally. You can state that you disagree, but do not argue. Disengagement, unlike almost anything else you can do, does not invite retaliation. Instead, it faces the narcissist with aloneness and lack of control, both of which are distinctly uncomfortable. The discomfort serves as a negative behavioral reinforcement.

Rule 3: Use Behavior Modification. Contrary to their image, narcissists are very needy, which makes it possible for you to give out positive and negative reinforcement to shape the narcissist's behavior. Emotional or physical disengagement is usually your most powerful tool. If the narcissist in your life has a secret need for you—say because you have a more accurate sense of other people and how to manage social situations—you may be able to use that need as leverage to demand respect from the narcissist. Don't say this out loud. Just do it. Give unspoken rewards for good behavior and disengage in response to bad.

Narcissists, like sharks, depend on signals to find their way. Lacking empathy, they are actually quite blind. If you go silent or speak without revealing much, the narcissist will try to provoke you in order to draw you out. If you persist in remaining quiet, the narcissist's need for clues from you will escalate and she may be more ready to engage in a silent negotiation, accepting your requirements to regain contact with you.

The possible liability of these moves is that the narcissist may turn to someone else to fulfill her needs. In that case, you have lost your leverage and there is not much else you can do.

Of course, these rules are much easier said than done, especially if your instincts were formed by growing up in a household with a narcissist. You may have to fight your own patterns of behavior in order to deal with the current narcissist in your life. If you succeed, you will sustain less personal damage. I can't guarantee that the relationship will survive, but if it does, it will likely be more tolerable for both of you.

Please remember that these "rules" are meant as helpful ideas. Amateur diagnosis is not always right, and no rule is right for every situation. Do refer to the disclaimer in the Overview at the beginning of this book.

THE FUTURE STARTS TODAY

*Encouraging words and the Scarsdale Psychother-
apy Self-Evaluation (SPSE), a universal tool for
evaluation of therapy effectiveness.*

In a nutshell, here's what we have learned: *A very large part of our life
is about feelings.* Having feelings, avoiding feelings, understanding
and accepting feelings. The hangups we all have, our dysfunctional
patterns, grow out of childhood needs to escape feelings that are beyond childhood coping abilities. Our great reluctance to face those
feelings is due to outdated dread that is as old as the feelings themselves. That is why crossing our personal Bridge will turn out to be
less painful and more rewarding than we imagine.

Now that we have adult desires and ambitions, we have outgrown
our dysfunctional patterns of reaction, and we can decide to change.
Granted, we have to go through the painful and uncomfortable feelings that we avoided initially, but this time we have adult support
systems, resources, and abilities.

The process is not mysterious, nor is it magical. You will need to take risks, fight your superego, challenge your defenses, and go far outside your comfort zone. You may have to grieve the loss of cherished childhood dreams and replace them with more realistic, healthy adult plans. Along the way, it will be your connections with others and your internal rechargeable battery pack of connection (Chapter 3) that will heal your pain and allow you to do the job of growing that awaits.

I wish you much growth and happiness!

The Scarsdale Psychotherapy Self-Evaluation (SPSE)

How do you know if your therapy is working successfully? The Scarsdale Psychotherapy Self-Evaluation (SPSE) found at blog.psytx.com is one way you can look at therapeutic effectiveness. Each item in the self-evaluation focuses on an aspect of therapy that is believed to be related to results. The intent of the self-evaluation is more to help you think about what is important in your therapy rather than to come up with a specific numerical value.

This tool is unique in that it is designed to be independent of the theory or school your therapy may follow. Instead, it is based on the universal processes and principles laid out in this book.

You will be asked to rate statements in three categories: The Therapeutic Relationship, The Tasks of Psychotherapy, and Do You Feel Safe in Therapy? In all there are eighteen items, each to be scored on a scale of 1 to 5 with 5 being the most positive.

You can also take the test online at blog.psytx.com. Please enjoy thinking about the things that count in psychotherapy.

Part One: The Therapeutic Relationship

Please give each item a score from 1 to 5, where 5 is most positive.

1. First few sessions felt "right" (Score_____) This has been shown to correlate strongly with overall success of therapy. If you tend to give too much benefit of the doubt or not enough when you first meet someone, ask yourself if your first impression of this therapist is better or worse than your first impressions of other people.

2. Therapist shows "accurate empathy" (Score_____) Empathy isn't just being nice. It is a natural connection that occurs when you are able to let the therapist in on your personal world and the therapist understands just what you mean on an emotional level.

3. Therapist warmth (Score_____) Therapist warmth has been confirmed through much research to be correlated with therapeutic success.

4. Therapist "realness" (Score_____) Humans are very sensitive to others being fake. Falseness or artificiality creates a barrier to any real connection and prevents empathy from working, while realness makes it easier for a patient to open up.

5. Therapist helps me take healthy risks (Score_____) Almost all change processes involve emotional risk-taking when doing so is not really dangerous. Effective therapists help you feel connected and safe and push you a bit to go ahead.

6. Therapist has a plan, a focus, and direction (Score_____) Effective therapies feel like they are going somewhere. If yours doesn't give you a sense of direction, then raise questions about it. Some therapists tell you explicitly what to expect and work with you to develop a kind of contract. In other traditions, you follow a method that in itself gives direction and focus. Whether it is said out loud or not, therapy should soon feel like it is leading you in a purposeful way towards what you want in life.

Part Two: The Tasks of Psychotherapy

Each of these items asks you to rate the performance of your therapy on one of several core tasks. Sometimes you may do a task without even noticing and sometimes you may have to work quite hard at it. There may be some overlap between tasks. Score how well your therapy is helping you do each task or mark "NA" if an area is not relevant to the work you are currently doing.

7. Stop "running" from feelings (Score_____) There are many ways we avoid feelings, and they all interfere with healing and growth. Negative behaviors, rationalization, keeping busy all the time, acting out instead of feeling, even anger can be cover-ups for pain. How well is your therapy helping you to stop running and to face your uncomfortable or painful feelings?

8. Healing your shame, fear, anger, and pain (Score_____) When you hold an uncomfortable feeling for at least ten seconds in a context of safety and connection, the feeling (or at least a portion of it) is transformed and no longer has the power to generate the distress it once did. This is what I call catharsis, the most common and important healing process in therapy. How well is your therapy helping you to use catharsis to heal your difficult feelings so they no longer hold you back?

9. Gain knowledge of yourself (Score_____) All therapies depend on some kind of understanding. Progressing from a vague sense to a clear concept gives us a handle on ourselves. How well is your therapy helping you to make sense of your problems and how you can heal and grow?

10. Reform your conscience or core values (Score_____) Our superego or conscience judges things according to strongly internalized templates. These templates include values, attitudes, ideals, and prohibitions. When we live up to them, we feel pride. When we don't we feel guilt or shame. The problem is that sometimes those templates are wrong or unhealthy. When they are, we may feel shame or guilt when we shouldn't. How well does your therapy help you identify and resist unhealthy values and judgments?

11. Voluntary Behavior Change (Score_____) Behavior patterns can undermine our lives by covering up feelings we need to face and by supporting unhealthy attitudes or values. Many kinds of dysfunctional behavior patterns can sabotage your life. Most of the time these started out as ways to shield you from feelings that once were too much to handle. How well is your therapy helping you to make healthy changes in behavior?

12. Reevaluate secret wishes and plans (Score_____) Do you repeatedly find yourself blocked from the things that are most important to you in life? Could you be sabotaging yourself? If so, you may have a secret world of wishes and plans in conflict with secret prohibitions. How well is your therapy working to help you clarify these issues and get unstuck?

13. Restart arrested development (Score_____) Regardless of your age, growing emotionally and maturing involve taking emotional risks, practicing new behaviors, and going through the feelings that result. Often pride and shame block us from recognizing areas of immaturity. How well is your therapy working to help you face areas where you need to grow, practice more mature behaviors, and go through the uncomfortable feelings that accompany change?

Part Three: Do You Feel Safe in Therapy?

Please give each item a score from 1 to 5, where 5 is most positive.

14. Therapist makes it safe to criticize or disagree (Score_____) This is important in any therapy, and may be the key to resolving unfinished business from the past that has been "transferred" to the therapeutic relationship. Therapists should put personal feelings aside and work with you to see what part of the problem is yours and what part is theirs. How well is your therapy working to help you resolve difficult issues with your therapist?

15. Therapist makes it safe to share highly personal material (Score_____) Many thoughts and feelings come up in therapy both from the past or in the present, including feelings related to the therapist. Therapists need to be respectful and professional while making it as easy as possible to make these feelings part of what you talk about. Sometimes the therapist's feelings and emotional reactions may be part of the interaction. These, too should be handled in a way that keeps the focus on your treatment.

16. Therapist only makes promises that can be kept (Score_____) Therapists can be tempted to promise more than they can realistically deliver. However, you need and deserve a therapist who will be reliable and firm, even if you are putting on pressure. When promises are broken, it is hard to forgive, and the relationship may be seriously damaged. How well does your therapist manage expectations and set limits?

17. Therapist avoids setting bad precedents (Score_____) Bad precedents are similar to unrealistic promises but are unspoken. For example, if your therapist goes along with you in avoiding an important task—say, not addressing a certain difficult area—you may feel better in the short run but see your progress blocked in the long run. How well does your therapist avoid setting bad precedents?

18. Therapist maintains safe boundaries (Score_____) Therapy is about you, not the therapist. The reason why therapists don't tell you too much about themselves is to avoid making the therapy about the therapist and his or her needs and to keep it focused on you. Physical boundaries are maintained to prevent arousing natural feelings that have the power to take the focus away from your healing and growth. If it feels as though your therapist is dealing with you in a way that is (or feels) inappropriate, or if his or her self-interest is getting in the way, then you can be hurt and your therapy damaged. Do you feel safe about the boundaries in your therapy? If you have questions, talk to an outside person you trust.

GLOSSARY AND BIOGRAPHIES

Glossary

Affect regulation: How we keep feelings at a level that doesn't overwhelm us. The first form of affect regulation we develop involves the use of empathic connection with the primary caregiver to soften the bumps and jolts of life through catharsis.

Amygdala: Almond-shaped groups of nerve cells located deep within the medial temporal lobes of our brains, one in each hemisphere. They are specialized for detecting potential dangers and pleasures.

Attachment: A fundamental human need for empathic connection starting in infancy and lasting throughout life. Problems in early relationships can damage readiness for attachment as well as the ability to go easily from connection to aloneness and back again.

Black Box Motivator: A part of our motivational apparatus that influences us to do what is required for survival of the species. It works mostly out of our conscious awareness and produces thoughts and impulses to steer our behavior. It has a profound effect on our lives but does not always steer in directions we might consider healthy.

Catharsis: Originally coined by Sigmund Freud and used here to designate the fundamental healing process by which raw, unprocessed feelings lose their power over us and are transformed when we share them in a context of connection and safety.

Connection distress: The discomfort we experience when our need for connection is thwarted or threatened. This feeling is a powerful driver of behavior as well as a trigger for us to internalize values.

Dissociation: The mind's circuit breaker. An automatic mechanism for splitting off consciousness of circumstances beyond the coping skills of the individual. Anything can be split off, including feelings, physical pain, and memories. The process is usually not voluntary and can last minutes or decades.

Dysfunctional pattern of reaction: A general formula to describe human mental problems. *Dysfunctional* means that the pattern causes you some loss or discomfort; *pattern* means that the *reaction* didn't happen just once but occurs regularly and can be expected to occur again if nothing changes; reaction can include feelings, thoughts, behaviors, perceptions, and any other products of the mind.

Hippocampus: A seahorse-shaped brain structure involved in moving explicit memories from short-term to long-term storage. Injury to the hippocampus can destroy the brain's ability to form explicit long-term memories.

"I" statements: You are the expert on your feelings and perceptions, and factual statements about your emotions and point of view are inarguable. They are also not threatening to your partner since they don't require action or change. They are very useful for communication as opposed to "you" statements, which tend to threaten.

Identification with the lost object: Internalizing characteristics of an important person in our lives triggered by the loss of that person.

Insight: Understanding of our own psyche. When put into words, insight can help us to understand and change our conscious and unconscious thoughts, feelings, motives, values, and goals.

Internal rechargeable battery pack of connection: A term used in this book referring to an internalized sense of connection to a person or world greater than oneself that enhances resilience and limits the depth of aloneness that the individual might feel. Equivalent to Margaret Mahler's concept of internalized libidinal object constancy.

Intervention: A planned event in which people close to someone suffering from addiction or other compulsive behavior come together in a caring way to confront the person's behavior and invite him or her to accept help.

Motivational Apparatus: A part of our mind that operates outside of consciousness to steer our behavior in directions that are presumably identified as good for the survival of the species. End products such as feelings of pleasure, pain, guilt, and pride as well as thoughts and impulses do enter into consciousness.

Narcissistic personality disorder: A severe personality disorder in which an individual cultivates and believes in a persona of superiority unrelated to his or her actual success. Behind this front is a life-and-death struggle to ward off humiliation that undermines empathy and any regard for the feelings of others.

Neural network: A grouping of nerve cells in the brain that function as a unit and that store and together represent a specific chunk of mental information.

Neurosis: Usually neurosis refers to milder emotional problems that can still ruin lives. In this book it refers to dysfunctional patterns in which we somehow defeat ourselves when trying to achieve our most cherished wishes.

Object constancy: A term for a child's ability to tolerate separation from the primary caregiver felt to be based on availability of an internal representation of the person.

Oedipus complex: Freud's term for a boy's conflict between the wish to compete with his father for his mother's affection and the fear of his father's punishment. Named after the title character in the play *Oedipus Rex*, written by fifth-century B.C. Greek tragedian Sophocles. Oedipus unknowingly kills his father and marries his mother.

Post-traumatic stress disorder (PTSD): A group of symptoms experienced by some people following a traumatic experience. Symptoms include distancing from feelings and/or the memory of events, avoidance of reminders of the trauma, breakthrough of fragments of memory in flashbacks or dreams, and hypervigilance as if feeling that the event could recur at any moment.

Psychotherapy integration: Combining techniques and ideas from more than one psychotherapy orientation in a way that is coherent and clinically sound. The field is associated with the Society for the

Exploration of Psychotherapy Integration (SEPI) as well as a scientific journal.

Secondary emotions: Unlike primary emotions (e.g., fear and sadness), which relate directly to experiences, secondary emotions (pride, shame, and guilt) reflect how our personal values shape the way we judge ourselves and others.

Schema: A learned pattern of reactions stored in implicit memory, whose aim is to avoid pain or anxiety and to increase comfort or pleasure.

Stockholm syndrome: When people who are held hostage grow to sympathize with, like, and even identify with their captors. It is believed to occur in about a quarter of victims of hostage-taking.

Superego (conscience): A part of our motivational apparatus, independent of our wishes and impulses, that uses pride, shame, and guilt—along with our Black Box Motivator—to convince us to follow its internalized standards even when we don't want to.

Transference: Freud discovered transference in the 1890s, when one patient thought Freud was the worst doctor ever, while another thought he was the very best. Freud realized that they were transferring onto him feelings they had felt early in life.

Biographies

Beck, Aaron (1921-): Beck is considered to be "the father of cognitive therapy." He developed systematic treatment options for depression and anxiety, as well as the Beck Depression Inventory.

Bowlby, John (1907-1990): Bowlby, a British psychiatrist and psychoanalyst, championed the then novel idea that children need emotional contact with caregivers in order to thrive.

Joseph Breuer (1842-1925): A prominent Viennese physician who took the young Freud under his wing and whose patient first suggested the technique of talk therapy.

Camus, Albert (1913-1960): Camus won the Nobel Prize for Literature in 1957. His most famous works are *The Stranger* and *The Plague*. He was also an existentialist philosopher and a journalist.

DiClemente, Carlo C. (1942-): See James O. Prochaska.

Ellis, Albert (1913-2007): Ellis originated rational emotive behavior therapy (REBT), an early form of cognitive-behavioral therapy.

Fonagy, Peter (1952-): Freud Memorial Professor of Psychoanalysis at University College, London, Fonagy has focused on the integration of research and theory, particularly in relationship to borderline psychopathology, violence, and early attachment relationships.

Fosha, Diana (1952-): Fosha developed accelerated experiential-dynamic psychotherapy and is the author of *The Transforming Power of Affect*.

Freud, Sigmund (1856-1939): Freud founded the field of psychoanalysis and pioneered talk therapy aimed at understanding and resolving the unconscious forces that drive dysfunctional patterns of perception and behavior.

Goleman, Daniel: Goleman, a psychologist and journalist, authored the highly influential 1995 book *Emotional Intelligence*, arguing that success in life depends on skill with emotions and relationships as much as cognitive ability.

Hearst, Patricia (1954-): Hearst is the granddaughter of newspaper publisher William Randolph Hearst and heiress to the Hearst fortune. In 1974 she was kidnapped by the Symbionese Liberation Army (SLA). She was later arrested for participating in a bank robbery with the SLA and served two years in prison.

Karen, Robert: Psychologist in New York and author of books on attachment and forgiveness.

Kernberg, Otto (1928-): Kernberg developed important theories about people with borderline personality organization and narcissistic pathology. He is a psychoanalyst and professor of psychiatry at Weill Cornell Medical College in New York.

Khabat-Zinn, Jon (1944-): Prominent teacher and proponent of mindfulness meditation and the integration of Zen into American medicine. Developed the Mindfulness-Based Stress Reduction program (MBSR).

Kübler-Ross, Elisabeth (1926-2004): Kübler-Ross wrote the book *On Death and Dying*, in which she described five stages that people go through when faced with death: denial, anger, bargaining, depression, and acceptance.

Mahler, Margaret (1897-1985): Mahler, a Hungarian physician and psychoanalyst, studied separation and individuation and described how children go through various stages of development on the way to acquiring a sense of identity.

Norcross, John C. (1957-): Distinguished researcher, teacher, and clinician who has focused on behavior change and psychotherapy. Collaborated with Prochaska and DiClemente. He has championed research demonstrating the crucial importance of the therapeutic relationship in psychotherapy success as well as what works to make lasting changes in behavior.

Piaget, Jean (1896-1980): Piaget was a developmental psychologist and philosopher who pioneered understanding of children's cognitive development.

Prochaska, James O. (1943-): Prochaska and Carlo C. DiClemente developed the transtheoretical model of behavior change, a method by which a therapist can assess whether a person is ready to change and then guide the person through adopting and maintaining a new, healthier behavior.

Schore, Allan (1943-): Leading researcher in neuropsychology and author of *Affect Regulation and the Origin of the Self*.

Shapiro, Francine (1948-): Shapiro is best known for her invention of eye movement desensitization and reprocessing, or EMDR. She is a licensed clinical psychologist, Senior Research Fellow at the Mental Research Institute in Palo Alto, and Executive Director of the EMDR Institute.

Siegel, Daniel J. (1957-): Siegel, Clinical Professor of Psychiatry at the UCLA School of Medicine, is the author of *The Mindful Brain: Reflection and Attunement in the Cultivation of Well-Being* and *The Mindful Therapist: A Clinician's Guide to Mindsight and Neural Integration.*

Stern, Daniel N. (1934-2012): Stern was a psychiatrist and psychoanalytic theorist specializing in infant development. He was the author of *The Present Moment in Psychotherapy and Everyday Life.*

Yalom, Irvin: Yalom, therapist and author of *The Theory and Practice of Group Psychotherapy,* a classic description of the therapeutic process, is Emeritus Professor of Psychiatry at Stanford University and writes both fiction and nonfiction.

Van der Kolk, Bessel: A pioneering researcher, clinician, and teacher specializing in trauma and PTSD since the 1970s. Recently published *The Body Keeps the Score: Brain, Mind, and Body in the Healing of Trauma.*

About The Author

Dr. Jeffery Smith is a native Californian and graduate of Stanford University. He went to medical school at UCLA and interned in Syracuse, N.Y. in internal medicine. He completed psychiatric residency at Albert Einstein College of Medicine.

In 1976, he began private practice in Scarsdale, N.Y. Dr. Smith was Chief Physician in the outpatient clinic of Bronx Lebanon Hospital until 1980. It was there in 1977 that he became interested in the area of dissociation and what is now called dissociative identity disorder. He cofounded a professional study group on dissociation in the 1990s.

In 1980, he joined the faculty at New York Medical College. There he was appointed Director of Alcoholism Services and in 1989 left to establish Cortland Medical, the first evening intensive outpatient program for alcoholism in Westchester County.

A Distinguished Fellow in the American Psychiatric Association, Dr. Smith was twice president of the Psychiatric Society of Westchester and served as Public Affairs Chair in the New York State Psychiatric Association.

He continues to serve on the clinical faculty at New York Medical College and teaches courses on psychotherapy technique and combined psychodynamic and behavioral treatment in the residency. He has written and lectured on psychotherapy, dissociative identity disorder, and addiction. His primary area of interest continues to be the process of change in psychotherapy. He authors a website, www.Psytx.com, which offers course material for psychotherapy teaching, as well as a blog on psychotherapy. He remains in full time private practice in Scarsdale, N.Y.

While an undergraduate at Stanford's campus in Tours, France, he met his wife Claude Smith, who is a partner at Just North, an interior design firm in Scarsdale. They have three children.

INDEX

acceptance 138, 224

accurate empathy 4

acting out 116

addiction 82, 204, 225, 236

adolescence 59, 268

affect regulation 172

aloneness 44, 110, 157, 187, 195, 264, 271

amygdala 126

anorexia nervosa 178

anxiety 35, 53, 66, 160, 204, 211

attachment 19, 273, 275

attitudes 174

automatic thoughts 4, 54, 70, 84, 88, 137, 227

avoidance of feelings 21, 34-94,

Beck, Aaron 189

behavior change 202, 226

behavior patterns 14, 92, 153, 202-239

biological factors 159

Black Box Motivator 87, 133, 178, 251

body work 20, 112, 128

Bowlby, John 274

brain 3, 26, 125

Breuer, Joseph 78, 79, 102

bucket method 99

catharsis 1, 15, 95-132

Cave, Bridge, and Village 10-15

Castles and Prisons 35, 48, 66

civil disobedience 192

cognitive-behavioral therapy (CBT) 18, 53, 142

compulsions 214

connection distress 186, 191, 193, 200, 265

conscience 22, 31, 47, 88, 131, 155, 167, 170-201, 221, 244, 260

denial 135

depression 68, 157, 217

development 24, 57, 259-299

DiClemente, Carlo 227

dialectical behavior therapy 19

displacement 136

dissociation 72, 217

dissociative identity disorder (DID) 77

Ellis, Albert 189

EMDR 19, 104

emotion-focused therapy 19

emotional intelligence (EQ) 20

empathy 20, 103, 142, 192, 195, 282

explicit 143-153, 223

Erikson, Erik 109

experiential therapies 20

exposure therapy 104

failed rites of passage 222

fantasy 136

Fonagy, Peter 120

forgiveness 138, 224

Fosha, Diana 104

free association 248

Freud, Sigmund 78

Good Will Hunting 135

grow graph 228

guilt 47, 88, 128, 170-199

helplessness and hopelessness 39, 68

hidden agendas 204, 218-225

hippocampus 144

hypnosis 75

I statements 98

ideals 48, 89, 155, 174, 267

ideas 14, 32, 133-169

identification with the lost object 184

implicit 122, 143, 147-180, 203, 231

inner child 21, 149, 166, 209, 235, 251

internal rechargeable battery pack of connection 109-122, 265, 279

imago therapy 19

impulses 46, 84, 151, 175, 213, 230-261, 290

inborn strategies 204, 210, 234

insight 123, 151, 152

internal electric fences 195, 250, 267

internalization 180, 184, 193, 267, 279

Kahneman, Daniel 141

Karen, Robert 275

Kernberg, Otto 285

Khabat-Zinn, Jon 142

Kubler-Ross, Elisabeth 40

logic 70, 147, 162, 173,

losing battles 70, 266, 280

loss and grief 45, 224, 255

Mahler, Margaret 110, 264

marijuana 25, 65, 289

medication 26

mental dysfunction 38, 51

mentalization 119, 122, 127

mind 3, 13, 27, 83-90, 148, 242

mindfulness 19, 118, 142

motivational apparatus 79, 260

narcissism 281

neural network 125

narrative 113

Norcross, John 227

obsessions 214

Oedipus complex 183, 246

Onoda, Lt. Hiroo 37

object constancy 108, 265

outflanking behavior 232

panic attacks 35, ,53, 212

parents 29, 61, 254, 268

Piaget, Jean 242

positive psychology 19

pride 47, ,88, 175, 261

Prochaska, James 227

projection 136, 284

post traumatic stress disorder (PTSD) 73, 111, 218

psychoanalysis 20, 142, 248

psychotherapy 22

quests 204, 240-258

reenactment 158, 163, 244

resilience 19, 142, 266

Rogers, Carl 4

Scarsdale Psychotherapy Self-Evaluation (SPSE) 301

schema 19, 203-212, 231, 264-273

Schore, Allan 173

secondary feelings 47, 174, 175

self-hatred 69

self-mastery 62, 269, 289

separation and individuation 264, 271

shame 47, 174, 262

Shapiro, Francine 106

Siegel, Daniel 120

someday 204, 241-258, 268

Stern, Daniel 107

stockholm syndrome 181

stress 63, 293

superego 172-201

surf the feeling 118

talk therapy 18, 55, 103, 248

templates 155, 174, 267

terrible twos 43, 70, 266, 280

therapy (see psychotherapy)

therapeutic relationship 20, 163, 190, 227, 248

thoughts 3, 31, 84, 133-169, 175, 183, 213, 243, 247

twelve step 5, 20, 237

values 14, 170-201

Van der Kolk, Bessel 112

Yalom, Irvin 93

words 6, 76, 92, 150, 231

70337275R00178

Made in the USA
Columbia, SC
21 August 2019